1-27-77

# MONEY IN THE AGE OF TIBERIUS

TO

R. E. Smith

# MONEY
# IN THE AGE
# OF TIBERIUS

## Cosmo Rodewald

MANCHESTER
UNIVERSITY PRESS

ROWMAN AND LITTLEFIELD

Published by
Manchester University Press
Oxford Road, Manchester M13 9PL

UK ISBN 0 7190 0616 3


USA

Rowman and Littlefield
81 Adams Drive, Totowa, N.J. 07512

*Library of Congress cataloging in publication data*

Rodewald, Cosmo.
  Money in the age of Tiberius.

  Includes bibliographical references and index.
  1. Money – Rome – History. I. Title.
HG237.R6   1976     332.4'937'6     76-948
ISBN 0 87471 823 6

Printed in Great Britain by
Unwin Brothers Limited
The Gresham Press
Old Woking Surrey
A member of the Staples Printing Group

# CONTENTS

# FOREWORD

IN BOOK VI OF THE *Annals* Tacitus describes a financial crisis at Rome in A.D. 33. When I tried to learn what lay behind this crisis, that is to say, find out what is known about money in the Roman world in the time of Tiberius, I discovered that little had been written on the subject that a student of history could readily understand. Numismatists have written many books for laymen about Greek and Roman coins, but for the most part they have not been much concerned with questions that social and economic historians ask. So I decided that the results of my own enquiries might be of interest, and that publication of these might stimulate those better qualified to do further work in this area.

To acknowledge my great indebtedness to numismatists in many lands I should need to place here a long list of names; I hope that my notes will show how much I owe them, even when I have ventured to disagree with some of their views on currency circulation. There remain those whom I wish to thank for important help that they have consciously given me, while emphasising that they are not responsible for any of my errors. Mr Michael Crawford—some of whose papers on Roman money, coming to my attention when my study was already under way, encouraged me by the similarity of their ápproach—has read, at two stages, most of what I have written and has contributed extremely valuable information and advice, though he is not to be regarded as endorsing any of my views, particularly on the significance of *aes* currency. Professor Theodore V. Buttrey, Mr John Crook and Dr A. H. McDonald have read one draft or another and have made many helpful suggestions, as have Professor Harold B. Matttingly and other members of the Northern English Universities Tacitus Seminar to whom I read a paper based on this work in May 1971. The text was substantially completed by August 1971, but I have since revised a number of passages; the last changes were made in March 1975.

The Editors and Publisher of *Historia*, who had accepted an earlier draft of a large portion of this book for publication as an *Einzelschrift*, generously released me from my commitment when the opportunity arose for me to have it published as a whole. The Trustees of the Tout and Little Funds facilitated publication by making a generous grant. The University of Manchester enabled me to lay the foundations of my study in 1967 by according me the rare privilege of a sabbatical term. Mrs M. Gissop, Mrs Patricia Lownsborough and Mrs D. Abel helped me to clarify my thinking by wrestling bravely with various portions of my manuscript. I have cause also to be most grateful to Mr Martin Spencer, Mr John Banks and the staff of the University Press.

Above all, I thank Professor R. E. Smith for unfailing help and encouragement at all stages of my work.

Cosmo Rodewald

Manchester, January 1976

CHAPTER I

# THE FINANCIAL
# CRISIS OF
## A.D. 33

DURING THE TWO CENTURIES before the birth of Christ, all the lands around the
Mediterranean came under the control of the Romans. Their power extended into
Europe as far as the Rhine and the Danube and into Asia as far as the Euphrates.
Some use was made of coined money over the whole of that area before the Romans
came; there were diverse currencies, based on a number of different systems. By
the middle of the first century A.D. Roman gold and silver had taken the place of
almost all other value currencies, and in much of the area Roman bronze and
copper had taken the place of other kinds of small change.*

So much is clear, but much else remains far from clear. What purposes had the
Roman government, and other authorities, in mind in deciding whether and when
to issue currency, and in what quantities and denominations? Was Roman
currency deliberately imposed, other currencies being deliberately suppressed?
Was there an increase in demand for coined money during this period, whether
as a result of Roman conquest or for other reasons? Was demand satisfied? Was
currency being exported from the Roman world in sufficiently large quantities to
cause a shortage already in the first half of the first century A.D.?

In the following pages an attempt is made to contribute to the answering of such
questions, taking as a point of reference an episode of which, as it happens, Tacitus,
Suetonius and Cassius Dio all give some account, although Greek and Roman
writers usually say almost nothing about monetary matters. This literary evidence
will be set alongside some of the evidence for currency circulation provided by the
coins themselves, and in particular by reports of coin finds; these have been
published in recent years in growing numbers, and in some countries in an increasingly systematic fashion, so that an enquiry of this kind can be somewhat
less speculative than it would have had to be twenty or thirty years ago.

The fullest and best account that we possess of the episode in question is given
by Tacitus in his narrative of events in Rome in A.D. 33.[1] It is, however, characteristically elliptical, so I have interposed a few explanatory sentences.[2]

Meanwhile a great pack of prosecutors bore down on those who were in the habit
of making their money grow by putting it out at interest in contravention of a law
passed by Caesar as dictator, which laid down rules for lending and for holding land
within Italy; it had long been disregarded, because private advantage takes precedence
over public welfare . . . But when Gracchus, the praetor to whom the court concerned
had been assigned, saw how many people were in peril, he felt obliged to make a
report to the Senate. The senators were alarmed, for there was not one of them who

* See the Preliminary note: Roman and Greek money (p. 75).

was innocent of such a charge, and they asked the Princeps for indulgence. Their request was granted, and eighteen months' grace was given to enable everyone to bring his personal accounts into line with the requirements of the law.

This led to a shortage of currency, as everyone's loans were called in at the same time, and also because so many people had been convicted [of other offences] and their property sold up, and the coined money thus realised was held in the *fiscus* or the *aerarium*.[3] To meet the situation [caused by the prosecution of those contravening Caesar's law], the Senate had decreed that everyone must invest two-thirds of the money he had out on loan on land within Italy. [According to Suetonius, whose account is quoted below, the Senate's decree also laid down that debtors must discharge two-thirds of their debts forthwith. Presumably the intention was to mitigate the debtors' embarrassment, while enabling the creditors to do what was being required of them. Tacitus' next words seem to presuppose that the decree did include such a provision.] But creditors were demanding repayment in full, and it would have been humiliating for those to whom the demands were addressed to diminish their credit by failing to make full repayment.

So at first people dashed about, begging for assistance, then the praetor's court began to hum with activity; and what had been devised as a remedy, selling and buying, produced a result opposite to what had been intended, since the lenders stored up all the money they had for buying land. [The decree had clearly been intended to ensure that there would be plenty of bidders for any land that a debtor might be obliged to sell in order to repay two-thirds of his debt, but those who had been expected to bid, in order to invest in land, instead took advantage of the grace they had been given.] The glut of property on offer caused a collapse in prices; the more heavily people were in debt, the more difficulty they found in selling, and many were turned out of their properties [having been unable to pay what they owed by the date that their creditor set]. Financial ruin brought with it an abrupt decline in status and reputation, until [Tiberius] Caesar came to the rescue: a hundred million sesterces were made available through banks, and loans were offered for three years free of interest [to enable debtors to repay their creditors], provided that the borrower gave the People security in landed property for double the amount. Thus confidence was restored, and gradually private individuals who would make loans began to be found. But the purchase of land did not proceed in accordance with the terms of the Senate's decree; what was begun energetically ended in carelessness, as usually happens in such cases.

Dio's account is briefer, but he adds a couple of details:[4]

Nerva [a leading senator] could no longer bear to associate with Tiberius, chiefly because he had revived the laws on loan-contracts which Caesar had enacted, for this was bound to damage credit and be very upsetting [since the inability of many respected citizens to comply with a sudden request for repayment of what they had borrowed would be exposed]. So he starved himself to death . . . After this Tiberius adopted a more moderate policy with regard to loans [a reference to the grant of eighteen months' grace to offending lenders?] and gave the public treasury twenty-five million [*sc. denarii*, the equivalent of one hundred million sesterces] to enable senators to make loans to applicants for three years free of interest. He also gave orders for the most notorious of those who initiated prosecutions to be executed, all on one day.

The only other reference to this episode is in Suetonius' life of Tiberius:[5]

There were only two occasions on which he made a public show of munificence, once when he advanced a hundred million sesterces free of interest for three years, and on another occasion when he compensated some owners of blocks of residential property on Mons Caelius which had burnt down. On the former occasion he was compelled to act when the people demanded relief at a time of great monetary difficulty, after he had laid down by senatorial decree that moneylenders should invest two-thirds of their patrimony in land and that debtors should forthwith pay the same proportion of their debt, for these measures were failing to solve the problem; while the other action was taken to relieve a dreadful situation.

Tacitus and Dio both assumed that their audience would be familiar with the provisions of Julius Caesar's law or laws on debt and landholding. Unfortunately we are not in that position, for there is no other explicit reference to this legislation, since it cannot be identified with his measures to reduce the burden of debt.[6] As the phrase which Tacitus uses to indicate the scope of the law, *de modo credendi possidendique intra Italiam*, meaning that it 'laid down rules for lending and for holding land within Italy', must have seemed to him to cohere quite naturally, one must suppose that the rule for lending was somehow bound up with the rule about holding land. The simplest hypothesis is that the rule for lending, the *modus credendi*, set the maximum proportion of a man's wealth that he might lend at interest, while the rule on holding land within Italy, the *modus possidendi intra Italiam*, fixed a corresponding minimum for landholding.[7] In that case the *modus credendi* need not have had anything to do with the rate of interest.

There are three objections to this interpretation. First, it has been said that the words *pecunias faenore auctitabant*, in which Tacitus describes the offence of which the lenders were guilty, imply that the way in which they were contravening Caesar's law was by charging illegal rates of interest.[8] I can not see that his words necessarily carry that implication: he uses the word *faenus* elsewhere to mean simply 'interest', not necessarily exorbitant interest. Secondly, it has been said that if the law was not concerned with the rate of interest, Tacitus' subsequent excursus on earlier attempts to control moneylending is irrelevant. But is it likely that Tacitus would have accepted quite so strict a criterion of relevance? Since an attempt was being made on this occasion to enforce a limit of some kind to the lending of money, it would be quite in character for him to use this as an opportunity to allude to other attempts that had been made in the past to control this unattractive practice.[9] Tacitus may well have chosen the rather ambiguous expression *modus credendi*, not only because this enabled him to describe the law in one neat, terse phrase, but also because its ambiguity opened the way to his *topos*. Legerdemain of this kind had no doubt served him well in the courts, as it has served many another barrister. The third objection is that a few lines further on Tacitus, using quite different words, mentions the passing of a senatorial decree on the same subject, the holding of Italian land. It is not so much that Tacitus uses different words (it was necessary for his purpose to state plainly the content of the decree), nor that the Senate was now establishing a rule resembling, if not identical with, one which, according to Tacitus, all the senators had been breaking (circumstances made this volte-face advisable, for otherwise lenders might have felt that they had protected themselves sufficiently if they called in their loans and hung on to the money—as did, indeed happen; moreover, Suetonius attributes the initiative to Tiberius). What is really disturbing is that the provision which Tacitus mentions was similar to one of the provisions of Caesar's law, if not identical with it, yet he says nothing of this similarity. However, this difficulty seems to me to be outweighed by the difficulty of explaining otherwise the composite phrase, *de modo credendi possidendique intra Italiam.*

No other source alludes to a Caesarian law on this subject, but it is in keeping with the action that Caesar took already in 49 B.C., when he revived an older law forbidding the holding of more than sixty thousand sesterces in coin, in order to increase the flow of money.[10] This rule may indeed have been incorporated subsequently in the law to which Tacitus refers, if that law was passed in 46 or 45, for there was evidently still a shortage of money at that time.[11] However, no allusion to the enforcement, or the continued existence, of such a rule can be found, so far as I can see, in any of the ancient accounts of events in A.D. 33, and it seems more likely that Caesar allowed it to lapse, having found that it had no effect on the money supply.

I can now turn to considering the substance of Tacitus' explanation of this shortage of currency. This does not seem to have been called into question until Tenney Frank published an article on the subject in 1935.[12] In this article Frank attempted to show that the causes which Tacitus mentions cannot have been the real causes of this *inopia*. On the one hand Tiberius was, according to Frank, 'not guilty of very extensive confiscations' before A.D. 33.[13] On the other hand there had been 'a contraction of currency . . . far more serious than can be explained' by the causes which Tacitus gives.[14] What, then, in Frank's view, caused the serious contraction of currency which he thought had occurred? His answer was that 'while Augustus increased the coinage for circulation very strikingly from 30 to 10 B.C., he in his last twenty years and Tiberius during his nineteen years of power before 33 coined relatively little and spent very frugally; so that, while gold and silver went abroad increasingly to pay for imports, the *per capita* circulation inside Italy was steadily decreasing for forty years'.

In order to decide whether Frank's criticism of Tacitus is valid, and whether his view of the crisis is acceptable, we need to examine the contentions on which his view rests. Is there reason to think that the shortage of currency in Italy was so severe that it could not have been due solely to the happenings to which Tacitus refers? Was there a gap, which had been growing wider for over forty years, between the amount of money that flowed into Italy from abroad and the amount that was being sent out of Italy to pay for imports? Could and should Augustus and Tiberius have remedied the situation by striking more coins? Had they been coining much less than Augustus in his first twenty years of sole power?

Let us consider first what can be said about the striking of coins in precious metals under Augustus and Tiberius. Frank was assuming that when some state in the ancient world produced a large amount of new coinage this must mean that the government was spending on a large scale, and conversely that when a government spent on a large scale the state was bound to produce a large amount of new coinage. He was also assuming that when a large amount of new coinage was produced there was necessarily a corresponding increase in the amount of money in circulation. In making these assumptions he seems not to have taken into account the possibility that during Augustus' last twenty-four years and Tiberius' first nineteen years of rule the government might have been making greater use of old coins than it had during the preceding twenty years. The impression of a reduction in governmental expenditure and of a contraction in the supply of new money that is derived from comparing the plethora of new issues before 12 B.C. with the dearth of new issues after 12 B.C. may therefore be wholly misleading. It can, I think, be shown that it is not only possible but probable that after 12 B.C. the Roman authorities went in more for reissuing old coins than they had previously.

The situation was this. A government could melt down and restrike as many as it pleased of the coins that came into its hands, but it was *obliged* to strike coins only when it wished to spend more currency than it had at its disposal; and in so far as it was not obliged to strike coins it might well prefer to reuse many, if not all, of the old coins that came into its hands, even alien coins, at least as long as they were not worn to the point of being unrecognisable. It is practically certain that all ancient governments did reuse old coins, especially old coins of their own, instead of withdrawing them. Unfortunately we can usually do no more than guess to what extent a particular government did so at a particular time. Mattingly could only ask: 'Were coins withdrawn after a stated term of years? Or were they allowed to circulate as long as they were not too worn?'[15]

The composition of hoards provides no evidence for governmental policy in this matter, for we cannot tell over how long a period or at what rate or on what principles of selection a hoard was accumulated.[16] It is, however, significant that in three 'packets' of coins lost by soldiers in Britain at the time of the building of Hadrian's Wall, a quarter of the *denarii* were republican.[17] This indicates that it must have been the policy of the provincial authorities, a policy surely approved by the central government, to reissue, for the payment of troops, old coins that these authorities received, for instance in the payment of tribute.[18]

Moreover, in Cicero's time it was still regarded as normal that the government should reuse non-Roman currency for official purposes, in appropriate contexts; this is shown by the proposal of the quaestors at Rome in 60 B.C. that the allowance of Quintus Cicero as governor of Asia should be paid out of a supply of *cistophori* (the tetradrachms struck by a number of Greek states in that region) which Pompey had acquired and had left in Asia.[19] Under Augustus, 'derartige Münzen fanden sich gewiss unter dem Schmelzgut der römischen Münze oder im Ärar massenweise',[20] and we have no reason to suppose that he broke with republican custom and treated them all merely as 'Schmelzgut', as bullion.[21]

The great advantage in reusing old coins was avoidance of the expenses incurred in melting down and restriking. In addition to the cost of making good any loss through wear, there would also be the cost of cutting the necessary dies and producing the coins. Evidence from the later middle ages and the early modern period shows that 'the cost is surprisingly high'[22] (and at the time at which these words are being written the British public has been asked to accept old bank notes 'for the sake of national economy' instead of asking for new ones). Moreover there would be the cost and the risk involved in sending old coins to the nearest mint from provinces in which there was no official mint, and in sending out new coins to take their place.[23] In the case of Roman gold and silver this would normally have meant, after 12 B.C., sending coins to and from Lugdunum, since in the view of most numismatists gold and silver were not struck by the Roman government elsewhere west of Asia after that date.[24]

There was an *economic* incentive for a government to fetch back and melt down old coins only if it wished to spend more money than it had in its possession and if it had at its disposal little or none of the metal that it needed for striking new coins of the same quality as those in circulation. In these circumstances it might decide to issue coins supposedly equivalent to those already in circulation but either of lower weight or of inferior composition or both, and it might get metal for this purpose by withdrawing those coins that came into its hands.[25] There is, however, no reason to think that Augustus or Tiberius did anything of this kind, either before or after 12 B.C.; for, if one leaves plated coins out of account, Augustan and Tiberian *denarii* appear to have been in no way inferior to the *denarii* already in circulation.[26]

We may conclude that it would not have been materially profitable for Tiberius, or Augustus, to strike new coins in metal obtained by melting down or restriking old coins of the same denomination, either before or after 12 B.C. And we have seen that there was no need for them to withdraw old coins, even coins of alien powers and denominations, so long as the old coins were recognisable and acceptable.

On the other hand, the melting down and restriking of old coins could be politically advantageous.[27] New coins, with new types, carry a message to all who use them, a message that, as has often been pointed out, could not in those days be conveyed to so large an audience in any other way. That is, no doubt, one of the reasons why so many Roman issues, relatively speaking, were put out during the civil wars that brought first Julius Caesar and then Octavian to supreme power. Large quantities of uncoined precious metal will have come into the hands of the potentates who were engaged in these struggles, but they must also have received or seized quantities of currency. This could quite well have been reused, and probably much of it was hastily reused;[28] but it is not unlikely that some of it was melted down to contribute to the production of the numerous issues through which they made known their achievements, the merits that they claimed to possess, the ideals to which they professed devotion and the benefits that they promised. However, one must remember that a large proportion of the coins that came into their hands during the widespread conflict must have been non-Roman, and that others will have been coins advertising their opponents; they had an even stronger political motive for melting these down than for melting down older Roman coins.

These same considerations would have been likely still to influence Octavian for some time after Actium. It is impossible to say how far he was in fact influenced by them. What can be said is that, when he had the opportunity, after he had attained supreme power, to transform his defeated enemies into non-persons by calling in their coins, he did not systematically do so.[29] This is shown by the great number of coins struck for his enemies, in particular Antony,[30] that have turned up on sites or in hoards dating from the reigns of Augustus, Tiberius and later emperors. But one can well imagine that in his earlier years of supreme power he may have given instructions for the melting down and restriking, as a general rule, of older coins that chanced to come into the hands of those working for him. On the other hand, there are grounds for suggesting that in his later years he came round to thinking that the political advantage to be derived from withdrawing and replacing old coins could not justify the cost, and that Tiberius held that view even more strongly. This is a question to which I shall return. The point that I want to make here is that the emergence of a plethora of new issues need not connote a corresponding increase in the supply of money (and that, conversely, the supply of money could be increased by the mere distribution of accumulated reserves).

For some years after Actium, however, Octavian was probably compelled to strike fresh coins, for he was spending lavishly to reward his supporters and to consolidate his position. In particular there was the whole mass of legionaries and auxiliaries to be paid; some of the legionaries presently began to be pensioned off, but in his early years that, too, meant spending more money to buy land. Much of what he was spending in the first years after Actium came, no doubt, as Frank argued,[31] from the plunder of Egypt. This will surely have included large quantities of currency,[32] but much of the currency will naturally have been Ptolemaic, and the Ptolemaic silver coinage produced for use in Egypt had sunk to a very poor quality in recent times.[33] It was therefore of practically no use outside Egypt and it was left behind by the conqueror, to be put back into circulation as the official currency of the new regime, until Tiberius created a substitute. The Romans must also have found some coins of good quality, coins struck in Ptolemaic dominions overseas, and precious-metal coins of foreign states, both in the royal stores and among the valuables confiscated from private individuals, and these were probably reused in areas in which they were familiar;[34] but there may not have been much good coin altogether, relatively speaking. However, there must also have been a large amount of uncoined gold and silver, and much of this gold and silver was probably turned into money during the next few years. Thus at this stage Octavian was almost certainly following in effect a policy of currency expansion.

One might expect such an expansion to bring about a rise in prices: and, if Orosius can be believed, 'the prices of real estate and of other things put up for sale' were indeed doubled 'as a result of the abundant supply of money' after the conquest of Egypt.[35] However, one may doubt whether he had good authority for this sweeping assertion, for Suetonius and Cassius Dio speak only of a fall in the rate of interest, from 12 per cent to 4 per cent according to Dio, and a rise in the price of land: a sharp rise, according to Suetonius, but he seems to imply that it was caused by the fall in the rate of interest, not by an expansion of the money supply; while the fall in the rate of interest was itself due as much, perhaps, to the restoration of peace.[36]

One factor that may in such cases limit the fall in purchasing power of a currency is the confidence that it commands.[37] A further factor is that of currency supply and demand: a large increase in the supply of gold and silver currency, even if it brings about a fall in interest rates (though in this case the fall may have had another cause) need not lead to a rise in prices if it is accompanied by an increase in demand, that is to say, an increase in economic activities requiring a supply of money; and there must have been an exceptionally rapid increase in private demand for Roman currency in these years, with the enforcement of peace throughout an Empire in which the production of other currencies had dwindled.[38]

From about 25 B.C. onwards, mints in the western half of the Empire were the chief suppliers of new gold and silver coinage. It has generally been held that the most productive of these mints were at first all situated in Spain, until in about 16 B.C. a mint was opened in Gaul, at Lugdunum, which soon became the sole centre of production. The multitude of new types used, especially down to 10 B.C. and above all on coins supposedly struck at Spanish mints between 25 B.C. and 16 B.C., shows that importance was attached to the conveyance of a large number of political messages, and this suggests that large quantities of *denarii* and even of *aurei*—though these will have been much scarcer—may have been melted down and restruck to make this possible. Moreover, both in Spain and in Gaul the silver that came to the Romans as tribute or as plunder will have included a good deal of local currency that had previously been in circulation. However, the reference of

Florus to the opening up of new mines by the Romans in north-west Spain at this time and the account by Cassius Dio of the accumulation of gold and silver in Gaul by Augustus' procurator, Licinus,[39] indicate that during this period the Romans acquired considerable supplies of bullion in this area without having to pay for them. It is also likely that some bullion was bought for the mints from the owners or concessionaires of established mines in these provinces, especially in Spain; but the coins into which it was made would also have constituted an addition to the currency in circulation.

So we may accept that between 25 B.C. and 10 B.C. the amount of gold and silver currency in circulation was being further increased. We have no evidence of a rise in prices during this period; if in fact there was no notable rise, this was probably the result of a continuing increase in private demand for money.

The coins produced at Rome by the *tresviri monetales* are a different matter. When they began to strike gold and silver again in 20–18 B.C., after many years of inactivity, their raw material may well have been derived entirely from the melting down of old gold and silver coins that reached the *aerarium*; for there was no source from which considerable quantities of bullion would have been reaching the *aerarium*, as distinct from Augustus' *fiscus*, unless by purchase, which would have required his assistance, and in permitting or promoting the revival of this mint's activity he was probably concerned to provide an outlet for the self-importance of reliably obsequious young *nobiles*, who through Augustus' influence were put in charge, rather than to increase the supply of currency.

Be that as it may, what concerns us here is that the size of the issue produced by the *tresviri* at this mint was relatively small. It is simply not true that it 'also poured out large issues from 18 to 12 B.C.', as Frank asserted. Nor is it true that this 'can readily be seen by using Mattingly's *Coins of the Roman Empire in the British Museum*'. All that can be learnt in this connection from that catalogue is that a great many new types were brought into use for gold and silver coinage between 31 B.C. and 12 B.C., some by the officials who were in charge of this Roman mint, others by those in charge of other mints in the eastern and western portions of the Empire, and that far fewer new types were brought into use in the following forty-five years.[40]

Does it necessarily follow that much less new money was being produced? So Frank believed.

This brings us to Frank's fourth basic assumption. 'If we compare the known issues of gold and silver during the first twenty years of the Augustan regime with those of the following forty years [9 B.C.–A.D. 32], we discover', he wrote, 'that the annual output during the later period fell to about 5 per cent of the issues of the former years, an amazing contraction over an extensive period. Unfortunately we do not know how large the various issues of coins were, but there are indications that there was some uniformity.'[41] He proceeded to expound two of these indications. One is that 'in Caesar's day the gold bullion of the Sacred Treasury was stored in uniform bars of $3\frac{1}{3}$ ounces (each good for 10 *aurei*, and worth 1,000 sesterces) while the silver bullion was stored in three pound bars, these also worth 1,000 sesterces each'.[42] To Frank 'this uniformity suggests . . . a custom of issuing standard amounts'. Even if the data concerning the storage of bullion are correct, this is an exceedingly tenuous thread of reasoning, especially as hundreds of three-pound bars would be needed for even the smallest issue of *denarii*. It is likelier that the metal was stored in bars of uniform weight merely for convenience of inventory.

The other indication is to be discerned, according to Frank, in the phenomenon that 'in years of very heavy expenses (e.g. in 90–87 and 83–80 B.C.) the coin types are very numerous', whereas 'from peaceful years the number of coins represented is relatively few and the various types are correspondingly few'.[43] Now, in the earlier years of the first century B.C., if an unusually large amount of money was being drawn out of the *aerarium* in a particular year to meet heavy military expenditure, it does seem to have happened that those who were in charge of the mint in that year were able to bring it about that much of the money was issued in the form of newly struck *denarii*, bearing types advertising their families or their ideals, whereas the use of so large a number of new types would have obviously been far less justifiable when a much smaller amount of money was being issued. And we do seem to encounter a similar phenomenon in the first twenty years after Actium, which were again years during which there was occasion to issue large quantities of coin. Augustus, that is to say, seems to have been following republican precedent in encouraging or permitting the creation of a large repertoire of types during these years. However, even in respect of the nineties and eighties the evidence of finds does not at all support Frank's thesis that there was 'some uniformity' in the size of individual issues,[44] and in relation to issues made under Augustus and Tiberius his thesis can easily be shown to be even more remote from the facts.

I will take just three examples. First, an issue made in 28–26 B.C. of silver *quinarii* which bear on the obverse Octavian's portrait and the legend CAESAR IMP VII and on the reverse a *cista mystica* surmounted by a figure of Victory, with the legend ASIA RECEPTA.[45] The incidence of these *quinarii* in chance finds, excavation finds and hoards[46] suggests that this issue was for some reason far larger than any single issue of *denarii* made in the years between Actium and 12 B.C.[47] Perhaps the production of this large issue of *quinarii* was an expedient to remedy in some degree the shortage of small change, as there were no official issues of *aes* in the early twenties.[48]

The second example is more familiar and more striking. One of what Frank called the 'very scarce' Augustan types dating from the years after 11 B.C., the reverse type representing his grandsons Gaius and Lucius,[49] is found on a vastly greater number of surviving *denarii* than any of the 'abundant' types belonging to the earlier part of Augustus' reign.[50]

The third example is the most remarkable of all. During Tiberius' reign only three reverse types were used for *aurei* and *denarii*. All three of these reverse types were accompanied by one unchanging obverse type, a laureate head of Tiberius, with one unchanging obverse legend, TI. CAESAR DIVI AVG. F. AVGVSTVS. But one of the reverse types, portraying a draped female figure, evidently a goddess, seated on a chair,[51] turns up incomparably more often than the other two, as many numismatists have pointed out;[52] and incomparably more often than any of Augustus' reverse types, apart from the type representing Gaius and Lucius. It is generally believed that the issue of *denarii* and *aurei* bearing this reverse type must have extended over the greater part of Tiberius' reign.[53]

These three examples will perhaps suffice to illustrate how seriously Frank was in error in supposing that each pair of types appeared on approximately as many gold or silver coins of a particular denomination as each other pair of types used for that denomination. Numismatists and collectors have of, course, been aware since the Renaissance that that was not the case, and it is strange that Frank fell into this error. However, in studies of Roman coinage written for the inexpert, it is often not made sufficiently clear how very greatly the size of issues under discussion appears to have differed, although this is of great importance, particularly when their political significance is in question.[54]

What Frank could have said is that, on an average, not more than $x$ coins can have been struck from each obverse die and not more than $y$ coins from each reverse die (and that not many fewer will have been struck, unless the issue was exceedingly small, involving only two or three reverse dies altogether). Thus sufficient patient study of dies can give us a more reliable idea of the relative size of issues than mere counting of surviving specimens, and can perhaps even enable us to determine approximately their absolute size.[55] C. H. V. Sutherland, for instance, has published calculations which suggest that the cistophoric issues of Augustus comprised altogether between two million and five million coins. Unfortunately no similarly detailed work has been done on other issues of this period, so there is nothing with which these figures can be compared.[56]

It has been suggested that, *faute de mieux*, one should count the published examples of issues.[57] It will be apparent that a few steps have been taken in this direction in the preparation of the present study, but it is not clear how reliable an indication of the relative size of issues one can obtain in this way. There are so many variables for which allowance has to be made; for instance: hoards are more common in certain times and places; silver was more willingly lost than gold; some coins are more likely than others to have been melted down; more gold, perhaps, than silver went into jewellery; finds have been more carefully recorded in region $A$, in which issue $x$ chiefly circulated, than in region $B$, the main area of circulation of issue $y$; and so on.[58] I have therefore made comparisons only between issues that seem likely, all things considered, to have had a similar survival rate.[59]

These comparisons suffice amply, I think, to demonstrate that we cannot accept it as a 'reasonable inference that during the orderly regime of Augustus the amount of coinage from year to year is probably quite fairly represented by the number of coin types now known'.[60] Evidently there was a contraction of the repertoire of types after about 12 B.C. and especially after 6 B.C. This is an interesting and surely significant phenomenon, but its significance must be political (or psychological) rather than economic, and need not be discussed here. What is important for our present purpose is that we can now see that the reduction after 12 B.C. in the number of issues of gold and silver coin has in itself no bearing on the *inopia rei nummariae* of A.D. 33. We have seen that Frank's attempt to draw from this reduction in the number of issues the conclusion that the government was hoarding more and spending less rested on misconceptions.

One misconception was that the Roman government could not spend on a large scale without producing a large amount of new currency, so that, if there was a decline in the production of coins, this would indicate a fall in government expenditure. We have seen that a fall in the rate of production of new currency could mean that the government was for one reason or another making more use of existing coins that had come into its possession instead of withdrawing and restriking them. We have seen that there was probably no financial advantage in withdrawing and restriking; rather a disadvantage. And if the government had so few political messages that it wished to convey on its gold and silver coins as it appears to have had in the later years of Augustus' reign, and under Tiberius, then there was no considerable political advantage. How little political advantage Tiberius could derive from maximising the circulation of his favourite reverse type is shown by the fact that numismatists cannot agree which goddess is represented, and whether an allusion to his mother Livia is also intended. (Pax and Iustitia have been the goddesses most strongly favoured, but the latest candidate is Concordia.)[61]

The other misconception was that there was 'some uniformity' in the size of issues: we have seen that this is wholly false. Indeed, the evidence of finds suggests that, although there were fewer issues from 10 B.C. onwards, the output under Augustus of new gold and silver coins, far from having 'dwindled to a miserable trickle', was perhaps larger, taking an annual average, than it had been before.[62] And the evidence of finds suggests that under Tiberius the average annual output of silver coins was not much smaller than it had been in the time of Augustus, and that the average annual output of gold coins was perhaps somewhat larger.[63]

Is there any other evidence to support Frank's view that 'Tiberius was probably to blame for a dangerous contraction of the currency'? There are some remarks by Suetonius. In his life of Augustus Suetonius tells us two things that may be relevant: firstly that Augustus made Tiberius heir to two-thirds of his estate (leaving one-third to Livia), and secondly that Augustus said in his lifetime that his heirs would not receive more than 150 million sesterces in all.[64] Then in his life of Gaius Suetonius says that the immense sums which Gaius spent in the first year of his reign included all of the 2,700 million sesterces of Tiberius: *totum illud Ti. Caesaris vicies ac septies milies sestertium.*[65] From these three scraps of information Frank drew the conclusion that Tiberius 'beginning with an inheritance of about 100,000,000 sesterces from Augustus, was able by frugality, if not stinginess, to leave his successor 2,700,000,000 sesterces'.[66] But we cannot really be sure that this is a correct picture of Tiberius' stewardship, even if we assume that all the figures are correct. In the last passage that I quoted, from the life of Gaius, Suetonius is clearly speaking of the whole amount that Gaius found that he had under his control when he succeeded Tiberius,[67] whereas in the two passages from the life of Augustus he is speaking of Augustus' personal fortune.[68] In the life of Augustus he goes on to say that Augustus left at his death a statement of the amount of money 'in the Treasury, in official purses and in outstanding revenues' (*in aerario et fiscis et vectigaliorum residuis*), but he does not say what that amount was. And that amount, or at least the part of it that was contained *in fiscis*, is the amount that we should have to combine with the amount of Augustus' personal estate in order to find out how much Tiberius added during the twenty-three years of his principate to what he had received from Augustus. (We have to add in the whole of Augustus' personal estate, since the portion of it left to Livia, one third, reverted to Tiberius after her death.) It might turn out that Tiberius added very little to what he had taken over. It might emerge that whereas Augustus had acquired a reputation for munificence because he had so much to spend, Tiberius acquired a reputation for stinginess because he had so much less, and was acutely conscious of having so much less. For one would imagine that the quantities of uncoined gold and silver that became available for minting under Tiberius without having to be paid for must have been smaller than in the time of Augustus: less must have been coming into the hands of the authorities as booty or by confiscation, less, also, into the hands of the Princeps, for instance by bequest.[69] If we set these considerations alongside the numismatic evidence, it seems to follow that although Tiberius will have been conscious of the need to be careful in his

expenditure, and will thus have gained his reputation for being stingy, he was, far
from hoarding gold and silver, spending as much as he could afford. The only
other way in which one could account for the volume of his coinage would be by
assuming that he was much more industrious than Augustus had been in melting
down and restriking old coins that came into his *fiscus* or into the *aerarium*; but, as
we have seen, this is not at all a plausible hypothesis. For one thing, such a policy
would have been wasteful (the proportion of coins coming in that appeared, on
one ground or another, unsuitable for reissue must have been much smaller by
now than it had been in Augustus' earlier years). Secondly, there was evidently
only one message that Tiberius was much interested in conveying to users of gold
and silver coin, if indeed he can be said to have been interested in conveying any
message at all through that medium.

It appears, then, that neither numismatic evidence nor the statements of
Suetonius entitled Frank to assert that hoarding by Tiberius was a cause of the
*inopia* of A.D. 33.[70] Tacitus, as we have seen, does not suggest that it was one of the
causes, although he would surely not have failed to say so if he had suspected
anything of the sort. A shortage might have arisen in Italy by this time if Tiberius
had been exporting money from Italy on a large scale to pay for bullion mined in
Spain to feed the mint at Lugdunum, for the money exported for this purpose
would not have been replaced, since the coins struck at Lugdunum were for the
most part put into circulation outside Italy. However, that is a possibility which
Frank does not appear to have envisaged.[71]

Reference to the possibility of a shortage arising in Italy in this way brings us back
to considering another of the major questions which Frank's article raised. Is there
any reason to suppose that in A.D. 33 there was in fact 'a contraction of currency . . .
far more serious than can be explained by Tacitus' reference to recent confiscations'[72] and to the calling in of loans?[73] In Frank's opinion the account of
Tacitus itself points in this direction: it is

reasonable as far as it goes, but it does not explain what induced the Senate and the
courts to revive Caesarian war measures half a century after they had come to be
generally ignored. Apparently the prevailing rates of interest had risen and land
values in Italy had been falling, and the land-holding aristocracy therefore decided
to raise land prices by creating an increased market for land by reviving Caesar's law.
If prices were falling and interest rates going up, the natural assumption would be
that there had been a contraction of currency, and one that was far more serious . . .[74]

In these sentences Frank seems to be putting forward one reason for his belief
that there had been a serious contraction of currency; such a contraction would
explain why the price of land was falling and interest rates on loans were going up.
But Tacitus does not say that the price of land was falling or that interest rates on
loans were going up. What led Frank to believe that they were? He presented no
evidence in support of either proposition. One can therefore only surmise that his
reason for supposing that there had been a rise in the rates of interest charged by
lenders was that there could not otherwise have been so many prosecutions. For
the normal rate of interest was well below 12 per cent,[75] which had been the legal
maximum,[76] and there is no reason to think that a lower maximum had since been
set. Determined investigators could no doubt ferret out information about loans
made at higher rates of interest[77] but if we are to believe Tacitus, it was not a
question of isolated cases: 'there was not one of the senators who was innocent of

such a charge' (*neque enim quisquam tali culpa vacuus*).[78] Is it credible that there had been such a steep rise in rates of interest that rates above the legal maximum were now being commonly charged? If we decline to believe this, it does not follow that we should think Tacitus guilty of gross exaggeration, for, as I have argued above, it is far from certain that the charging of an illegal rate of interest was the basis of any of the accusations to which Tacitus refers.[79]

What of Frank's other assertion, that land values had been falling? From the rest of what he says in the passage quoted above, it would appear that his chief reason for believing that they had been falling was that it would explain the determination of the Senate and the courts, regarded as the instruments of the landowning aristocracy, to enforce a law that promoted investment in land. There clearly must have been some reluctance to invest in Italian land, if failure to do so in sufficient measure was, as I have suggested, the offence, or at least one of the two offences, with which people were being charged. This must surely mean that they found the ownership of Italian land less profitable—or more troublesome without being significantly more profitable—than other forms of investment. That could be because the price had been pushed too high in the last decades B.C., when many greatly enriched persons had been putting some of their new wealth into land for safety, and had not fallen back substantially since then. In such circumstances those who had land would have been glad to keep it but people with fresh wealth to invest would not have been so willing to pay high prices, now that peace, favouring other profitable activities, seemed to be firmly established. One may add that it does not follow from what Tacitus says that failure to invest sufficiently in land, if that was the ground of the accusations, was a new phenomenon: if anything, the contrary is implied. No doubt there had always been a good many men of means who could have been prosecuted on this account, just as there had no doubt always been cases of the lending of money at exorbitant rates, when there was poor security. What is hard to believe is that no senator was guiltless: but that would be equally hard to believe in respect of loans at illegal rates.

However, Frank's notions about the enforcement of Caesar's law seem to rest on a misreading of Tacitus. According to Tacitus, what set events moving was not any initiative taken by the Senate or the courts but the onset of 'a great pack of prosecutors' (*magna vis accusatorum*). It was the *accusatores* who in the first place 'sought to revive Caesarian war measures'; and, if his account is right, neither Sempronius Gracchus, the praetor in charge of the relevant court, nor the Senate, to whom Tiberius referred the matter, welcomed the revival; quite the contrary; and the Senate's reaction was to seek the Princeps' pardon (*veniam a principe*) for their transgressions of the law. But the haste with which senators and others had meanwhile proceeded to call in transgressing loans caused a shortage of currency (*inopia rei nummariae*); and no doubt there was, at this stage, a collapse in land values, as debtors struggled to sell. It was in this context that the Senate decreed, as an emergency measure, that debtors need repay forthwith only two-thirds of loans that they might be called on to repay, and that lenders must invest two-thirds of the amounts that they had been lending in Italian land. Presumably it was hoped, as I have said, that in consequence better prices would be offered to those who were compelled to sell land in order to repay loans that had been called in; or that creditors would be glad to accept land at a decent price in part payment (which would come to the same thing).[80] What will have moved the Senate was, of course, not merely sympathy with the sufferers but distress at the diminution in value of their own land-holdings, especially among those of the richer senators who felt themselves to be primarily landowners and only incidentally money-lenders.[81] Perhaps it was also hoped that money would thus be put back swiftly into circulation.[82] But the decree did not have these effects: the dearth of money was not remedied, and debt-laden landowners were not helped, for the money-lenders (*faeneratores*), having called in the whole amount of their transgressing loans, simply sat on their money (if they got it)[83] and held off from buying land.[84] No doubt they were hoping for a fall in prices—rightly, as it turned out. Presumably the eighteen months' grace that Tiberius had recommended that they should be given to conform with the law *de modo credendi* was believed to cover also their rearrangement of their affairs to conform with the senatorial decree, which, according to Suetonius, Tiberius himself had proposed.[85] They proceeded to ensure the maximum benefit for themselves by doing without the period of grace where the calling in of loans was concerned while taking advantage of it in respect of investing in land.

There are, as I have said, points in Tacitus' story that are puzzling. This is partly because he is concerned not to explain the underlying economic significance of these happenings but to use them, like so many other episodes, as an illustration of the character and conduct of the senatorial order and of the relations between its members and Tiberius. But if we discriminate between what we can and what we cannot reasonably expect Tacitus to tell us, we are still left with one important thing that he does not explain, although we might have expected him to do so: he does not reveal the aims of the *accusatores*.

The reason for his silence can hardly be lack of information, unless we are to suppose that what Dio seems to tell us [86] on the subject is a post-Tacitean invention. Dio's account is so abbreviated that by itself it would be quite incomprehensible, but he appears to imply that the man behind the *accusatores* was Tiberius himself, inasmuch as it was he who 'revived the laws on loan-contracts which Caesar had enacted'. In so doing, he disregarded, according to Dio, the warnings of his *amicus* Cocceius Nerva, who foresaw that this would cause damage to credit and would be very unsettling.[87] It is surprising that Tacitus omits this story, if it was in circulation already in his time, for he could easily have told it in a manner damaging to Tiberius, so as to support the interpretation of Tiberius' character that he had adopted, especially as according to Dio it was this disregard of his advice that chiefly drove Nerva to suicide—an event which Tacitus describes in some detail,[88] to the credit of Nerva and the discredit of Tiberius. However, the silence of Tacitus is perhaps not a sufficient reason for rejecting Dio's assertion that Tiberius 'revived' the Caesarian law. Indeed, one is tempted to believe that he had tacitly if not explicitly incited the *accusatores*. For this would have been a characteristically Tiberian act: it was altogether right that senators, and others, who had lapsed from the best republican standards of conduct should be brought to order, regardless of uncomfortable consequences for *them*[89]—Nerva had perhaps emphasised the inconvenience that would be caused to members of the upper classes, and the damage to their credit, and probably Tiberius had not foreseen how serious the effects would be, for landowners of more modest means also. When these effects had become fully apparent, it was Tiberius who 'came to the rescue'—and proceeded to throw the blame on the luckless *accusatores*, if Dio is to be believed. It is interesting that Tacitus gives Tiberius due credit: 'thus confidence was restored'

(*sic refecta fides*); although he concludes his account of the episode with a characteristic comment on the futility of attempts to legislate against human appetites.[90]

The way in which Tiberius rendered help was, according to Dio, by giving the
*aerarium* a hundred million sesterces, to be used for interest-free loans for a period
of up to three years.[91] Tacitus, whose account is otherwise much more detailed,
does not state explicitly that Tiberius gave the money to the *aerarium*, but he
clearly means to imply that he did,[92] and Suetonius in his very brief allusion also
implies that Tiberius advanced the money.[93] This means that he must have had in
hand in his *fiscus* at least one hundred million sesterces not needed for current
expenditure. This would not be at all surprising, in relation to Frank's estimate
that the annual income and expenditure of the state was between four hundred
and five hundred millions. (Frank described this as income and expenditure of the
*aerarium*, and in law it probably was, but most of it will have arisen within the
sphere for which the Princeps was responsible, so that the largest amount of spare
cash would be likely to be found in his *fiscus*.)[94] The availability of such an amount
would not in itself be evidence that expenditure was falling so far short of income
that an excessive amount of currency was being accumulated by the Princeps or in
the *aerarium*, causing a public shortage.

According to Frank, 'Tiberius very soon after the crisis began the policy of
bringing gold and silver mines into the Fiscus'.[95] In his view this shows 'that
Tiberius realised the cause to be monetary stringency'.[96] That is building a great
deal on the one piece of evidence of such a policy that he adduces: 'a few months
later, when Sextus Marius, the rich mine-owner of Spain, was condemned to
death on a charge of treason, his mines were confiscated and assigned to the
imperial treasury'.[97] More substantial evidence can perhaps be found in Suetonius,
for in giving a list of 'robberies' (*rapinae*) perpetrated by Tiberius in his later years
he makes the statement that many communities and individuals were deprived of
'their rights with respect to mines and revenues' (*ius metallorum ac vectigalium*).[98]
But one is tempted to suspect that, so far as mines are concerned, the only basis
for Suetonius' generalisation may have been the one instance recorded by Tacitus.[99]
And even if there were other instances, his statement does not seem, on closer
examination, to provide any considerable support for Frank's interpretation of the
currency crisis.

It may be that the leasing or concession of confiscated mines would, in the long
run, bring the state larger revenues than the taxation of their previous owners.
But it is not easy to see how the bringing of mines under direct state control could
in the long run increase significantly the available supply of precious metals (unless
one supposes that the mines concerned had been exploited very inefficiently by
their private owners; but this is nowhere suggested). And it was only by somehow laying his hands on additional precious metal that Tiberius could expand the
supply of gold and silver coinage. The fact that he confiscated the mines of Marius,
and the possibility that he may have confiscated the mines of some other private
owners, are surely, then, of greater political and moral than economic significance. Admittedly, the agents of the *fiscus* could lay hands on whatever stocks of
refined metal the owners might have in hand, and this would have served as a
stopgap if Tiberius was in reality faced with 'the exhaustion of the bullion then
obtainable by the treasury', which is what, according to Frank, impelled him to
confiscate. But surely bullion was obtainable just as easily and simply without
confiscation. Why should it have been any more difficult in A.D. 33 than at any

other time to buy it from the owners of private mines and from the concessionaires of state mines ?[100]

One possible explanation would be that the state had no resources at all at its disposal at that juncture: no bullion, no currency. That was surely not what Frank meant to suggest. It would mean that the reserve which Tiberius left at his death must have been built up entirely during the last few years of his reign. The only other conceivable explanation would be that Tiberius was indeed sitting on a great mountain of currency but was so determined not to put any of it into circulation, either directly or by the purchase of gold and silver, that he chose to confiscate mines in order to obtain a trivial windfall of bullion to feed the mint. That is credible, considered by itself, but again it is not what Frank meant to suggest. More probably, the confiscation of Marius' mines was not closely connected in anyone's mind with the currency situation.

It remains to mention a further difficulty involved in Frank's view of the currency crisis. The help given by Tiberius 'apparently ended the crisis': those are Frank's words.[101] Now if the crisis had been caused, as he believed, by a diminution of governmental expenditure and if it was 'apparently ended' by an issue of governmental loans, which were a kind of expenditure, and if, as he seems to have supposed, the paying out of money by the government normally involved the minting of coins, we should on his view expect the numismatic evidence to indicate the production of a new issue, with a new type or types, precisely at this juncture— whether or not confiscated bullion played a part. But Frank was not able to point to any significant new issue of gold or silver coins that can be plausibly linked with this crisis or attributed to the last years of Tiberius' reign, and I have not seen any evidence or argument put forward since Frank wrote that would lead one to suppose that the bulk of the great Tiberian issue which I have mentioned should be attributed to the last years of his reign.

However, as matters stand at present, we cannot rule out the possibility that *denarii*, and *aurei*, were being struck in larger quantities during the last four years of Tiberius' reign than during the previous nineteen years. It is therefore possible that a considerable part of this great issue was produced, or put into circulation, precisely at the time at which the government was making loans to debtors in distress. Likewise some part of it may have been put into circulation in A.D. 37, on the occasion when Tiberius distributed a considerable sum of money in gifts to the owners of buildings in Rome that had been destroyed in a serious fire.[102] Clearly large quantities of gold and silver coins must have been handed out by government officials on each of those occasions. But on both occasions old coins could have been used. It is noteworthy that in any case no use was made of either of these splendid opportunities to advertise in some new way the concern of the Princeps, or to proclaim any of his merits or achievements. The neglect of these opportunities exemplifies the lack of interest in publicity, or the changed attitude to it, that was suggested above as the main reason for the relative paucity both of issues and of new types ever since 10 B.C.[103]

Having evidently found no evidence of an increase in monetary output during Tiberius' last years, Frank suggested that 'the heavier minting of gold and silver by Caligula and Claudius was made possible by Tiberius' expropriations of mines'.[104] Here again he appears to have been misled by the relative number of issues and to have failed to take into account their varying size. Unfortunately, evidence for the output of gold and silver coinage under Gaius and Claudius is even scarcer than for output under Tiberius, since there are even fewer relevant hoards. What might accurately reflect output under Claudius would be a number of hoards buried during the reign of Nero but before his currency reform, which reduced the weight of the *denarius*;[105] I know of only one. In later hoards Claudian and Gaian coins are even likelier to be misleadingly scarce or wholly absent than are coins of Augustus and Tiberius, simply because they would have been fresher and heavier, on average, at the time of the reform, and therefore would have been the most obvious candidates for the melting pot. Hoards including coins of Claudius but no later coins are of some use for our purpose, although even they will be misleading, since the latest reign covered by a hoard is as a general rule less well represented, other things being equal, than the previous reign.[106] The evidence of such hoards suggests strongly that even if Gaius began his reign with what Frank described as 'a large emission of new coins in all metals', average annual output both under Gaius and also, if due allowance is made for this distorting factor, under Claudius was smaller than under Tiberius.[107] Finds of coins of Augustus, Tiberius, Gaius and Claudius at Vindonissa, a Roman camp occupied from *c.* A.D. 17 onwards, point to the same conclusion.[108]

# CHAPTER II

# THE TRIUMPH
# OF THE
# *DENARIUS*

'GOLD AND SILVER WENT ABROAD increasingly to pay for imports.'[109] In mentioning this among the causes of the scarcity of money at Rome in A.D. 33, one of the phenomena that Tenney Frank may have had in mind was movement of money out of Italy into the provinces.[110] The growth of demand for Roman money outside Italy but within the Empire is a feature of this period which has attracted much less attention and investigation than it deserves. It was surely of great importance.[111] It had four main causes.

For one thing, the area under direct Roman rule, which had been expanding ever since the earliest days of Roman coinage, had expanded more rapidly than ever before in the fifty years following the first consulship of Julius Caesar; and within this area, whatever the reasons may be, what in fact happened was that the production of other precious-metal currencies sooner or later ceased. It is commonly assumed that production ceased because, as a rule, the Romans forbade it.[112] It seems to be supposed that, as successors to the Hellenistic monarchs, they adhered to the doctrine propounded in a work once mistakenly attributed to Aristotle, the *Oeconomica*, the author of which has been thought to imply that only the monarch has to concern himself with the issue of currency, a doctrine which seems to be implicit in a letter sent by the Syrian king Antiochus VII Sidetes to the Jewish prince Simon Maccabaeus, in which he says 'I permitted you also to make coins of your own as currency for your territory'.[113] But already at the time at which the passage in the *Oeconomica* is thought to have been written, 'whatever the theory, the fact was that there was a supplementary coinage from the cities'.[114] It has not been proved that the Romans took a stricter line. There is no evidence that the Roman authorities decreed, before or during the period that concerns us, that Roman coins only should be used for all transactions within the Roman state,[115] let alone that Roman coins only should be used for all transactions in states subject to Rome or allied with Rome.[116] On the contrary, not only the use but also the production of non-Roman silver coinage (to say nothing of base metal) appears to have continued in Spain and in Gallia Narbonensis after these lands came under Roman rule, and perhaps also in Gallia Comata (the Roman name for the whole of Gaul outside Narbonensis).[117] So, although the Romans could obviously have forbidden a subject community to strike silver coins, or indeed any coins, if they had wished, and could have deterred a community that was supposedly allied or free, if it lay within their sphere of control, one may doubt whether minting was forbidden, or explicitly discouraged, as a general rule or in many individual cases.[118] It seems not unlikely that most states in the east gave up minting silver voluntarily.[119] Their pride,[120] which had taken so many blows, was not strong enough to offset the expense, for whereas those Iberian and Gallic communities, for instance, that continued to mint silver, may have still had supplies of ore under their own control, there were few, if any, eastern cities that had silver resources of their own in the first century B.C.[121]

Besides, Roman undervaluation of precious-metal currencies that did not conform to the *denarius* system made it more costly for holders of such currencies to meet obligations expressed in Roman currency, in particular payments to tax-collectors and moneylenders.[122] Moreover, when the amount of an obligation was not merely expressed in Roman currency but had to be actually paid in Roman currency, the holder of foreign currency had to pay commission to a banker.[123] And there were other factors. One may apply, *mutatis mutandis*, the comments of M. I. Finley on the factors favouring Athenian currency in the fifth century B.C.: 'Tribute was paid her in her own coin . . . Her imperial agents and garrisons abroad, and her armies generally, were undoubtedly paid in Athenian coin, too. Such factors weakened other coinages within the empire, except for small coin for local use, and help explain why some of the subject-states closed their mints before (sometimes many years before) the coinage decree.'[124]

Even in Spain the extinction of native silver currency was complete by the time of Augustus. Hoard evidence shows that Roman silver had been circulating there in considerable quantities since the Second Punic War, but it had circulated along with local silver.[125] The minting of silver by Spanish communities probably ended with the suppression of the Sertorian revolt;[126] and after the middle of the first century B.C. local silver hardly occurs in hoards at all.

In Gaul, too, the production of local coinages in precious metal had nearly ceased by Augustus' time, though here the penetration of Roman money was more recent. The evidence suggests that before and even during the Caesarian campaigns Roman money hardly circulated at all among the natives of Gallia Comata.[127] There is only one recorded hoard containing Roman coins that is clearly pre-Caesarian,[128] while finds at Mont Beuvray (Bibracte), a Gallic settlement occupied until nearly the end of the first century B.C., included very few pre-Caesarian Roman coins, most of which might well have arrived during or after the Caesarian campaigns.[129] Even in Narbonensis Roman money does not appear to have circulated among the Gauls to any considerable extent before Caesar's time,[130] except perhaps on the coastal route to Spain.[131] A good many republican coins have been found at Vieille Toulouse, evidently an important trading centre in the first century B.C., to judge from finds of non-Roman coins, pottery, etc.[132] but here again there is no telling when they arrived.

It would seem, then, that if in 75 B.C. Roman businessmen were really playing as dominant a part in commercial transactions in Gaul as Cicero asserts,[133] the *nummi* that they were handling must have been mostly non-Roman, just as the absence of *denarii* from hoards of the period of Caesar's campaigns shows that the Romans must have used local silver in their dealings with the Gauls.[134] Production in most areas, apart from Aquitania, continued down into the time of Caesar both in Gallia Narbonensis and in Gallia Comata.[135] Minting of silver at Massalia may have ceased early in the first century,[136] and the traditional gold coins of the north and east and the *monnaies à la croix* of the south-west[137] were declining in quality during the first half of the century, partly, it is suggested, because of lasting damage done to the Gallic economy by the Cimbric invasions, but in the Rhône valley and in the region between Rhône, Loire, Seine and Rhine tribes that had friendly relations with Rome (especially, it seems, the Aedui, the Arverni, the Sequani and

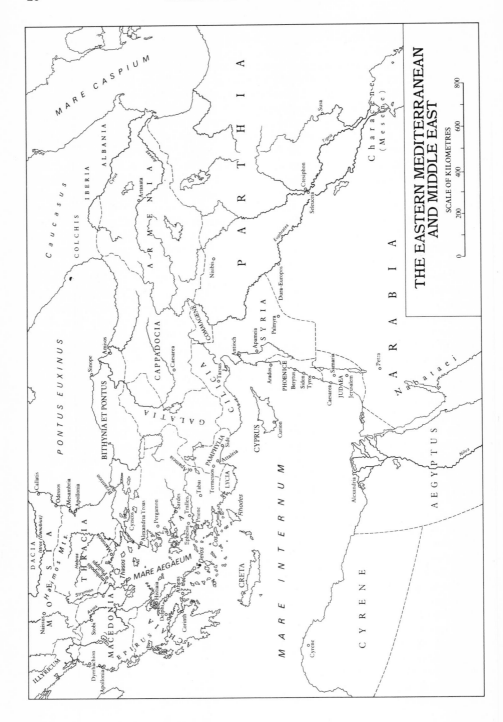

THE EASTERN MEDITERRANEAN
AND MIDDLE EAST

SCALE OF KILOMETRES

the Lingones) began to produce adaptations of the *denarius*, normally of about half its weight (though initially heavier in some cases), which are therefore sometimes described as *quinarii*.[138]

During the Caesarian war the production of coins of this kind spread over a larger area, but probably the ultimate effect of the war was to reduce greatly the number of silver and gold, or quasi-gold, coins in circulation: either they were buried during the war and not recovered or they passed into Roman hands, as booty or as tribute, and were melted down.[139] After the conquest coining of silver seems to have continued in some districts, but probably only for a few years, while from this time onwards there are numerous hoards containing, or consisting of, *denarii*, reflecting their increased circulation.[140] There is, however, still a large proportion of Gallic silver in three considerably later hoards.[141] But by the time of Tiberius the circulation of Gallic gold and silver had clearly ceased to be quantitatively significant.[142]

In central Europe, likewise, production of native coins of precious metal seems to have ceased by the time of Tiberius. It is difficult to assign dates to Celtic coins, or coins of Celtic character, struck in central Europe, for although some of the types are evidently derived from Greek or Roman coins, which provide a *terminus post quem*, few of the coins have been found in contexts that provide a certain *terminus ante quem* for their minting, or in hoards with Greek or Roman coins (which in any case provide only a *terminus post quem* for the hoard's deposition), and attempts to associate the beginning or the ending of production of an issue or a series with historical events are hazardous.[143] However, it seems to be generally agreed that, after minting of Gallic coins had ceased, Celtic coinage is not likely to have continued in other regions, for its social basis had by then disintegrated.[144]

Minting of precious metal had also come to an end almost everywhere in the Empire east of the Adriatic.[145] Several major coinages had continued (with interruptions in some cases) down into the first century B.C.: the drachmas of Apollonia in Illyria, Dyrrhachion and Rhodes, and the tetradrachms of Athens, Thasos, Byzantion (in the name of Lysimachos), the states of Asia Minor that struck *cistophori*, Side, the Seleucid kings of Syria, and the Phoenician states, Aradus, Sidon and Tyre. Then Mithridates VI of Pontus, needing a great deal of money for his enterprises, seems to have sponsored the production of tetradrachms, not only in the name of Lysimachos at Byzantion but also in the name of Alexander the Great at Odessos and Mesembria, and of gold staters, bearing his portrait, at Histria, Tomis, Callatis and Odessos, in addition to producing coins on a large scale in his own name.[146] But the frustration of his ambitions put an end to these issues, and most of the other major series came to an end before the middle of the century. At Apollonia and Dyrrhachion production of silver appears to have continued a little longer,[147] but it seems that only Aradus, Sidon and Tyre maintained their issues of silver down into the reign of Augustus, and by then only those of Tyre were of major importance.[148] Meanwhile, some coins that had been abundant in the second century and had continued to circulate for a time in the first century, such as the triobols of the Achaean League, widely used in Greece, and the tetrobols of Histiaia, found from Phoenicia to the Danube and the Rhone, must have gradually disappeared from circulation.

The second cause of a growth of demand for Roman currency was that trade with some lands that had until recently been outside the Empire and were now under Roman rule, in particular Egypt and Gallia Comata, grew considerably.[149]

Thirdly, the spread of town-based civilisation within the Empire meant that the demand for coined money, for local use also, gradually increased. To speak of a transition from a barter economy to a monetary economy would, however, be to exaggerate, and to oversimplify. There were on the one hand regions such as Gaul and Spain in which there had been some use of coined money for some of the purposes that money can serve since long before the time of Augustus, and in such regions what occurred was a gradually increasing use of coins, not only as a standard of value and a mode of storing wealth, but also as a means of exchange and a mode of payment, in local as well as external trade, for retail as well as wholesale transactions.[150] But there were other regions in which coins began to be used in trade merely to supplement and facilitate barter.[151]

Finally, the Roman authorities now needed to have much more money at their disposal to meet their own needs. Above all, there was a much larger standing army, the members of which were, moreover, paid at a much higher rate than before the Civil Wars. This meant that more money was needed for pay, and also to provide land or gratuities for those whose term of service had expired. But more was needed also for other purposes, such as donatives, *congiaria*, the payment of officials and the more extensive commissioning of public works.

These were probably the only needs that the authorities took into account in regulating the size of issues of gold and silver coin, for it would have been practically impossible to quantify the private needs that we have noted, even if anyone had thought of doing so (or to satisfy them directly, even if anyone had wanted to do so), but it would have been possible to calculate with some accuracy how much was required for *stipendium*, salaries, contracts with *publicani*, *frumentationes*, *congiaria* and suchlike expenditure. In fact we have no evidence from the Republic or the early Empire indicating explicitly the purposes for which coins were struck or the ways in which, once struck, they were put into circulation.

However, Mattingly has listed what appeared to him as the likely 'occasions of coinage';[152] above all, wars, but also the foundation of colonies, and, in the later Republic, 'the distributions of cheap corn to the populace or the celebration of games . . . Probably, if we could trace the occasions of all Republican issues, we should find that the vast majority fall under one or other of these headings.' There is perhaps some confusion here between the occasions chosen for new issues and the needs for new money which the authorities consciously tried to satisfy: in other words, between the political and the economic purposes of Roman coinage. It is essential to bear in mind that it served both purposes. A foundation, for example, provided, in itself, an 'occasion' in a rather different sense from that in which a war provided an 'occasion'. For a war, coins would be struck, normally, only in so far as there was a need; those that were available in the *aerarium*, or in the *fiscus* of the officer who was to conduct the war, could be used without being restruck. 'The foundation of colonies was certainly accompanied by special coinages; we are certain of the fact in the case of Narbo Martius': but here, although the foundation provided an *occasion* (and, in the case mentioned, probably the site for a new mint), yet even if 'it was only natural that the colony should be started in life with a supply of Roman coinage' (to enable the authorities to buy goods and services at the outset ?), this would surely not have constituted, in itself, a *need* so large that the *aerarium* could not cover it out of its existing resources. A distribution of cheap corn might likewise be an occasion to be celebrated; it might or might not involve also a need for fresh coin—to pay the corn merchants the difference between their price and what the authorities received from the purchasers. 'In the case of the shows, the burden fell on the magistrates, who received special permission from the Senate to commemorate their munificence by special coinage.' Presumably they had to provide the mint with the necessary metal: and presumably what they provided was very often money which they owned (or borrowed). On the other hand, major public works might be occasions for coinage in the sense in which wars were occasions, in the sense, that is to say, of giving rise to a need for new money; public works should then be added to Mattingly's list of occasions, to make it more or less complete for the republican period.

But it is possible that generals sometimes struck coins when there was no necessity for them to do so, simply as a means of self-advertisement: and may not some moneyers have struck coins at Rome for the same reason, if they were willing to meet the expense involved in turning old money into new?

Under the Principate there were the same material needs, but on a larger scale; and similar occasions; and for a time moneyers were perhaps still permitted to gratify, within limits, their desire for self-advertisement. There is no reason, that is to say, to suppose that there was any abrupt change in the purposes of Roman coinage. (It is in this light that one must interpret statements such as Sutherland's on the activity of the mint at Lugdunum between the closure of the mint at Rome and the death of Augustus: 'its purpose was to supply the whole Roman world with gold and silver coinage.'[153]) Most of the material needs are set forth by Statius (for whom these are already expenses that the emperor himself had to meet) in a passage that has received more attention than would have been given to it if there were not such a dearth of literary evidence: the army throughout the Empire, the populace of Rome (he is referring to distributions of imperial largesse, the *frumentationes* and *congiaria*), the temples, the waterways (or the fleets?), the roads, the emperor's residence, the statues, the mint.[154] The mint, of course, does not really belong in the same list as the others, for it had to be fed only in order that the other expenses could be met. To feed it, however, bullion had to be purchased.

In republican times, it was presumably the duty of the *quaestores* to report to the Senate, annually and in emergencies, what Roman and non-Roman money and what bullion was on hand in the *aerarium*, and what requirements could be foreseen, and it was then for the Senate to give whatever instructions seemed appropriate, including instructions for the purchase of bullion and instructions to the *tresviri a.a.a.f.f.*, the annually elected officers who were in charge of the mint, to strike so many coins of such and such denominations, using either coins that were supplied to them or new metal, as the case might be (though, as I have suggested, they may also have had freedom to restrike old coins unnecessarily at their own expense). Outside Italy, it was presumably the duty of the *quaestor* concerned to keep the *imperator* to whom he was attached similarly informed.

Under Augustus and Tiberius there need have been no formal change in these arrangements. Writing under Domitian, Statius regarded it as the duty of the secretary appointed by the emperor to keep his accounts, the *procurator a rationibus*, to supervise all the revenues and expenditures that he lists, and to control accordingly the operations of the mint, but one may doubt whether any one man yet had this responsibility fifty years earlier. Already Augustus, however, had his *procuratores* everywhere, operating no doubt with much greater efficiency than the *quaestores*; that was what made it possible for him to compile and present imperial accounts (*rationes imperii*).[155]

In considering heads of expenditure, we have already encountered the chief ways in which the authorities could put new money into the hands of users: which were also the only ways in which they could add to the volume of currency in circulation. This seems sometimes to be overlooked; it is an important point, especially as machinery did not exist to organise an expansion of credit. It is, however, conceivable that, if bankers reported a commercial demand for coins of a particular denomination which they could not satisfy, a supply of these might be produced and issued to the bankers in return for coins of other denominations.

Except in that very limited way, it was impossible, as I have said, for the authorities to satisfy the expanding private needs for currency that I have discussed. However, one of these private needs, the replacement of other silver currencies, would have been effected to some extent automatically, so to speak, in so far as non-Roman silver and gold coins that came into the hands of the authorities were melted down and restruck. Meanwhile the new money that was put forth to meet the need for more money for the army and for contractors would, of course, as it came into circulation, help to meet other needs also.[156] Indeed, if these other needs had not existed, the increase in government expenditure would have meant inflation. However 'good' the coinage and however great the confidence it commanded,[157] prices would have risen,[158] especially as the soldiers and the pensioners and the Roman proletarians who were having money handed out to them contributed little or nothing to the production of goods in return.

But whether within the reigns of Augustus and Tiberius the increased supply sufficed, accidentally, to meet all the increased needs, it is impossible to tell (although further research into the size of issues might ultimately narrow the range of uncertainty). In Mattingly's view, 'the existence of local imitations of Imperial coinage, particularly in the West under the early Empire, seems to point directly to a failure in supply'.[159] In fact, there do not appear to be many Augustan or Tiberian coins in precious metals that can confidently be classed as local imitations.[160] Plated coins, if they are not official, might be so described, but there was obviously a different incentive for producing them.

One expedient which Roman authorities began to use in the eastern Mediterranean already in the republican period for satisfying their own needs for currency, and one whereby they did consequently to some extent satisfy private needs, was by sponsoring the revival of several of the major coinages that had lapsed. During the second century B.C. and again in the first decades of the first century they promoted the production of tetradrachms in Macedon and on Thasos.[161] These, in particular the Thasian tetradrachms, became the main monetary instrument of trade between the Aegean and the peoples of Thrace and Dacia,[162] but they did not make much contribution to currency circulation within regions then under Rome's control. Subsequently, in the fifties of the first century B.C., Roman authorities went some way towards providing substitutes for two other major coinages that had finally petered out in the previous decades, cistophoric and Seleucid tetradrachms. They, and the issues instituted later at Caesarea in Cappadocia, are the coinages that Mattingly had in mind when he remarked that 'the provincial silver of the East, supposing it to have served a really useful end, should have been coined with far greater regularity than we find to be the case'.

The first sponsored cistophoric tetradrachms bore no indication of Roman overlordship apart from the governor's name; then, after large issues in the thirties advertising Mark Antony, *cistophori* were struck in considerable abundance in the name of his victorious rival between 28 and 18 B.C. It does appear strange at first sight that thereafter none were produced until the reign of Claudius. One explanation is that those struck under Augustus 'would have provided Roman Asia with a bulk of coinage sufficient to last a long time',[163] but we do not really know whether Rome's subjects found the supply adequate, for the fact that they continued to circulate down into the reign of Vespasian is obviously no proof. It may be that they were struck not 'for the province of Asia' nor 'for commercial purposes',[164] in the ordinary sense of these phrases, but simply to provide for Roman armies stationed in or near the province, and for officials who had to purchase supplies, now that the days of harsh requisitioning were over, coins that would appear familiar to the inhabitants and would therefore be readily acceptable. That they should thus 'reach the busier urban areas of Asia Minor'[165] was a natural consequence; if in consequence they served the 'really useful end' of facilitating trade in general, this was probably not their purpose.

The same may be said of the coins struck under Roman rule at Antioch in Syria. Here, probably from 57 B.C. onwards, coins were struck which looked like Seleucid tetradrachms, the chief currency of the region, and bore the name of a recent Seleucid monarch, Philippos Philadelphos, who had actually reigned from 97 B.C. until his death in 84–83 B.C. Production of these pseudo-Seleucid tetradrachms continued until 16 B.C. Then from 6 B.C. onwards there were issues of explicitly Roman tetradrachms, bearing the name and portrait of the emperor.[166]

Like the *cistophori*, these Syrian tetradrachms may well have been produced primarily to meet the needs of Roman forces, but indirectly they would have helped to sustain the monetary economy of the Levant. However, once they had thrown off their Seleucid disguise they do not seem to have been produced in large quantities before the time of Nero. Perhaps it soon became known that they were of poor quality, so that people preferred *denarii* or Tyrian tetradrachms if they could get them.

Finally, the didrachms and drachmas of Caesarea.[167] The drachmas were first struck in A.D. 32–34, 'probably in preparation for the campaign of L. Vitellius against the Parthians'.[168] Thereafter there were issues under Gaius and Claudius and, on a larger scale, under Nero, for Corbulo's campaign. Presumably someone working for Tiberius had the idea that the provision of coins of Greek denomination, but smaller than tetradrachms, would be welcome to Roman forces stationed in this region and to those furnishing supplies, and subsequent minting was no doubt geared to these needs. The existence of productive silver mines in the Taurus near Cybistra made the arrangement all the more natural.[169] Even so, these coins also were of poor quality, and it seems to have been only after Nero had reduced the weight of the *denarius* and the mint at Tyre had ceased to produce tetradrachms that the mint at Caesarea began to make a notable contribution to currency circulation.[170]

In sum, it does not seem likely that any of these pseudo-Greek coinages were intended to meet the same needs as had been met by the coinages that ceased, or that they did in fact suffice to do so. That the coins were given a familiar appearance was a concession to the conservatism of those who would be required to accept them.[171]

Excavation finds suggest that in the old Greek world the gradual extinction of Greek silver coinages resulted in a gradually increasing demand for *denarii*. Among silver coins of the period 133 B.C.–A.D. 69 found on Delos, outside hoards, twelve republican and four Augustan *denarii* have been reported, but only nine Greek silver coins, tetradrachms of Mithradates.[172] For the Athenian agora the corresponding figures are twelve republican, two Augustan and two Tiberian *denarii*, and (to 1936) two Athenian new-style tetradrachms;[173] for Corinth, five republican *denarii*, one of them plated, but no Greek silver of this period.[174] Similarly, the only silver coin of this period mentioned in reports from Thasos is one republican *denarius*. It is less surprising that excavations in the west at Elis, Corcyra and Dodona yielded, from this period, only a few republican *denarii* and *quinarii*,[175] and that at Phoinice ten republican *denarii* were found, as against two drachmas of Apollonia and one of Dyrrhachion.[176]

Such sites in western Asia Minor as have yielded any silver confirm the impression. At Troy the only silver coins of the late republican and early imperial periods that were found were one republican *denarius* and one of Tiberius.[177] Among the miserably few coins found at Larisa on the Hermos the only silver later than the fourth century B.C. was one of Antony's legionary *denarii*.[178] At Sardes also the presence of *denarii* is notable, considering the scarcity of silver.[179] Priene presents a similar picture: Regling remarked that 'der republikanische Silberdenar zeigt durch sein mehrfaches Auftreten an, wie er seit Bildung der Provinz Asia allmählich die Herrschaft in Edelmetallumlauf statt und neben dem Cistophoren antritt'.[180]

It must be admitted that many of these Roman coins from excavations in the Greek world could have arrived long after they were minted; in that case what the finds would indicate would be poverty in the Greek world during the period that interests us. But some hoards have been published also: and these show that although there was strong attachment to Athenian tetradrachms and in some cases to *cistophori* for so long as these continued to be available (indeed, in the many hoards from Attica and Delos—none of which extend beyond *c.* 80 B.C.—there are no *denarii* at all), *denarii* begin to appear between 150 and 80 B.C., and they are already the dominant silver coins in the majority of the not very numerous hoards of the old Greek world and Macedon with terminal dates between 80 and 30 B.C.[181]

Increasing reliance on *denarii* is reflected also in finds from lands outside the old Greek world that had used Greek coins to satisfy their needs, supplemented in some cases by coins of their own modelled on them. In the parts of Thrace and Moesia that lie within present-day Bulgaria—a country whence there is fortunately a steady flow of reports, some very brief, some detailed, of hoards and other finds—*denarii* do not yet figure in hoards that appear to have been closed before the middle of the first century B.C., but thereafter they rapidly become the dominant element. A few Thracian and Moesian silver hoards from the second half of the century still have a large local or Greek element, but on the other hand there are many consisting solely of republican *denarii*.[182] Evidence from the Levant is much scarcer, but the data available suggest that from the end of the century *denarii* were seeping in even there, partly taking the place of Seleucid silver.[183]

Such are the reasons for suspecting that during the century or so that preceded the principate of Tiberius demand for currency had been increasing within the Roman frontiers and that supplies had not been increasing in proportion, had even perhaps diminished.

Could pressure of demand in the provinces have brought about a shortage of currency in Italy? *Prima facie*, this seems quite likely. The city of Rome produced very little, materially speaking, in return for what it consumed. Moreover, 'Italy as a whole, with its numerous cities, was', to quote Rostovtzeff, 'a gigantic and rich market for the rest of the civilised world',[184] and, as A. H. M. Jones has said, 'the vast sums which came into the hands of senators and equites from the Empire were partly spent on luxury goods and slaves, and as these were mostly imported from abroad, much of the money returned to the provinces and other foreign countries'.[185]

But, granted that 'there is no trace of an attempt to secure a favourable balance of trade',[186] Rostovtzeff's opinion was that, although 'we have no statistics, what can be gathered about the industrial productivity of Italy shows that the largest part of the import was covered by a corresponding export' of goods, at least in the Julio-Claudian age: 'most of the ships which imported goods from the provinces sailed back with a valuable return cargo.'[187] For one thing, 'the Romanisation of the barbarous western provinces no doubt produced a limited and temporary demand for such Italian products as wine and olive oil and some Italian manufactured products':[188] these would have paid, for instance, for the iron of Noricum. 'It was only as a result of the spreading of production to the various provinces, taking place during the first century A.D., that the trade balance of Italy became seriously adverse.'[189] Moreover, although the provinces were no longer being so ruthlessly pillaged, revenues continued to flow in from property owned by Romans resident in Italy. Already under the Republic 'upper class Romans used their surplus wealth to acquire provincial lands', and under the Principate

the land hunger of the Roman aristocracy . . . increasingly extended to the provinces . . . Thus there began an increasing flow of rents from provincial estates to owners domiciled in Italy. These rents must have been considerable, a factor in the economy of the Empire comparable with the imperial revenues . . . If Pliny's income, about a million a year, be taken as an average [two generations, that is, after the time of Tiberius] the total rental drawn by six hundred senators would have been 150 million *denarii*, of which an increasing proportion was drawn from the provinces. We have no figures for the state revenues under the Principate, but at the end of the Republic they were under 100 millions.[190]

There were also the profits arising from trading, banking, moneylending and tax-collecting operations in the provinces financed by Italian investors.[191] In the east the activity of Italian businessmen seems to have been waning, but this was offset by expansion in the west.[192]

We must, of course, bear in mind that even if there was a favourable balance on private account, the government had to send money out of Italy to buy corn for free distribution and to pay for the administration, defence and equipment of those parts of the Empire that could not cover the cost out of their own revenues. In particular, Tiberius and his advisers may well have found that, after the spoils of conquest had been consumed, normal revenues from the western provinces did not suffice to cover the cost of the Spanish bullion that was needed for the mint at Lugdunum, on top of the cost of the administration and defence of these provinces.[193] But the resultant outflow of public money from Italy to the west should surely have been at least balanced by the flow of public money into Italy from profitable subject territories.[194] Here one thinks especially of Egypt, where, after the stock of booty had been exhausted, the surplus would have been increasing as efficient exploitation was resumed.[195]

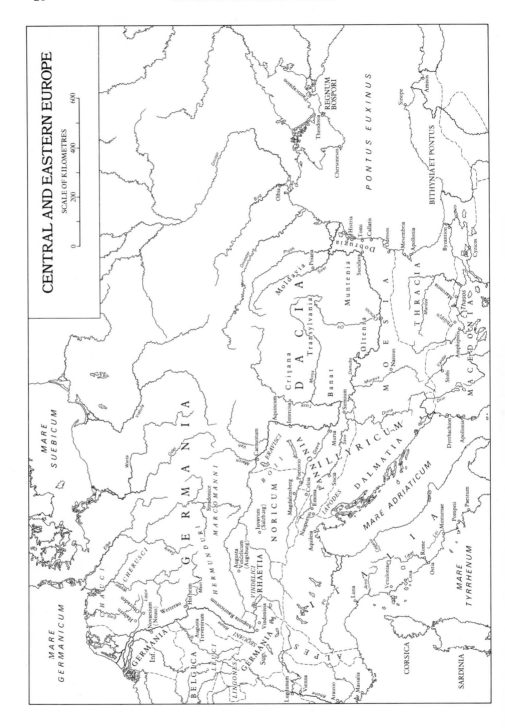

# CHAPTER III

# AD EXTERNAS
# GENTES

TIBERIUS WAS THE FIRST MAN to draw public attention to the export of currency from the Roman Empire to peoples outside it. According to Tacitus, he mentioned the phenomenon with distaste in a speech in the Senate in A.D. 22:[196]

What am I to tackle first, if I set about imposing restrictions and cutting things back to old-fashioned standards? The boundless sprawl of our country houses? Our swarming tribes of servants? The masses of silver and gold on our tables? Our marvellous displays of sculpture and paintings? The garments that make men and women indistinguishable, and the jewellery of our womenfolk, for which we make over our money to peoples outside our domains, or even to our enemies—to pay for stones?

It is evident from the context that Tiberius was speaking as a moralist and not as an economist; and it was certainly as a moralist that Tacitus thought it worth while to record this criticism of a phenomenon that by his time had no doubt grown more conspicuous.[197] For him it was one of the symptomatic evils of the imperial age.

Modern writers, however, have been more interested in the economic and in particular the monetary significance of this outflow of Roman currency. This is what Tenney Frank most probably had in mind when he referred to the sending of gold and silver abroad as a cause of the shortage of currency in Italy in A.D. 33. The implication of his reference to it is that much of this money did not return. Either it was retained for use as currency in non-Roman lands or it was treated as bullion and hoarded or melted down. He is not the only scholar to have maintained that this had already become a serious matter early in the first century A.D.[198] So it is seems desirable to examine the available evidence, in the hope of narrowing the limits of plausible hypothesis.

In the time of Augustus and Tiberius the flow of currency across the frontiers of the Empire must have been almost entirely along the channels of trade. Some Roman currency must have fallen into German hands when Roman armies, in particular Varus' legions, were defeated beyond the Rhine,[199] some, perhaps, into Arab hands with the débâcle of Gallus' enterprise;[200] some Romans captured in Germany or Arabia may have been ransomed (though not necessarily by means of a cash payment); but, so far as we know, no subsidies were paid to barbarians by Augustus or Tiberius,[201] there were hardly any instances of barbarians serving in Roman armies and returning afterwards to their homelands,[202] and although there were successful barbarian raids across the Rhine and the Danube, none of them, so far as we know, touched any places in which considerable quantities of coin would be found.[203] So the question is whether it seems likely that the outflow of gold and silver from the Empire along the channels of trade was large enough, in relation to the total amount in circulation, to have been among the causes of a shortage of currency in the Roman world, and in Italy in particular.

In the days of the Roman Republic there was a belt of tribal peoples in Europe, along the western and northern fringes of the urbanised and Hellenised Mediterranean world, including Iberians, Celts, Thracians and Dacians, who had for some time accepted coined money from the Mediterranean world in payment for goods and services. Indeed, already in the second century B.C. (and in south-western and south-eastern Europe probably earlier) all of these peoples were also making coins of their own for their own purposes.[204] But the Germanic tribes lay beyond this belt, beyond the Celts and the Dacians, and before the end of the first century B.C. they had not grown accustomed to receiving money.

There was some circulation of coins of Celtic type in the first century B.C. outside the area of fully developed late La Tène civilisation, in the centre and north-west of what was later Germania, in the region between upper Weser, Lippe, Main and Rhine, and also in the adjacent regions, westwards across the Rhine and eastwards in Thüringen, regions marked by a similar culture and varying degrees of La Tène influence, and west of the Rhine and in the Wetterau there was some minting of coins of Celtic type during this period. But although the population was probably not Celtic throughout this area, it does not follow that it was as yet wholly or even partially Germanic.[205]

Coins of Celtic type are also found in regions, further east and north, that would by common consent be regarded as already dominated by Germans in the first century B.C., but in insignificant numbers.[206] So are coins of the Roman Republic, but few of these in contexts which make it unlikely (and most in contexts which make it probable or certain) that they arrived in imperial times. A few, however, might have been brought by Celts;[207] Celtic traders visited German lands in the first century B.C. from Gaul[208] and probably also from the south, and brought some goods from the Mediterranean world.[209] It was the push of the Romans northwards and the migration of the Germans southwards and westwards that changed the situation, causing the collapse of Celtic civilisation and the cessation of Celtic coinage[210] and bringing Romans and Germans into direct contact.

At the time at which Tacitus wrote the *Germania*, the remoter German tribes, according to him, still relied on barter, but those who lived nearest to the Roman frontier were gladly accepting Roman coins of precious metal, and especially silver, to facilitate commercial transactions. He insists, however, that they did not in the least covet precious metal for its own sake; they thought no more of the gold and silver plate that had come into their possession than they did of earthenware.[211]

The assertion that the Germans did not in the least covet gold and silver must be treated with the same caution as any other statement in the *Germania* carrying an implicit or explicit moral for the Romans. In fact, the contents of graves of the early imperial epoch show that, although this was a time of relative poverty for the Germans, some of them did possess and did not despise objects of silver (and more rarely of gold). Evidently their possession and use constituted a status symbol.[212] This being the case, it may be that some of the *denarii* and *aurei* that reached Germany were melted down, for there is evidence for the manufacture of jewellery and silverware. However, none of these products can be confidently assigned to the Julio-Claudian period.[213]

But is there any reason to think that Roman coins were being used by Germans as money, in commercial transactions, already in the time of Augustus and Tiberius ? Finds in free Germany, and beyond, of Roman products that can be assigned to the first century B.C. and the early decades of the first century A.D. do not constitute evidence for the circulation of Roman coins, since they could have been obtained by pure barter or by gift, and might have passed in those ways through many hands, then and later.[214] However, evidence that coins were already in use in some parts of Germany early in the first century A.D. can perhaps be found in Tacitus' often quoted words that those Germans who used coins favoured old coins with which they had long been familiar (*serratos bigatosque*).[215]

*Denarii serrati*, with notched instead of smooth rims, had been struck by the Roman authorities on a number of occasions between *c.* 115 B.C. and *c.* 60 B.C., for reasons which we can only guess. What sort of *denarii* Tacitus had in mind in referring to *bigati* is less clear, for although a considerable proportion of the *denarii* struck between the middle of the second and the middle of the first century B.C. might be called *bigati* for the reason that their reverse types included a representation of a *biga*, a chariot or car drawn by two horses or other creatures, it is not apparent why Germans should have preferred these to the numerous *denarii* of the same epoch bearing other reverse types. But whatever coins Tacitus was intending to refer to, he must have supposed, and must have assumed that his audience would understand, that *bigati* were at least as antique as *serrati*.

His use of these archaic designations may be a sign that he was borrowing from an account of Germany composed long before his own time: which would mean that the use of Roman coins in trade went back quite a long way. However, it is possible that he employed this recherché terminology in order to report as vividly as possible what someone who had visited Germany in his own time had told him about the attitude of Germans to money; and in that case his statement need not imply that there was any considerable circulation of Roman money in Germany before, say, the reign of Claudius, for at that time, and down into the reign of Nero, republican *denarii* still formed a large proportion of the silver currency, and there were a good many *serrati* and *bigati* among them[216] If some of the Germans who lived beyond the Rhine became familiar with Roman silver during Claudius' reign, they may well have discovered quite quickly that many Caesarian and imperial *denarii* were of base metal, coated with silver. Their liking for *serrati* could reflect an innocent and mistaken belief that coins with notched edges must be of silver through and through; but in any case they had good reason for believing that both *serrati* and *bigati* were less likely to be of base metal than *denarii* of the Republic in its last decades and of the Julio-Claudian emperors.[217]

There is, however, some evidence from other writers, Cassius Dio and Velleius Paterculus, which may be thought to imply that some of the Germans living between the Rhine and the Weser had become accustomed to the use of coined money well before the end of Augustus' reign.

First, there is Dio's account of Varus' conduct when he became legate of the Rhine army in A.D. 6 or 7 and of the events leading up to it:

I shall now relate what had been happening in Keltiké during this period [Keltiké is Dio's name for the whole area, lying beyond the bounds of organised Roman provinces, that was occupied by German tribes]. The Romans were holding portions of it: not as a whole, but whatever parts of it happened to have been subdued: which is why no mention of this has entered the historical record [he seems to mean that the achievement had not arisen out of any momentous, memorable victories]. Soldiers of theirs were wintering there and people were being settled together in towns; the barbarians were changing over to Roman ways, they were holding regular markets and peaceful gatherings . . . Without realising it, they were changing. When Quinctilius Varus became governor of Germany [the Roman province so called, west of the Rhine] and, on the strength of holding that office, took charge of the affairs of the people of Keltiké as well, he was anxious to change them more completely; he treated them as if they were actually slaves to the Romans, and in particular tried to exact payments from them such as he would demand from subjects. This they would not tolerate. . . .

In what form would payments have been exacted ? The Greek word χρήματα which Dio uses can denote money, but more often it comprehends all forms of movable property, and it seems likely that if Varus really did make such demands they were for payments in kind, on the basis of some quite rudimentary assessment of means. However, the other steps towards provincialisation which Dio describes might well have involved initiation into the use of Roman money.[218]

One may hesitate to accept Dio's account of Varus' conduct, noting its similarity to Velleius' rhetorical portrayal of his activities, more appropriate to the Syria he knew than to Germany.[219] But there remains the description of Romanisation in progress before his arrival. This we can accept 'only if we postulate military occupation by units of native auxiliary forces in the vast area beyond the region where archaeological evidence attests the existence of Roman military establishments in the period before A.D. 9'.[220] It has recently been argued[221] that something of this kind can and should be postulated, and in particular that after the capitulation of the Cherusci to Tiberius in A.D. 4 some of them had been enrolled in regular auxiliary units of the Roman army under the command of Arminius, who, as Velleius says, in describing the events of A.D. 9, 'had been associated with us constantly in previous campaigning, had been granted Roman citizenship and had attained equestrian rank'.[222] If so, these Germans would have received pay in Roman money for several years: leaving most of it, probably, on deposit, against their retirement, like other soldiers, but surely drawing small amounts of *aes*, and perhaps occasionally a few *denarii*, to pay for comforts and trinkets.[223]

If a portion of the Germans did become habituated to the use of Roman money, some through being employed as auxiliaries, others through frequenting markets, if not through being taxed, their habituation was brief. However, the experiences of these years may have hastened their acceptance of Roman money as an instrument of trade with the Empire; even those who had detested it as a symbol of servitude might well have been willing to use it for that purpose once the overwhelming victory over Varus had appeased their resentment of the attempt that Rome had made to enslave them.

In considering the coin evidence itself, we must leave out of account a group of *denarii* and several groups of *aurei* found near what was probably the scene of Varus' defeat, and also, of course, coins found on or close to the sites of Roman camps or forts.[224] We must also exclude most, if not all, coins found beyond the Rhine and the Danube but within the Limes,[225] since there are few, if any, coins found in that region of which it can safely be said that they arrived before the Flavian occupation. The most extensive other evidence comes from a comparatively small area in the north-west of free Germany, north of the Lippe, in the Ems valley and the adjacent parts of modern Holland—a region to which the influence of Celtic civilisation, evident elsewhere in western Germany in the late La Tène period, did not extend and in which coins of Celtic type are not found.[226] Here eight hoards, comprising republican and Augustan and, in two cases, Tiberian *denarii*, but no later coins, have been found at places well away from any Roman site. Two other hoards with Augustan terminal dates have been found further east, just beyond the Weser, at Bingum and at Franzburg near Hanover.[227]

This might mean that some Roman currency was in commercial circulation in the north-west of free Germany by A.D. 33, whereas probably almost none had been in circulation a century earlier, before Caesar's conquest of Gaul. Some of it might have come overland from the Rhine, up the Lippe valley, where there is other evidence for the beginning of Roman trade with Germany, but some of it might have come up the Ems and Weser valleys from the sea, and might thus constitute evidence of the first steps, from the Gallic side, towards that 'large-scale traffic with Eastern Germany, Norway and Sweden . . . in the age of Claudius and Nero',[228] which proceeded by sea from the mouth of the Rhine as well as overland via Carnuntum. The absence from free Germany of finds of the later Julio-Claudian period, and the scarcity of hoards of the remainder of the first century and much of the second, might well be the result simply of greater peacefulness in these regions, after the disturbances in the time of Augustus and Tiberius.

On the other hand, all the Augustan and Tiberian hoards mentioned above were found close to routes followed by Roman military expeditions, in particular those of Tiberius in A.D. 4–5 and Germanicus in A.D. 15–16. So it may well be that they have no connection with trading activities.[229] It is perhaps worth adding that there is a concentration of isolated finds of Augustan coins, and Celtic coins, along a line from Hessen into Thüringen and thence down the Saale to Magdeburg, though the total number involved is small,[230] for here again one may note the coincidence with the route followed by a German army, that of Drusus in 9 B.C.[231]

Another possibility is that these finds do reflect activities of Roman traders, but at a considerably later date. According to Willers,[232] the Augustan *denarius* (*RIC* I Augustus 7) in the Niederlangen hoard was in such a poor state that the hoard could not have been buried before the middle of the first century A.D., and, since the coins in the Bingum hoard were mostly in poor condition, he suggested that this might be true of it and the Onna, Feins and Denekamp hoards also (he had no information about the state of the coins in these hoards). The absence of coins of Gaius and Claudius was, he thought, no bar, as their *denarii* are scarcer 'und kommen in unserem Norden fast gar nicht vor'. Subsequently he went further, placing the burial of all these five hoards late in the first century A.D. or early in the second,[233] and later he expressed the same view about the Franzburg hoard.[234] He saw in them proof of Roman trade with free Germany—at that period. It is certainly conceivable that Romans trading with Germany at that time used the oldest *denarii* they could get, in deference to known German wishes; in particular, the curious composition of the Niederlangen hoard, which so strikingly confirms Tacitus' statement, could have resulted from careful selection.

There are also the isolated finds, which include some Julio-Claudian *aes* coins,[235] but many such coins remained in circulation for a long time. So it may well be that none of the republican, Augustan and Tiberian coins which have been found in free Germany bear witness to the use of Roman money by Germans in the time of Tiberius; they may reflect military activity under Augustus and Tiberius, they may be relics of the attempt to make Germany between Rhine and Elbe into a province, or they may have arrived considerably later.

Since the material evidence is ambiguous, we are left with the implications of the literary evidence. This, as we have seen, suggests that already in the time of Augustus some of the Germans living between the Rhine and the Weser became accustomed to the use of Roman money. However, it also suggests that the resultant demand could have been of importance only during the dozen years or so of abortive provincialisation that preceded the Varian disaster. Under Tiberius only a quite insignificant quantity of Roman currency would have been involved, for it seems likely that, in so far as Germans beyond the Rhine were using coins in his time, they were using them simply to facilitate trade with the Roman Empire, rather than for exchanging goods with one another,[236] and there is no reason to assume that the goods which the Romans obtained from the Germans exceeded in value, in the eyes of those concerned, the goods which the Romans were glad to take from them.[237] Moreover, such transactions need not have involved the use of large amounts of money: there would probably still be an exchange of goods, but now sometimes accompanied by a cash adjustment.[238]

The area beyond the Danube frontier, to the north of Rhaetia, Noricum and Pannonia, had been predominantly Celtic in the first century B.C.—or, since 'we should be on our guard in attempting to make too sharp a distinction between Celts and Germans',[239] perhaps we should rather say that it lay within the sphere of late La Tène civilisation. Bohemia was indeed, alongside Gaul, the region in which this civilisation reached its fullest development,[240] and it is generally agreed that it is with the presence there of the Boii that we must associate the production of distinctive gold coins during the second century and the first half of the first century B.C. One variety was imitated by other Celtic or Celticised peoples over a wide area to the west and south, from the Moselle and the Black Forest to Croatia.[241] Here we have an example of the abundant evidence from this period for lively contact over long distances between areas that bear the impress of late La Tène civilisation, contact which probably included trade rather than a mere exchanging of gifts: but this evidence is provided by the finding of various artefacts far from their place of manufacture,[242] by stylistic similarities between artefacts produced in widely separated areas,[243] and, in the case of coinage, by similarities of type, as in the instance just mentioned,[244] rather than by considerable finds of coins far from the area in which they were minted.

To judge from finds, most varieties of Celtic coins circulated only, and all varieties circulated mainly, in a very limited area. In most hoards more than half the coins are of only one or two varieties. Moreover, in many Celtic series there are wide variations of weight among coins of the same variety: 'considering their inconstancy of weight . . ., it is not clear how they could have served as a measure of value.'[245] Some varieties of Celtic coinage have been found distributed over certain regions in sufficient quantities to suggest that they were used in trade within those regions, but it seems doubtful whether long-distance trade in Celtic Europe depended on money, or involved its use to any important extent.[246]

An ingenious hypothesis has recently been put forward, designed to reconcile these phenomena with the common belief that at all times and in all places the main object of producing coins is to facilitate trade. It has been suggested that traders who engaged in long-distance trade in the Celtic world gave the coins as pledges to those who placed goods in their hands, and then, after bartering these goods at their destination, returned and took back the coins, in exchange for goods that they had brought with them. It is suggested that the minting of these coins was in the hands of traders, not princes: and that that is why many of them bear no names.[247] Another suggestion of a similar nature is that the Celtic coinage of Bohemia and Moravia was in the hands of 'die Herren der Werkstätten' (who were, as such, it is said, virtually a nobility), and that it was only in the final Slovakian, or North Pannonian, phase that it came to be issued by 'die politischen Machthaber'.[248]

However, it would seem to be simpler, and more in accord with what we know of coinage in those parts of the Mediterranean world with which Celts, Thracians and Dacians came into contact, to suppose that the coins were at all times struck by princes, partly in pure emulation of Mediterranean monarchs, partly as a means of storing wealth in a form that was not perishable and could easily be hidden in time of trouble, partly to provide a convenient 'official' medium for paying craftsmen, traders and others for relatively small consignments of goods, or for services, and for receiving in return dues that were owing to them. (It might be added that most Greek issues also circulated in a very limited area, having been produced, probably, for similar reasons.) Even if the weight of some varieties was so variable that weighing was necessary, these 'official' pieces would still be more safe and convenient than bullion, or barter, for such transactions. The reason why many of the coins bear no names is that the Celts were much more attached to images than to words.

Anyhow, whatever had been the role of coins in Bohemia, Moravia, Slovakia and the adjacent regions during the La Tène period, the defeat of the Boii by the Dacians between 60 and 50 B.C., the pressure of migrating German tribes, and the breaking of links between Gaul and regions to the east, as the Rhine was transformed into a barrier and Gaul was drawn more fully into the Roman sphere, together brought about the collapse of La Tène civilisation, and thereafter economic life seems to have sunk to a more primitive level, the change being, of course, most marked in Bohemia.[249]

Meanwhile, Roman rule reached the Danube a generation later than it had reached the Rhine, and economic development within the frontier, in an area that had moreover been less highly civilised (except in south-eastern Noricum) than Gaul, or Bohemia, was correspondingly backward. At the same time the Danube too became to some extent a barrier.[250] Consequently there was probably less trading activity across and along the middle and upper reaches of the Danube in the time of Augustus and Tiberius than there had been in the late La Tène period, so that probably even less Roman money than before was being taken for use beyond the frontier in this part of the world.[251] Even within the frontier there was seemingly not much use of money in the northern parts of Rhaetia and Noricum in the time of Augustus and Tiberius, except where the army was concerned.[252] Probably the farthest point that was reached in the time of Augustus and Tiberius by considerable quantities of Roman coinage flowing northwards from Italy for the purposes of trade was the Noric *oppidum* on the Magdalensberg, reached via Aquileia.[253] That was not a new traffic, but the Roman occupation of Noricum probably led to an increase. Moreover, this is an area in which Roman coinage, including *aes*, was needed and used in increasing quantities from the time of

Augustus onwards, to replace the native Celtic-type silver coins, tetradrachms, worth about two and a half *denarii*, and minims, worth about one-sixth of a *denarius*, which had been produced since about 70 B.C., and had circulated mainly in south-eastern Noricum and southern Pannonia, as production of these evidently ceased, for one reason or another, in the time of Augustus.[254]

There was also, of course, the long-established amber route running eastwards from Aquileia to the Danube at Carnuntum and then up the March,[255] and at this time toilet articles of amber were being manufactured in Aquileia, for distribution in the Empire, probably in larger quantities than ever (Rostovtzeff classed them among articles of everyday use, as distinct from luxury articles).[256] But before the reign of Nero the Romans themselves evidently knew nothing of the route beyond the Danube,[257] and there is no reason to think that the traffic across Germany involved as yet any use of money: barter may well have brought amber all the way to Aquileia, or at least as far as Nauportus or Celeia.[258] The fact that Celeia was a *municipium* already in the time of Claudius[259] would suggest that there had been a *conventus* of Roman citizens there as early as the reign of Augustus. The earliest published hoards from sites near to this route that include Roman coins, which might reflect their use in trade along this route, have terminal dates between 31 B.C. and 2 B.C.; but they could equally well reflect Roman military activities.[260] Tacitus tells us that in A.D. 19 there were Roman *negotiatores* resident among the Marcomanni, where 'eagerness to make their money grow' had brought them.[261] This is quite in keeping with the archaeological evidence.[262] Probably, however, they made their profits mainly 'by the exchange of goods',[263] selling at a high price in the *canabae* at Carnuntum, or further inside the Empire, goods that they had received from the leading men of the Marcomanni in exchange for wares that they had obtained at a lower price on a previous visit to the frontier; for in Bohemia, the region where the Marcomanni had gained the ascendancy, in place of the Boii, and in the adjacent regions, very few finds of Augustan or Tiberian coins have been recorded, to set alongside the few republican finds.[264]

Coins of the Flavians are more numerous in Bohemia, coins of the second century A.D. much more numerous. The rate of increase is similar to that in finds of single coins at Carnuntum[265] but although it is tempting to associate the few Augustan and Tiberian coins that have been found at Carnuntum with the known presence of a legion almost throughout Tiberius' reign, they and the few found in Bohemia might equally well have arrived much later. Only hoards with pre-Claudian terminal dates can be regarded as reliable evidence for the travel of Roman coins across the Danube into Bohemia before Claudius' time, and the only such hoards to have been recorded consist entirely of republican *denarii*.[266] For Moravia, the area in which the Quadi were living, through which ran the route from the Danube to the Oder, the data are similar.[267] So are those for Slovakia, through which ran the route from the Danube to the Vistula.[268] Most of the Slovakian finds were made either very close to the Danube or on the route northwards up the Váh valley towards the Vistula.

In Poland only a few isolated finds of republican and early imperial coins had been recorded, from the Carpathian foothills and the Vistula, Oder and Warta valleys,[269] until in 1968, at Połaniec in the Vistula valley, some hundred miles east of Krakow, a pot hoard of 148 *denarii* was found (of which all but one were recovered) extending down to Augustus' issue in honour of Gaius and Lucius, the richest hoard yet found in any of the parts of Europe that were never included in the Empire.[270] But although Połaniec lies on the amber route, it may well be that 'the appearance of these coins should be ascribed not to trade but to migration processes and the shifting of their owner onto Polish territory, maybe in connection with events taking place in Pannonia or in the Marcomannic state, or in connection with the wars waged by the Romans against the Germans.'[271]

Except at Stradonice, Roman coins do not seem to have been found in close association with Celtic coins anywhere in the middle trans-Danubian area that we have been considering.

However, the pre-Caesarian hoards from Bohemia mentioned above show that Roman coins were reaching this region in the Celtic epoch, as may the fact that all the datable single republican coins from Bohemia are also of the eighties B.C. or earlier, with the exception of one *denarius* of Julius Caesar.[272] But it seems not unlikely, and it is consistent with the find-evidence to suppose, that there was less use of money in this region between the collapse of Celtic power, c. 60 B.C., and the Flavian epoch than there had been before. It was suggested above that traders visiting the Marcomanni in the time of Augustus and Tiberius concentrated on purveying luxuries to the aristocracy by barter. Money is far more likely to have been used where trade had become intensive enough to include goods of comparatively small value in proportion to their bulk, such as pottery; and finds of pottery indicate that, as one would expect, trade of this kind did later become a link between the Empire and the regions just across the frontier from Carnuntum, Moravia and Slovakia. The finding of coins close to the Danube in Slovakia suggests that such trade may have been just beginning in the first half of the first century A.D., but the scantiness of the finds shows that it was not yet important.

Pannonia was another of the main areas of production and circulation of Celtic coins during the first half of the first century B.C.,[273] but production there of such coins seems to have ceased (except perhaps in the upper Save valley, which lay within the Noric currency sphere) soon after the collapse of the power of the Boii.[274] No Celtic coins, whether of Boic or of Noric or of East Celtic kinds, are present in any of the hoards from Pannonia which contain Roman coins.

The two earliest Pannonian hoards containing Roman coins have terminal dates in the forties of the first century B.C.; the next four terminate with coins of Augustus, Tiberius or Gaius. These six hoards were all found in the far north-east, in the region of Budapest. In this region it appears that coins of a new kind were being produced for a short time during the first century B.C., for coins modelled on *denarii* occur in one of the two earliest hoards and in two of the others; they occur also in a hoard found to the north of this region, across the Danube, and there have been isolated finds.[275] Many of them bear legends which have been convincingly interpreted as showing that they were produced by the Eravisci, an Illyrio-Celtic tribe which had been pushed by the Boii into the region between Lake Balaton and Budapest.[276]

In the light of this evidence it has been suggested that Roman money made its appearance in this region as a result of Octavian's Illyrian campaign of 35–33 B.C., which, it is said, opened up communications with Aquileia through the land of the Iapodes. A demand for money was thus created, but the Romans, after mastering the region, failed, to judge from the evidence of finds, to satisfy this demand until the Flavian period.[277] But this view seems to rest on an overvaluation of the results of Octavian's campaign.[278] Moreover, does the production of local imitations point unmistakably to an unsatisfied demand, that is to say, does it show that a ruler, or a body of traders, having learnt the advantages of the use of coins for making and receiving payments in certain circumstances, found that they did not have at their disposal as many as they wanted ? That is indeed the accepted explanation of some of the imitations that have been made of widely circulating coins, for instance imitations, with Aramaic inscriptions, of Athenian tetradrachms in the Persian Empire in the fourth century B.C.[279] But one can imagine at least two other motives: first, the desire to use to the greatest advantage a supply of silver or gold (one may think of the coins produced by obscure tribes in silver-producing regions on the borders of Macedon and Thrace late in the sixth century B.C. and early in the fifth, many of which went to satisfy the demand for 'guaranteed' silver in Egypt[280]); second, the desire of a ruler or a tribe for self-assertion. It would be natural to take as model, for weight-standard and general aspect, a coin with which people would be familiar.

It is possible, then, that the Eravisci produced these coins, not after Octavian's Illyrian campaign, but already in the fifties, during the last period of power of the Boii, which was perhaps also a good time for the Eravisci.[281] (In Dacia, as we shall see, the production of imitations of *denarii* most probably began even earlier.) But the evidence from Pannonia, taken as a whole, does not suggest that, after the upheavals during the reign of Augustus, there was much demand for Roman money north of the Save valley in the time of Tiberius, except to meet the army's needs.[282]

The one route in Pannonia along which there was probably some regular flow of money before the middle of the first century A.D. in the service of civilian trade is the route from Nauportus down the Save valley, via Siscia, to Sirmium, especially after the campaigns of Agrippa and Tiberius had extended Roman control to the whole of this region. Thereafter this route rapidly became one of the most important in the Empire, providing by far the most convenient communication between Italy and the middle and lower Danube.[283]

Previously, Greek and Roman coins seem hardly to have found their way into the region between Noricum and Sirmium. In the first century B.C., if not before, there had been some circulation of Celtic coins, of the Noric sort in Slovenia and Croatia, and of the East Celtic sort in Serbia, but trade had probably been conducted mainly by barter.[284]

Meanwhile, such trade as there was between Italy and the region around and beyond Sirmium before the opening up of the route through Nauportus, and such money as was used in that trade, had probably for the most part followed one or another of several difficult mountainous routes from the Adriatic coast to the Drina, Save and Morava valleys. That is what is suggested by the distribution of numerous and abundant finds of coins of Apollonia and Dyrrhachion in Dalmatia, Bosnia, Hercegovina, Albania, Macedonia and Serbia.[285] If so, the trade must have been in goods of great value in proportion to their weight and bulk.[286]

Evidently it was also a trade in which, so far as money was used, *denarii* had been gradually taking the place of the coins of Apollonia and Dyrrhachion (although production of these seems to have continued until, if not beyond, the end of the republican epoch);[287] it was thus that the Eravisci were led to making imitations of *denarii*. Subsequently the opening of the easier route through Nauportus and down the Save will have led to an increase in trade between Italy and the lower Danube valley and thus to an increase in the amount of Roman money used in this trade.[288]

Beyond Sirmium it was relatively easy for travellers to make their way into the region, roughly coextensive with present-day Romania, lying to the north of the lower Danube. This region, which was occupied by two peoples often confused by the Greeks and Romans, the Celticised Dacians and the Thracian Getae, had an economic and monetary history rather different from that of Central Europe. Here too there had been local silver coinages, but these had derived their types from coins that had been making their way into the region, from the Black Sea coast and up the Danube or from the Aegean across the Balkans, since the fourth century, above all the silver tetradrachms of Philip II, but also those of Alexander and Philip III and the gold staters of Lysimachos.

Attempts to date either the beginning or the end of these derivative coinages (which are sometimes classed with East Celtic coinages but sometimes described as Geto-Dacian) are beset by difficulties and controversies which cannot be fully examined here. Some have held that few if any of them began to be produced before the first century B.C. and that minting of them continued at several places in Dacia through the reign of Burebista (c. 60–44 B.C.), the ruler who briefly united the Dacian tribes.[289] The other view is that quasi-Macedonian coins began to be produced in this region towards the middle of the third century and that minting of a variety of derivative types was carried on thereafter at a number of workshops, under the auspices of different tribal chiefs, until the tribes were united by Burebista.[290] It is suggested that he then put an end to these coinages: which would help to explain why none of the pseudo-Macedonian coins have been found in excavations of fortresses in the Hunedoara region associated with his rule. What, if anything, he put in their place is a question to which we shall return.

Another foreign coin of which numerous imitations have been found in Dacia is the spread-flan tetradrachm of Thasos.[291] These imitations date, seemingly, from the first half of the first century B.C. They clearly must have been produced, at least for the most part, in Thrace, where they are also found in large numbers.[292] However, the originals seem to have circulated in Dacia in larger numbers than the imitations.[293] Those of them that were struck in the second century B.C. are often found in association with the tetradrachms of the First Region of Macedonia, the other coinage that the Romans sponsored in that part of the world; those that were struck in the early years of the first century, and imitations of these, which seem to have been produced over a longer period, are frequently accompanied by republican *denarii*.[294]

The great majority of Dacian finds of these tetradrachms of Thasos and Macedonia Prima have occurred either in southern and central Muntenia, between the Danube and the Transylvanian Alps, or beyond this region, within Transylvania. Since very few have been found in Oltenia or in the Banat, the Strymon valley is not likely to have been a route along which they travelled northwards. More probably they reached the lower Danube either from the Black Sea or by way of the Hebros valley and the Shipka pass. The numerous finds both of originals and of imitations throughout Thrace, where they are by far the commonest coins of their time, suggest considerable use of this overland route.[295] It seems surprising that much use should have been made of a route across the Balkan range, but the routes from the Adriatic to Dacia, which were certainly in use, are even more difficult. Wine and oil, which were Thasos' chief exports, can hardly have been imported into Dacia, or grain exported thence, by the route through Thrace, but perhaps gold and slaves were the chief Dacian exports.[296]

It was mentioned above that tetradrachms of Thasos and imitations of these are often found in Dacia in association with *denarii*. So are drachmas of Apollonia and Dyrrhachion. Some of these mixed hoards contain no *denarii* struck after 70 B.C. (assuming for the moment that the *denarii* in question are genuine Roman coins), and the same is true of a number of hoards consisting wholly of *denarii*.[297] So *denarii* were almost certainly beginning to reach Dacia before 70 B.C. (What is puzzling is that they hardly ever occur in hoards with the local quasi-Macedonian coins mentioned above, for it is generally agreed that production of these—which, like *denarii*, are often found with imported Greek coins—continued well into the first century B.C.[298])

It has also been pointed out that hoards which extend down into the second half of the first century B.C. or beyond contain more *denarii* struck between 124 and 100 B.C., and far more struck between 99 and 75 (and especially between 94 and 85), than *denarii* struck between 74 and 50.[299] This too has been taken to show that Roman money was reaching Dacia in large quantities already by 100,[300] and that it was arriving in much greater abundance between 100 and 70 than during the next twenty-five years or so.[301] However, it seems likely that many of the *denarii* struck in the second century and in the nineties and eighties of the first century that have been found in Dacia in hoards with a considerably later closing date did not arrive until long after they were minted, rather than that they had been circulating, or reposing, in Dacia for many years before the hoards in which they occur were deposited. So it may be that the fluctuations in representation of issues of successive decades that have been noticed in Dacian hoards are at least partly a reflection of fluctuations in the volume of Roman monetary output during the second and first centuries B.C. and are therefore not a reliable indicator of fluctuations in the rate of arrival of *denarii* in Dacia.[302]

Some of the *denarii* found in Dacia probably came by the same routes, across Serbia and, in some cases, north-western Bulgaria, as the drachmas of Apollonia and Dyrrhachion which are also found in abundance in Dacia and are associated with *denarii* in many hoards.[303] But the distribution and composition of hoards containing *denarii* suggests that it was at the same time, or not long afterwards, that they began to arrive by the same routes as the tetradrachms of Thasos. It has however been suggested that the Mithridatic wars will have encouraged greater use of routes from the Adriatic.[304]

What can be asserted with confidence, given the great number of Dacian hoards containing republican but not imperial *denarii*, is that well before the time of Augustus *denarii* had taken over the rôle that Greek coins, and local coins derived from them, had previously played in the life of Dacia.[305] Moreover, the find evidence suggests *prima facie* that in republican times, and especially during the last pre-Caesarian decades, Roman silver was reaching Dacia in far larger quantities than any other region beyond the frontiers, and indeed than many regions within them: it suggests also that the volume of Roman money in circulation beyond the lower Danube was as large then as at any time before Trajan's conquest of Dacia, if not larger.

It is not easy to decide why foreign currency had reached a region like Dacia in such relatively large amounts, and had been so extensively imitated, before the time of Augustus. Most scholars have taken it as axiomatic that the drachms of Apollonia and Dyrrhachion, the Thasian tetradrachms and the Roman *denarii* that have been found in Dacia had, generally speaking, been brought to the region—

and to the other parts of barbarian Europe in which they occur—as instruments of trade, to be used in payment for goods, even if many of them were taken out of circulation for long periods, as a means of storing wealth.[306] The fact that copies and imitations were made lends weight to this explanation. However, one must not overlook the possibility that some part of the money from Mediterranean mints found in the parts of south-eastern Europe occupied by Celtic, Illyrian, Thracian or Dacian tribes was brought as booty, as tribute, as ransom, or as mercenary pay.[307] Celts are known to have obtained large sums from chiefs and states in south-eastern Europe in the third century B.C.,[308] and similarly Dromichaites, for instance, clearly did well out of Lysimachos for himself and his subjects, [309] while at an earlier date Sitalces had presumably paid in one way or another for the help of Getan cavalry.[310] To come nearer to the period with which we are chiefly concerned, there was the help given to Antony by the Getan chieftain Dicomes,[311] and there was Koson, otherwise unknown, whose name appears on silver and gold coins, bearing a type derived from a *denarius* of c. 55 B.C., that have been found in large numbers in southern Transylvania, with scattered examples elsewhere.[312]

Alternatively, or additionally, it could be suggested that the Dacians obtained some of their Greek coins and *denarii* in raids on their Thracian neighbours across the Danube, of which we have evidence, particularly for Burebista's time.[313] But if one were to rely too much on such an explanation, one would run into difficulties.[314] For one thing, it seems to presuppose that in Burebista's time such coins were in circulation in northern Thrace and eastern Illyria; if in these regions, why not in Dacia? For another thing, tetradrachms of Athens, for instance, are found in Thrace; why are there none among the numerous Greek coins that reached Dacia?[315]

It may therefore be accepted as likely that in so far as the silver coins that we have been considering were produced outside Dacia, many, even most, of them were brought to Dacia in the course of trade. Moreover, the fact that so many *denarii* and other coins have been preserved suggests that they were usually valued by the owners as money: probably not, generally speaking, in the sense of being kept constantly in circulation to facilitate a flow of trade, but in the sense that they were seen as a form of wealth that could be converted, without loss, into goods, or services, if or when need arose.[316] It does not at all follow that those which came from outside Dacia were brought, as Pârvan and Mitrea assumed, by citizens of the states that minted them. A safer hypothesis is that those who traded into Dacia used whatever money they found most readily available and readily acceptable. Among these traders there may have been many Romans, especially after the extension of Roman citizenship over the whole Italian peninsula in 90–89 B.C., and before that many Italians: but there is no explicit, or implicit but cogent, evidence of their presence.[317]

Even if Greek and Roman silver coins reached Dacia in payment for exports, and even if these were subsequently used to some extent by the Dacians to pay for imports from the Greco-Roman world, it would not follow that they were normally used also for trade within Dacia. Progress towards a monetary economy, to the point of the use of small change for small transactions, has been thought to be indicated by finds in recent years on several sites in the Danube valley. Finds made during excavations, and by chance, on the site of a Geto-Dacian *oppidum* at Zimnicea included a small number of base-metal coins of the fourth, third and second centuries,[318] and there have been chance finds on several other sites,[319] including a very little Roman *aes* of the first century A.D.[320] However, too much must not be made of these isolated finds, comprising so few coins produced over so lengthy a period of time. It is more significant that in the period with which we are concerned there seems to have been no regular local production of coins of small denominations,[321] such as were produced by the Celts in some parts of central and western Europe, and almost no import of Roman *aes* before the conquest.

It must be added that there is reason to suspect that from the outset some of the Greek and Roman silver money that reached Dacia was melted down to make jewelry for Dacian chiefs. A hoard found in 1953 at Stăncuta near Galati consisted of thirty-four *denarii*, to *c.* 60 B.C., fifty Thasian tetradrachms and three imitations; also two silver bars, together weighing 312 g. The bars were shown by chemical analysis to have been made from Roman and Thasian coins. Here, then, we seem to have the stock-in-trade of a workshop in which coins were melted down for the manufacture of silver objects. A silver bar and seventy republican *denarii*, together with a gold bracelet, are similarly the known contents of a dispersed hoard found in Transylvania.[322] However, the comparative rarity of finds of this character suggests that the amount of currency that was taken out of circulation in this way was relatively insignificant.

One indication that the Dacians were interested in coins as money is that otherwise they would not have troubled to produce coins of their own; it is unlikely that this was purely a gesture of self-assertion, and if part of their object was to market native silver as profitably as possible, that would imply that they recognised the advantages of coined money: but the quasi-Macedonian coins were in fact too variable in weight and composition to be suitable for export to the Mediterranean world, and furthermore there is no evidence of silver mining in Dacia before the Roman conquest.[323] During the first century B.C., as the supply of Greek coins dwindled, local production of coins derived from Greek models evidently ceased, sooner or later, but *denarii* began to be imitated instead.

Some Dacian imitations of *denarii* are fairly easy to recognise, by peculiarities of style and execution; they have been detected in a number of Dacian hoards of republican *denarii*. The great majority of them are modelled on *denarii* struck before 70 B.C.[324] Like those attributed to the Eravisci, they seem to have been, generally speaking, of good silver.[325] A die imitating, with seemingly intentional variations, the reverse die of a *denarius* of C. Marius Capito, a moneyer in *c.* 79 B.C. (*CRR*, 744), was found in 1876 in Transylvania, providing clear evidence of local manufacture of such imitations.[326] Later, three other such dies were found, two in Transylvania, one on the site of the Dacian fortress at Poiana in Moldavia, and recently ten dies for striking *denarii* were discovered, together with four faulty blank dies, on the site of another Dacian fortress, at Tilişca, near Sibiu, in Transylvania, these ten having been very closely copied from *denarii* struck between 150 B.C. and 70 B.C.[327]

To judge from the proportion of hoards that included some recognisable and recognised imitations, and the proportion of such imitations in these hoards, it would appear that these imitations were accepted as currency, whether inadvertently or with open eyes, by those who accumulated the hoards; but until recently it seemed reasonable to suppose that they constituted a relatively unimportant auxiliary to currency circulating within Dacia, from the time at which *denarii* became the chief currency until the Roman conquest. So far, however, we have been considering imitations that can be recognised without much difficulty. Recently it has begun to be suspected that recorded finds may include other imitations, or rather copies, so close that they have not been recognised. The Tilişca dies, being such faithful copies, gave rise to this suspicion.[328] Then in 1969 a hoard of 122 republican and Augustan *denarii*, with a terminal date in 8–6 B.C., which was discovered at Breaza in Transylvania, was found to include four pairs of precisely identical coins (*CRR*, 724, 784, 906, 1009) and one identical trio (*CRR*, 1185).[329] It is, of course, possible that these three pairs and this trio had in each case remained together since leaving the mint, but in view of the diversity of date, and place, of minting of the *denarii* in question, it is infinitely likelier that these coins had all been produced at one and the same time and place, in Dacia, from moulds copied from official *denarii*, not long before the hoard was deposited.

In the light of these discoveries we must now reckon with the possibility that many of the *denarii* found in Dacia that have been regarded as genuine are in fact copies. One reaction has been to suggest that it was under the auspices of Burebista that faithful copies of *denarii* were produced, to serve as a currency for all the Dacian tribes, after their union under his rule had put an end to minting by individual tribal chiefs of variously stylised imitations of foreign coins, including, in recent times, the *denarius*.[330] (To make this hypothesis cover the implications of the Breaza hoard, it has to be supposed that the policy of producing precise copies of *denarii* was maintained by others after the disintegration of his realm.) But is it really likely that a national leader who, if circumstances had been less hostile, might have earned a place in history, if not alongside Philip of Macedon, at least alongside some of Philip's notable predecessors, would have put a stop to coinages that had at least something of a distinctively national character, only to replace them with utterly slavish imitations of alien coins? One can accept that Burebista or his advisers might have been sufficiently interested in trade with the Roman world to think it advisable to ensure that coins struck under his auspices conformed with the Roman monetary system (although one could as readily believe that such a man was not at all interested in trade), but this could have been done by producing coins of the same standard and character.[331] It could indeed be argued that this was done, for it is not impossible chronologically to attribute to his reign most of the imitations of *denarii*. But is it not as likely that a reformer ,who decided that the Dacians ought to do without wine, a corrupting foreign invention, decided that they ought also to do without coined money?[332]

What the discovery of dies at Tilişca and of groups of identical coins at Breaza does clearly show is that by the time of Augustus there were some Dacian craftsmen who could and for some reason did cut dies with which they could strike faithful copies of *denarii*.[333] But it does not follow that a large proportion of the *denarii* that have been found in Dacia and that have hitherto been regarded as genuine are likely to be local copies. For if copies were produced on a considerable scale, one would expect the same types to occur frequently in hoards, especially within a certain area, a phenomenon which has not been observed among *denarii* found in Dacia. In particular, the types corresponding to the Tilişca dies do not seem to have turned up significantly more often among Dacian finds than elsewhere in the Roman world. It is true that not many coins could have been struck from the Tilişca dies, but if their maker had operated on a large scale, constantly striking *denarii*, one would not expect him to have kept choosing new types to copy as dies became unusable, and in fact two of the dies are of the same type. (The same can be said of coins cast in moulds.)

So it seems reasonable to go on believing that most of the *denarii* found in Dacia are genuine, unless and until the contrary is shown to be more probable, and that the copies represent, if not purely private enterprise, at least not a major national effort.

In any case, whatever the extent, the purpose and the circumstances of the production of close copies of *denarii*, Romans into whose hands they came would presumably have accepted them as genuine. So there may be almost as many of them lurking among supposedly genuine *denarii* found within the Roman world as among those found in Dacia. And if they were produced on a large scale, it follows that less Roman currency was drawn across the Danube frontier than finds have suggested.[334] Coins produced in Dacia might even have been making a modest contribution to currency circulation within the Empire.

A further possibility that we must bear in mind, in view of the discoveries that we have been discussing, is that dies or moulds copied or made from genuine *denarii* were used to produce plated coins. Here the incentive is obvious, for there would be a good chance of successful deception. One hoard, from Moldavia, shows that this was sometimes done. It comprised some twenty-five coins, fourteen of which came into official hands and have been examined. Eleven of these are plated, the other three are of base silver. Four of the plated coins are close copies of republican *denarii* (*CRR*, 770 and 774), six, and the three of base silver, are close copies of worn legionary *denarii* of Antony (*CRR*, 1225 and 1241), one is a copy of a *denarius* of Vespasian.[335] But the circumstances of the find suggest that all these copies were made at the same time, quite possibly after the Roman conquest of Dacia. There seems to be no evidence for the production of plated copies at an earlier date.

Our examination of the evidence from Dacia has so far disclosed no grounds for suspecting any additional demand for Roman money in the time of Augustus and Tiberius. It has indeed been argued that after the death of Augustus there was actually a diminution of intercourse between Dacia and the world south of the Danube, resulting in a contraction of the amount of Roman money employed in trade in this area. *Denarii* of the reigns of Tiberius, Gaius and Claudius are disproportionately rare, in relation to the lengths of their reigns, in those Dacian hoards of known or partially known composition in which the latest identified coin is post-Augustan but pre-conquest. It has therefore been suggested that during these three reigns there was an interruption of commercial contacts between Dacia and the Roman Empire and that this was the result of the Dacians' fear of their powerful neighbours and of Rome's creation of barriers between themselves and the Dacians, when fifty thousand Getae were settled south of the Danube in Moesia after the successful operations of Sextus Aelius Catus.[336]

If this were so, it would mean that there was a diminution in the demand for *denarii* in the time of Tiberius in a region in which they had been much used. However, there is another possible explanation of this phenomenon. The period between the death of Augustus and the accession of Domitian was a period of peace on the Dacian frontier, so far as we know, so it is only to be expected that fewer hoards should have been deposited, and left unrecovered, during this period, than during the troubled periods before and after; and this is what the Romanian evidence indicates.[337] Data relating to republican hoards from Dacia have been mentioned above.[338] Turning to hoards of imperial date,[339] we find that the latest *denarius* is of Augustus in twenty-four hoards (thirteen the contents of which are completely known, five the contents of which are largely known, and six the contents of which are partly known); these hoards, taken together, naturally comprise a good many Augustan coins (though, as is normal, republican coins predominate; and for the same reason it is quite possible that a few of these hoards were deposited under Tiberius, even though they are not known to have contained any of his coins). The number of hoards in which the latest known coin was struck between the death of Augustus and the accession of Vespasian is three (one completely known, to Gaius, one largely known, to Tiberius, and one partially known, to Gaius). Finally, the number of hoards in which the latest known coin was struck between A.D. 75 and the conquest is thirteen (four, four and five); it is not surprising that, in this region and elsewhere, hoards deposited during this period, well after Nero's reduction of the *denarius*, contain few imperial *denarii* struck before the reduction. One could cite numerous post-Neronian hoards from other parts of the Roman world which contained republican *denarii*, but none of Tiberius, Gaius or Claudius: some of them containing a number of Augustan *denarii*, some one or two of Nero, some none struck between Actium and the reign of Galba or Vitellius or Vespasian.[340]

Thus, hoard statistics do not entitle us to assert (or to deny) that trade across the Danube into Dacia declined under the Julio-Claudians, nor indeed do they enable us to draw any firm conclusions about fluctuations in the volume of Roman money reaching Dacia.

In the east, the age-old land route between the Mediterranean world and further Asia by way of the Euphrates and Tigris valleys had been practically abandoned in the late Hellenistic age, as a result of 'the hostility between the Parthians and Seleucids . . . combined with the anarchy prevailing on the Euphrates'.[341] But after the Romans had gained control of Syria, Palmyrene merchants organised a caravan route from Syria to the mouth of the Euphrates which avoided its upper reaches, where at the best traders had to pay heavy dues to the tribal chiefs through whose lands they passed,[342] and which may have also wholly avoided Parthian territory.[343] It was in this context that Palmyra became a flourishing trading town 'already under Augustus and Tiberius'.[344]

Did the development of this trade create a new demand for Roman currency at this time? We can not be certain, for there is no numismatic evidence from any point along this route; but such evidence as there is from other parts of Syria and from the regions further east gives no hint that it did. Thus, among the ninety coins, mostly *aes*, of dates ranging from 175 B.C. to A.D. 1377, found on the surface during excavations at Tell Rifa'at, a mound 35 km north of Aleppo, that is to say well within the province of Syria, the earliest Roman coins are an *as* of Nerva and a *denarius* of Trajan; the only earlier silver coin is a Seleucid tetradrachm, of Philip Philadelphos.[345]

The excavations at Dura-Europos, which constitute our chief source of numismatic evidence for the region adjacent to this frontier, tell more fully the same story. They yielded no pre-Neronian Roman silver (with the exception of three of Antony's ubiquitous legionary *denarii*, which persisted in circulation after other pre-Neronian *denarii* had disappeared). The earliest imperial silver coins were three *denarii* of Nero.[346]

Those who engaged in such trade as there was between Syria and Parthia in the first century B.C. and the first century A.D. presumably used Arsacid drachms and tetradrachms and Seleucid tetradrachms,[347] including the pseudo-Seleucid tetradrachms that were struck at Antioch, probably from 57 B.C. until at least 16 B.C., evidently with Roman consent, in the name of Philip Philadelphos.[348] Fifty of these Parthian coins and thirty-two of these pseudo-Seleucid coins were found at Dura, and many have been found elsewhere in the Parthian Empire.[349] However, 'the popularity of the imitations of Philip seems not to have extended to their immediate successors'[350]—the tetradrachms bearing the name and portrait of the Roman emperor which were struck at Antioch under Augustus from 6 B.C. onwards and in smaller quantities under Tiberius, Gaius and Claudius.[351] Whereas the absence of Julio-Claudian *denarii* from the finds at Dura may be explained by the fact that earlier imperial *denarii* that had not been lost before Nero's reign would have tended to disappear afterwards, this would not account for the absence of earlier imperial tetradrachms. Perhaps they were shunned for as long as possible, here as elsewhere, because of their poor quality.[352]

For official Roman *aes* there was probably even less demand beyond the eastern frontier under the Julio-Claudians. Dura has yielded the only finds of which I am aware: four *asses* and eleven *dupondii* of Augustus and two *asses* and twenty *dupondii* of Tiberius from official mints in the East.[353] For comparison, finds at Dura of *aes* struck by local authorities during these two reigns comprised seven *dupondii* and five *asses* of Antioch, one *as* of Berytus, two units, fifteen halves and nineteen quarters of Seleuceia on the Tigris, one unit of Apamea, four small *aes* coins of Judaea, and perhaps two or three other *aes* coins that cannot be closely dated. But this high proportion of official Roman *aes* is exceptional. Finds elsewhere, taken with the evidence from Dura, show that the main sources of supply of small change for this area at this period were the civic mints of Antioch and Seleuceia on the Tigris.[354]

Even at Antioch, where some, at least, of the coins belonging to official issues were produced, official coins were outnumbered in finds by the civic *aes* of Antioch.[355]

Interruption of the routes across the Euphrates evidently created greater interest in the first century B.C. in the more northerly routes into further Asia, by way of the Black Sea, particularly the route along the south of the Caucasus from the Black Sea to the Caspian, an interest which may have remained strong down into the Flavian period.[356] Quite abundant finds in the region traversed by the western part of this route, the region known to the Greeks as Colchis, now western Georgia, indicate that not merely the inhabitants of the Greek settlements on the coast but also the natives of the hinterland had become accustomed to the use of coined money long before the first century B.C., at least for transactions for which coins of precious metal were appropriate or for the storage of wealth.[357] In the fifth and fourth centuries B.C. silver coins, mostly quite small, coins commonly described by numismatists as hemidrachms, were produced locally in considerable quantities, but from the third century onwards the local mint or mints for some reason went over to producing imitations of gold staters struck in the name of Lysimachos, and later also of staters in the name of Alexander, these two being by then predominant among coins imported into Colchis. Production of these imitations continued for a long time, the types gradually becoming more distorted and the gold more heavily alloyed: Lysimachos staters were still being imitated in the first century B.C., while Alexander staters, said to be freshly minted, have been found in graves of the Antonine epoch.[358] Alexander staters also made their way eastwards, to the interior of Colchis and into Iberia and Albania, along the route to the Caspian, and into Armenia. Already before the time of Augustus, however, *denarii* had begun to arrive. Initially they may have come overland with Roman armies, the first of which had been led to this region by Pompey in 65 B.C., but gradually they took over the role of the Alexander staters, the largest share being taken, it would seem, by the Augustan issue honouring Gaius and Lucius, which was also imitated locally on a small scale.[359]

Here again, then, we have evidence of an expansion of the area in which Roman silver coins were used as currency, an expansion beginning before the time of Augustus and continuing through the first century A.D. (but with coins of Caesarea making a contribution alongside *denarii* in the latter part of the century).[360]

On the other hand, there is no good reason for supposing that in the time of Augustus and Tiberius Roman coins of precious metal were travelling along these routes eastwards, out of the Empire, in important quantities as articles of export, never to return, or that Greek coins were being drained away in this fashion.[361] That is to say, there is no evidence that the goods that were coming into the Roman world across the Caspian and the Euphrates at this period were of notably greater value than those that were going out.

Our only literary evidence for such an outflow in the Julio-Claudian period seems to relate solely to trade by the more southerly routes: trade with Arabia, and trade with India and East Africa either through Arabia or by sea from Egypt.

Before the time of Augustus, if Strabo is to be believed,[362] very few ships travelled from Egypt to India or to east Africa. Goods that came to Italy and the west from those regions reached the Mediterranean through Arabian hands (with the exception, of course, of those that came from India and other parts of Asia by the more northerly routes).[363] Under Augustus and Tiberius trade with Arabia naturally continued (most of it probably going as before by way of Petra),[364] and although the Arabians had coinages of their own,[365] this trade presumably involved by now some use of *denarii* and *aurei*.[366] No Roman coins of this period have in fact been found in Arabia, so far as is known, but, although there was a market in Arabia for a variety of goods from the Mediterranean world,[367] in exchange for the goods which the Arabians supplied, as producers or as middlemen, it is possible that some of the *denarii* and *aurei* which travelled there were melted down, whether for restriking or for other purposes.[368] According to Strabo gold and silver were among the products for which the Nabataeans were partly though not wholly dependent on imports,[369] and elsewhere he says that it was believed in the Roman world that the southern Arabians had accumulated large quantities of gold and silver by taking these in exchange for aromatics and precious stones.[370] He also quotes from Artemidoros a reference to the vast quantity of gold and silver articles that the Sabaeans and Gerrhaeans had amassed 'from trade' already by that time.[371] The Arabians, and the Parthians, may indeed have been the enemies whom Tiberius had in mind when he deplored the sending of Roman money 'to peoples outside our domains or even to our enemies'[372] in payment for precious stones, for there was no reason to describe the Indians as enemies. In the hinterland of the Red Sea coast Arabia possessed considerable resources of gold and smaller resources of silver, which are known to have been exploited later, in the eighth and ninth centuries,[373] but, apart from Strabo's statement that for gold and silver the Nabataeans were not wholly dependent on imports, there is no evidence that these were exploited in earlier times. It is possible, then, that from the time when the *denarius* and the *aureus* became the chief international currency of the Mediterranean, the Arabians may have been consumers and not mere users of Roman coins, having previously been consumers of Greek coins.

Meanwhile, the direct sea route from India to Egypt had, according to Strabo, begun to be busy in the time of Augustus,[374] and by the time of the elder Pliny imports to the Mediterranean world by this route had become, if we can believe what Pliny tells us, at least as valuable as imports from Arabia. He says that the sea route to India is worth describing, since fifty million sesterces are sent annually to India from the Empire in payment for goods,[375] and elsewhere he asserts that India *et Seres paeninsula illa* (Arabia) take at least one hundred million sesterces annually from the Empire.[376]

Modern scholarship has paid much more attention to this sea route than to the overland routes,[377] partly because of the impressive, and in some ways puzzling, finds of Roman coins in southern India which have been recorded on various occasions since the eighteenth century. Information about most of these finds is tantalisingly inadequate, and in some cases exceedingly sketchy, but some seventy (not including finds in Ceylon) have been recorded reliably enough to be taken into account.[378] None of these finds appears to have included any Roman coins other than *aurei* and *denarii*. Only five were made in the north, all in the neighbourhood of the north-west frontier; they comprise one isolated *denarius* of Tiberius and four small hoards, two of *denarii*, two of *aurei*, all with closing dates in the second century A.D.[379] They have been interpreted as relics of a transit trade linking the easy sea route from Egypt to India with the overland China road beyond, since 'the Kushana kingdom produced little that the luxury markets of the west desired'.[380]

To what extent *denarii* and *aurei* may have been drawn into the running of this trade up the Indus valley by the time of Tiberius we can only guess, but it is perhaps significant that neither of the hoards of *denarii* was lost before the reign of Hadrian, neither of those of *aurei* before the reign of Antoninus Pius. The region had gold and silver of its own.[381]

Of the thousands of Roman coins found in southern India, only six *denarii* are from the excavation of an ancient site, Chandravalli, in Mysore.[382] Nearly all the others were found in hoards, mostly in Madras, Mysore and the small states of the extreme south. Almost all the *denarii*, including half a dozen very large hoards, ranging in size from two hundred to 'thousands', would appear *prima facie* to have been deposited or lost in the Julio-Claudian period, since the latest recorded are of the early years of Nero's reign.[383] The great majority of those *denarii* which are identified in the records by more than a bare name belong either to Augustus' or to Tiberius' most prolific issue, with the latter far outnumbering the former.[384]

Almost all the *aurei*, on the other hand, including half a dozen hoards of from ten to five hundred coins, seem to have been lost from Nero's reign onwards,[385] although the same two issues of Augustus and Tiberius are again the most abundantly represented.[386] The majority of the *aurei* are known to have been defaced by a cut across the emperor's portrait;[387] there may well be other unrecorded instances of this.[388]

But the strangest feature of these strange finds in Southern India seems hitherto to have escaped comment: the almost total absence of pre-Augustan silver (and gold: but that is less remarkable) from hoards of imperial date. There is none even in large hoards that are seemingly of Augustan or Tiberian date: an unparalleled phenomenon.[389] One can see how strange it is if one compares the composition of some of the published hoards from Pompeii, or the 'foundation' hoard inserted by two business partners into the cellar walls of their premises on the Magdalensberg, in which, of thirty-three Roman silver coins, twenty-nine were republican, three of Augustus and one of Tiberius.[390]

Evidently some special factor must have influenced the composition of these Indian hoards. The natural conclusion to draw is that for some reason the Roman currency used in this trade was in some way manipulated. This seems all the likelier when one remembers that *denarii* and *aurei* probably did not circulate in Egypt, whence, according to the generally accepted view, those who brought these coins to India had come.[391] If they did not circulate, one may suppose that those who came to Egypt from other parts of the Roman Empire had to surrender on arrival their whole stock of *denarii* and *aurei* to bankers acting for the state, receiving local currency in return at a fixed rate of exchange.[392] It would follow that those leaving Egypt to trade elsewhere must have been allowed to obtain a supply of *denarii* and *aurei* from the bankers at more or less the same rate of exchange.[393] It might have been easy to organise a black market to circumvent this control: but for those going to India there would be no point in circumventing it if the bankers provided them with currency of satisfactory quality: and in fact 'the quality of the Roman silver in the hoards is almost uniformly good'.[394] This finding is one of the most valuable results of first hand study, for it should finally kill the legend that the very numerous *denarii* found in India commemorating Gaius and Lucius Caesar 'are nearly always plated'.[395] The absence of plated coins from Indian finds is not as remarkable as the absence of republican *denarii*, since most of the finds are hoards: but it is noteworthy, especially as plated examples of the two varieties of *denarius* that have been found in the greatest numbers in India are indeed common—everywhere else.

If the predominance in Indian finds of Augustan and Tiberian *denarii* in general, and of two issues of particular, may have been brought about artificially, one must observe exceptional caution in using them as evidence in any discussion of the circulation of Roman currency, or of the relative size of different issues, or of the extent to which coins of precious metal were flowing out of the Empire at any given period. But why should anyone have engineered this predominance? The obvious explanation is that these issues had somehow acquired in southern India a popularity similar to that of *serrati* and *bigati* in Germany or of certain Macedonian coins among the Celts, to mention only two parallels;[396] and it would be most likely that the *denarii* concerned gained this popularity in or soon after the time of the emperors that they portray.[397]

Consequently this peculiar characteristic of the finds in southern India constitutes no reason for abandoning the generally accepted view that they bear witness to the opening and the subsequent expansion of direct trade between the Roman Empire and India by the sea route: Strabo, as we have seen, mentions that this route had become important shortly before the time of his visit to Egypt.

Bearing in mind our initial *caveat*, we can perhaps discern in the numismatic evidence the signs of a change from almost exclusive use of *denarii* to almost exclusive use of *aurei*; a change which would appear to have occurred after this trade had been running for forty or fifty years.[398] Whether the Southern Indians came to dislike *denarii* or to prefer *aurei* for any positive reason, we can only guess. What is important for our present purpose is that the change must have been made possible, even if it was not wholly caused, by the increasing scale of transactions. Moreover, the *aurei* were habitually defaced; they were treated, that is to say, not as currency, but simply as a commodity, with no thought even that they might be used again to make purchases from visiting traders.[399] It is possible that the increase in the middle of the first century A.D. in the volume of imports into the Roman Empire from India to which this evidence seems to point resulted from the opening up of the direct sea route from Aden across the Indian Ocean to southern India, for some hold that it was not until about A.D. 40 that traders from Egypt had sufficient knowledge of the monsoon to voyage direct from the Red Sea to the Indus, and not until after 50 that they began to make direct voyages to the Malabar coast.[400] However, Sir Mortimer Wheeler, on the strength of his discoveries at Arikamedu, a trading station in the extreme south, in the area of the most abundant finds, holds that direct voyages must have begun before the end of Augustus' reign.[401] But, if they did, it still remains possible that imports into the Roman Empire from India in the time of Tiberius did not substantially exceed exports to India of goods, as distinct from coin.[402] Indeed, it becomes likelier. Traders going direct from Egypt to the Malabar coast would be able to take with them bulky wares, which Arabian middlemen might not have been interested in buying, but which the traders from Egypt might have found that they could sell, or barter, most advantageously to Indians unfamiliar with them. The author of the *Periplus Maris Erythraei* mentions as exports to the Malabar coast not only a great quantity of coin but also pottery, glass, wine, craftsmen, soldiers, masons, singing boys and girls[403]—and the finds at Arikamedu provide confirmation, so far as confirmation is possible.[404] This expansion of exports led to an increase in the supply available within the Roman Empire of hitherto rare luxuries; and this in turn led to an inordinate increase in demand, not balanced by an increase in the demand in India for the goods which the traders had been so successful in selling in moderate quantities.

That is what the coin evidence indicates: in Nero's time the demand in the Roman world for the products of southern India, or for products from further east that could be obtained there, was well in excess of the demand there for Mediterranean products other than gold. This will be the state of affairs described by the author of the *Periplus Maris Erythraei*.[405] He says that in the Punjab and at Barygaza in the Gujarat there was a demand for silver as well as gold (including, at Barygaza, silver and gold coin),[406] but he names only gold, not silver, among the commodities exported to southern India, stating that a great quantity of gold plate went to the Malabar coast.[407] Again, it will be to the increased trade since Nero's time, involving, as it seems, during his reign, and probably still under Vespasian, much export of gold coin, that Pliny refers when he remarks that the sea route from Egypt to India merits description, 'since India absorbs at least fifty million sesterces from our Empire every year in return for the goods she sends us'.[408]

It is interesting that the amount of this particular commodity reaching southern India declined sharply after the reign of Vespasian, to judge from the coin evidence. Thereafter, during a period at which, to judge from other evidence, Roman trade with India was very active, export of gold coins remained at this reduced level.

But it does not follow, as is often assumed, that less gold was being sent to India.[409] Once it had become clear that bullion was what was wanted, bullion, probably, was sent.[410] It would have been wasteful to go on sending *aurei* in large quantities, to be defaced, for somewhere along the line the additional cost of their production had to be met.

But we must return to the age of Tiberius. As we have seen, the evidence suggests that trade between the Roman Empire and India was then on a more modest scale. Probably much less precious metal was being used, much less, in terms of value, lost. How important the loss was, how large, that is to say, in relation to the total volume of currency circulating within the Empire, we can only guess; but it seems most unlikely that it was a factor of any importance in the currency crisis of A.D. 33.

# CHAPTER IV

# THE ROLE
# OF *AES*

IT REMAINS TO CONSIDER *aes* coinage, which so far has been mentioned only incidentally, for we have proceeded by examining Frank's explanation of the currency crisis of A.D. 33, and he made no mention of *aes* in this context. It may be thought that there was no reason for him to mention it; the supply of small change has no bearing on a currency crisis. However, if the official minting of *aes* under Augustus and Tiberius was as important a factor in the currency situation as the minting of silver, as I shall try to show, it follows that what Tiberius did or failed to do about the minting of *aes* needs to be taken into account in considering whether his monetary policy caused a serious shortage of currency in Italy or elsewhere.[411]

It must first be emphasised that one could make no progress towards estimating the importance of *aes* coinage by counting the contents of the major public and private collections of which catalogues have been published, for the simple reason that collectors and curators do not normally acquire sixteen examples of coin *x* for every example of coin *y* just because coin *x* turns up sixteen times more often among coins on offer.[412] Nor would it be of much use for this purpose to count all published examples, even if it were practicable to do so, for there has been far more publication of hoards than of other finds, and gold and silver were hoarded far more often than *aes*.[413]

Valuable evidence can be derived from those collections whose owners or keepers deliberately preserve all the coins they can get that have been found in the surrounding district;[414] but coins contained in such collections are seldom published.

Here, moreover, one comes up against a major difficulty. Even if all the finds of single coins known to have been made in some area were most diligently recorded, the record might misrepresent the role of *aes* coinage. On the one hand, people were no doubt readier to shrug off the loss of *aes* coins;[415] but on the other hand many *aes* coins that people find may never come to the attention of scholars, because they are of no obvious value; and we can hardly assume that these two factors cancel each other out. However, such publications as do exist of all the finds known to have been made in a particular area are of some value for our purpose and reference is made to such data in the following pages.

Turning to finds made on individual sites, which are likely to be less difficult to evaluate, we may first note that finds that have been made in the beds of rivers include a high proportion of *aes* coins. Those of which details have been published are from the Mayenne in north-western Gaul, and from two rivers in Italy, the Cesano, near Suasa, and the Liri at Minturnae.[416] But it cannot be assumed that these give an accurate reflection of the circulating medium. Coins are not thrown into a river at random. They were evidently thrown into the Mayenne, and probably also into the Liri, as votive offerings. Thus the fact that the Liri 'produced a large number of victoriates and *quinarii*' does not show that 'these issues must have been larger than catalogues suggest'. A prosperous but careful merchant who felt that he must cross the river's palm with silver might well use the smallest silver coin he had (one may compare the numerous fractional pieces of republican *aes*—the reluctant offerings of poorer travellers ?). For the same reason, the fact that 'almost 10 per cent of the Republican pieces found are of silver' does not provide 'evidence for the relatively frequent use of silver in common transactions during this period'.[417]

Probably the most nearly reliable indication of the composition of currency in everyday use is provided by careful and detailed reports of finds made in the course of the excavation of settlements, the more extensive the excavation the better. Reports of excavation finds in the eastern provinces bring out clearly the predominance of *aes*;[418] so do reports of finds in Spain and Morocco. But as most of the pre-Claudian *aes* found on sites in these areas is local, reports from these areas do not help us to estimate the relative importance of the issues of gold and silver put out by the Roman government under Augustus and Tiberius and the official issues of *aes* during the same period, which is one of the things that we should like to determine. However, they serve to remind us that, precisely because this local minting of small change continued in many of the provinces, the production of a given quantity of official Roman *aes* made a larger contribution to currency circulation in the areas, including Italy, in which official *aes* was the predominant form of small change than was made in these areas by the production of gold and silver coinage of equivalent value—since the official gold and silver were, as we have seen, wanted, and did in one way or another seep into circulation, throughout the Empire, instead of remaining largely concentrated, like official *aes*, in a smaller area.

The largest mass of evidence for the role of official *aes* in the Julio-Claudian period has come, so far, from the excavation of military sites on the Rhine and Danube frontiers. Reports of excavations, and of coin-finds in general, on and near such sites[419] show 'ein eindeutiges Vorherrschen von Bronze und Kupfer im täglichen Verkehr'.[420] This is for our purpose an important finding, even though it does not, of course, necessarily follow that *aes* was equally predominant in civilian life: 'man möchte gern wissen', as Dietmar Kienast has said, 'ob der Geldumlauf im gallisch-germanischen Grenzgebiet typisch ist für den jeweiligen Münzumlauf der Zeit oder bedingt wird durch die Anwesenheit grösserer Truppenkörper an der Grenze'.[421] Moreover, there are not very many adequate excavation reports even from this military zone.[422]

What we chiefly need, to set alongside evidence from military sites, are more reports relating to civil settlements in Italy and in the most closely assimilated adjacent regions, based on systematic excavation. It is therefore particularly regrettable that coin finds at Pompeii still await comprehensive publication, while repeated misfortunes have caused increasing confusion and losses.[423] However, from published samples of the finds and from what has been said of these by those who know them as a whole, it is clear that *aes* was what was used by the inhabitants of a prosperous Roman town in ordinary daily life.[424] Meanwhile, we must make the most of the few reports that we have of extensive and thorough excavations of sites in this area, outstanding among which are the reports from Minturnae and from the Magdalensberg, an important trading centre in Noricum. On both these

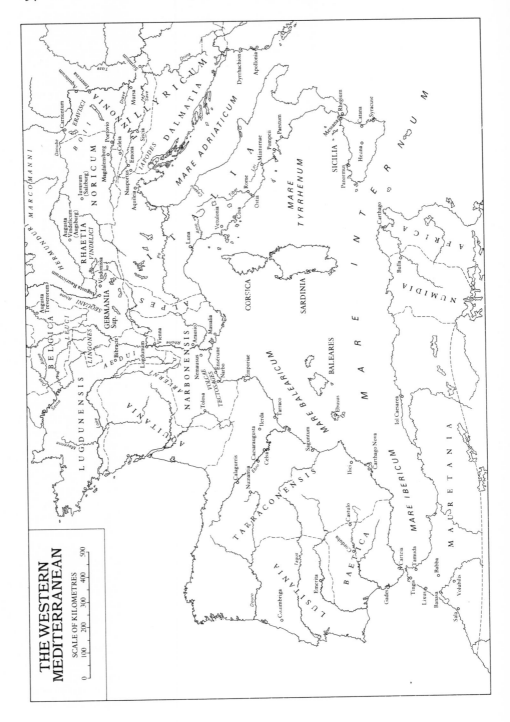

sites the *aes* found is of greater value than the silver.[425] Reports of excavation finds in Italy, though the finds are mostly scanty, likewise give the impression that silver was used even less in daily life under the early Empire in other, less bourgeois Italian towns than it was at Pompeii.[426]

In assessing evidence from the excavation of settlements, one must still allow for distorting factors: that people were more apt, as already mentioned, to resign themselves to the loss of coins of small value,[427] that those employed on digs tend to be more scrupulous about turning in *aes* coins,[428] and, in the case of military sites, that much of the silver due to the men was retained as voluntary or compulsory savings and thus generally protected from loss. All these factors would promote over-representation of *aes*, but after having made due allowance for them one is still very far from having explained away its predominance in settlement finds. And this predominance is what one would, *a priori*, expect: *denarii* would not have been of much use to those wishing to buy or sell goods or services in small quantities.

All in all, the data suggest that the purchasing power of the *aes* put into circulation by Augustus and Tiberius may well have been not much less, in the areas in which it formed the main small-change medium, than that of the silver which they put into circulation in the same area. It would follow that minting of *aes* was almost as important a factor in the total currency situation in Italy, and certain adjacent regions, as the minting of silver—indeed, more important, if one is considering circulation and shortages, since velocity of circulation makes a great deal of difference. 'If we want to know how much money has been used in the course of a year to make payments', says a modern economist, 'the answer is the total amount of money in existence multiplied by the average number of times it has changed hands in the course of the year.'[429] Although *aes* travelled more slowly from one region to another,[430] it probably circulated much more rapidly, at least in towns and in the neighbourhood of camps. 'Coins move round with surprising rapidity, not staying in one person's pocket or purse or till for more than a very few days on the average. Banknotes circulate less rapidly':[431] for coins one may substitute *aes*, for banknotes *denarii*.

It was suggested above that what those in charge of the main mints of gold and silver outside Rome at this period had chiefly in mind in fixing the size of issues was the army's need for coin, rather than the convenience of civilians. The same is even more likely to have been true of the official *aes* mints outside Rome. Certainly one of the chief ways in which the army was in effect provided for was by the production of a large quantity of *aes*. Among published coins of known provenance, the largest quantities of official Augustan *aes* from Gallic mints and of Tiberian *aes* generally, and of *asses* in particular in both cases, have come from excavations on military sites along the German frontier and from chance finds in that region.[432] The evidence of finds thus tends to show that Mattingly's assertion that in the Augustan currency system 'the *as* was designed particularly for the soldier's pay'[433] is correct in respect of mints outside Italy, although pay had long been reckoned officially in *denarii* and although large payments (for example, of a soldier's savings on his discharge) were no doubt actually made in *denarii*, or *aurei*.[434]

We have seen that finds indicate that *aes* coinage was also 'employed for the more diverse needs of civil life in a thousand towns and cities from end to end of the empire'.[435] But the fact that it was thus *employed* does not make it less likely that what the Roman authorities chiefly, if not solely, took into account in settling the production of *aes* coinage outside Italy were the army's needs.[436] This supplying of the army's needs meant, in effect, satisfying a great new demand for money, or rather a demand that had been growing greater down through the first century B.C., with the increasing size and professionalisation of the army, and more recently with the contraction of opportunities for plundering and requisitioning as means of satisfying men's wants. Hundreds of thousands of men who if they had remained farm workers would have handled money hardly at all thus became accustomed to its everyday use.

Some part of the small change that was produced by the government to satisfy the army's needs will, of course, have passed gradually into general circulation. It will thus have encouraged and facilitated movement towards a monetary economy in some of the regions in which troops were stationed; it will have created, that is to say, a need for additional small change, increasing the risk of a shortage. However, one must beware of entertaining exaggerated ideas on this subject.[437] It is in fact not easy to point to any area in which there have been finds that would entitle us to assert that the presence of troops led, during the reigns of Augustus and Tiberius, to the emergence of a substantial civilian demand for coined money for everyday transactions, or to substantial growth of an existing demand of this kind. The presence of a small quantity of Augustan and Tiberian *aes* in a few finds in areas in which there had been little or no previous use of coins of base metal or of low value, such as northern Noricum, constitutes no proof that any of it was circulating among the native population already in their time. It is to a growth of demand in the Flavian period that the evidence points more clearly. In parts of Pannonia and Rhaetia there had been a proportion of small silver coins of quite low value among the Celtic coins produced locally in the first century B.C.[438] But whatever functions these little coins may have performed while Celtic civilisation still flourished, it appears that the inhabitants of Pannonia and Rhaetia hardly wanted, or at least had hardly begun to get, Roman *aes* coins to take their place under the Julio-Claudians, for there have been very few finds of pre-Flavian *aes* outside Roman military stations, and these few concentrated in the frontier zone. This suggests that beyond the immediate neighbourhood of Roman camps there was little use of money between the conquest and the Flavian epoch, perhaps less than in the preceding decades.[439]

In still more backward areas, one may doubt whether there was at this time any demand at all for coins of low value, outside Roman camps. In Moesia, for instance, where two legions were stationed during the reign of Tiberius,[440] no finds whatsoever of Tiberian or earlier Roman *aes* have been reported, and finds of Greek *aes* seem to be very rare, except on the coastal fringe, in or near the territory of Greek colonies.[441]

To the south of the Haimos range, in Thrace, quite large quantities of the *aes* of Philip II and Alexander III have been found, even in districts far from the Aegean and the Black Sea, but in such districts hardly any *aes* occurs that was struck during the three centuries or so after Alexander. Perhaps the Celtic invasion reduced life to a more primitive level, at least monetarily, from which there was no recovery, so far as the use of money was concerned, until after the Roman conquest of Moesia.[442] But in Thrace as in Moesia Greek *aes* of these centuries is found in the neighbourhood of Greek colonies: and one substantial find of early imperial Roman *aes* has been reported: a somewhat surprising find, since it occurred close to the Black Sea coast—in an area, that is to say, in which one would expect any need for small change to be met by the Greek city states, especially Mesembria and Apollonia, or by the puppet kings of Thrace. At Ajtoska Banja, a spa with waters already highly esteemed in antiquity,[443] situated about twenty miles west of Anchialos, on the route inland from there and from Mesembria, building operations in 1910 involved digging down through the level of the Roman *thermae*. In the course of the digging thousands of coins were found, nearly all of *aes*, most of them below the stone floor of the Roman basin. Evidently visitors had thrown them into the spring for luck. Most of them were dispersed, but some three thousand were saved, 2,204 of which were not too damaged to be identified, approximately if not precisely. Nearly one thousand were Roman; six hundred of these were certainly, and another two hundred probably, pre-Neronian.[444]

This is pre-eminently a case in which coins reflect the movement of persons rather than goods, but since it is unlikely that a large proportion of visitors to the spa had travelled from the western half of the empire, one must ask whether the increasing number of official Roman coins points to considerable use of official Roman *aes* by civilians in this part of the world already well before the time of Nero. Was this one region within the Greek sphere in which the coinage of Greek city states or other local authorities had for some reason ceased to constitute an adequate supply of small change for civilian use? Or is it more likely that this was the only congenial spa which Roman soldiers and administrators serving on the lower Danube could reach during short spells of leave? Unfortunately there are no other finds with which this unusual find can be compared, for the nearest sites at which there have been considerable coin finds about which information has been published are Thasos, which belonged fully to the Aegean Greek world, and Histria, lying only just inside the Empire. However, it is perhaps worth mentioning that at Histria some six hundred Greek *aes* coins of the period 350–50 B.C. have been found, but only three certainly pre-Flavian Roman *aes* coins, while reports from Thasos mention only six Roman *aes* coins, 'of Augustus'.[445]

On the whole, then, it does not seem likely that the advance of Roman rule to the Danube created any considerable new demand for *aes* coinage before the death of Tiberius.[446]

To judge from the evidence of finds, Roman *aes* did not spread beyond the imperial frontiers, except where a lively trade grew up along the frontier, involving numerous small transactions; and there is in fact no frontier area of which one can say, on the strength of finds either of coins or of *terra sigillata*, that a local trade of this kind developed already in the Julio-Claudian period.[447]

It was in regions in which there had been local issues of small change which had dwindled or ceased altogether by the time of Tiberius that civilian demand for Roman *aes* became an important new factor. In Gaul, for instance, during the first half of the first century B.C., Massalia had continued to produce large quantities of *aes* coins, which circulated widely along routes followed by traders, especially in the south, but production seems to have ceased by the end of the first century B.C., and in the following years the supply of this popular medium must have steadily dwindled.[448] Meanwhile Gallic tribes were not only producing silver (and adulterated gold) in greater quantity, and greater variety, than ever before, but some tribes that had previously coined only in precious metal now began to issue *aes* or potin coins. Circulation of these base-metal coins seems to have been almost entirely local: they were presumably used in small-scale trade. During the Caesarian war of conquest this minting of base metal increased, and it continued in some areas after the conquest: some struck *aes* copied from *denarii*, but also several varieties of cast potin. In particular, the potin coinage belonging to this period that has been attributed to the Leuci circulated in large quantities over a very wide area, forming, as Pink says, a kind of *Verkehrsgeld*.[449] But Augustus may well have wished that Roman soldiers and officials should not be as dependent on these tribal coins as they perhaps had been in Caesar's time, and in the twenties the supply of official Roman *aes* must have been growing steadily scarcer, in Gaul as elsewhere, since hardly any was being produced. However, Roman needs were satisfied to some extent, to judge from finds, by large *aes* coins, of traditional Roman character, produced during the early twenties by the colonies at Lugdunum (Copia), Arausio ( ?), Vienna and Nemausus,[450] coins which the Roman authorities no doubt did use for official purposes. For some reason these issues were not maintained for long, but from the late twenties the same needs were met to a larger extent by the production at Nemausus of a long series of rather smaller coins which continued, with intermissions, through Augustus' reign.[451] These coins of Nemausus circulated abundantly in the following years in the Roman army; they are, indeed, now commonly regarded by numismatists as constituting an official issue, but they also circulated abundantly among the Gauls.

Not long after the initiation of this major Nemausus series an *aes* mint was opened at Rome, but at first this seems not to have had much effect on currency circulation in Gaul.[452] Then in 12 or 10 B.C., profuse supplies of *aes* began to emerge from the official mint at Lugdunum and perhaps from a subsidiary mint or mints,[453] and continued to emerge down to the end of Augustus' reign, perhaps with a break between 2 B.C. and A.D. 10.[454] The effect on currency circulation in the Rhine army is reflected in the finds from Neuss, occupied from *c.* 15 B.C. The excavations of 1955–62 yielded eighty-six coins or half-coins of Copia and Vienna, 110 of Nemausus' main series, sixty-seven struck at Rome before the official mint opened at Lugdunum and 523 of the Lugdunum series.[455]

Meanwhile minting of some of the base-metal Gallic coins had probably been maintained until about the time of the opening of the Roman mint at Lugdunum: in the words of Colbert de Beaulieu, 'Roman policy aimed at leaving to the tribes the outward signs of their autonomy, the better to veil the true realities',[456] and the circulation of surviving Gallic coins certainly went on for much longer: relatively large numbers were found at Haltern and Neuss, and twenty-two even at Vindonissa, not occupied before *c.* A.D. 17.[457] But the Gauls must have had to rely increasingly on Roman *aes* as time went on.[458] Ritterling may well have been right when he suggested[459] that the circulation of Celtic coins may have been explicitly forbidden by Tiberius, perhaps disturbed by the persistence of Gallic nationalism, for they are almost completely absent from finds in the temple area at Augusta Treverorum, although one might expect this area to have been frequented mainly by native worshippers.[460] They are strikingly absent also from the finds at Hofheim, a camp occupied in A.D. 15,[461] but this in itself could be taken to signify a ban merely on their circulation in the Roman army: which would also, however, increase the demand for official *aes*.

Even in a purely material sense, Roman *aes* seems not to have been a wholly satisfactory substitute. The imperial mints, in particular Lugdunum, produced fractions of the *as* only on quite a small scale, to judge from the proportion among surviving coins,[462] while the colonial mints produced no small *aes* coins at all. Since at this time there were probably still many goods and services that could be bought for a *quadrans*, one would think that the great scarcity of small coins must have caused considerable inconvenience. Here we seem to have evidence of the indifference of the Roman authorities to 'the diverse needs of civil life', especially the needs of those of modest means.'[463]

It has indeed been suggested that the *aes* and potin coins produced by Gallic *civitates* after the conquest may represent chiefly an attempt to meet local demand for coins smaller than the *as*.[464] It was presumably also to meet unsatisfied demand for smaller change that the practice grew up of halving *aes* coins,[465] a practice for which there is evidence also from other parts of the Roman world, especially Italy and Sicily.[466] This practice must have been at least tolerated by the authorities, for half coins have been found in large numbers on the sites of Roman camps along and beyond the Rhine and at Oberhausen behind the Danube frontier. It had evidently become well established in this area before 10 B.C.: of 175 identifiable *aes* pieces found at Oberaden, a camp abandoned *c.* 12–8 B.C., at least forty-eight were halves.[467] There is no clear evidence from any region that provides an earlier *terminus ante quem* for the emergence of the practice, but it is compatible with the evidence, and *a priori* reasonable, to suppose that it originated in the twenties of the first century B.C., if not earlier.[468]

The great majority of the coins that were halved were coins that had been struck as *asses*, and there does not seem to me to be sufficient reason to doubt that the intention, and the result, of halving them was the production of *semisses*.[469]

The practice may have begun, or become prevalent, somewhat earlier in Italy than in Gaul and Germany, where the Gallic tribal coins were available, but the quantity of halves found in the frontier zone suggests that here the demand either came to be larger than it ever became in Italy or lasted longer or both: which would not be surprising, in view of the previous use of Gallic coins and the cessation of Gallic minting.

The practice certainly continued on the Rhine frontier, if not elsewhere, far down into Tiberius' reign, since halves have been found of Augustan *asses* bearing countermarks that had been impressed on the coins during Tiberius' reign before they were halved, and of Tiberian *asses* belonging to issues thought not to have been produced before A.D. 23 at the earliest. But such halves form only a tiny proportion of all halved coins, and only a tiny proportion of the unhalved coins in these two categories. A survey of the whole of the evidence suggests that in this area the practice reached its peak in Augustus' later years and the early years of Tiberius' reign. Probably rising prices led to its gradual cessation.[470]

From our point of view, the importance of this phenomenon is that it reinforces the impression given by the rest of the find evidence that the increase in civilian demand in Gaul for Roman *aes*, and in military demand, that was engendered partly by the dwindling of local supplies of small change and partly by the Roman presence itself was by no means inconsiderable.[471]

The production in Gaul of local copies of official Julio-Claudian *aes* coins has been seen as an indication that after the cessation of local coinages the demand for *aes* among the civil population soon, indeed, far outran the available supply. Thus, for instance, in publishing a Flavian hoard of 212 early imperial *aes* coins discovered at Puy-de-Dôme, one tenth of which appear to be of local manufacture, Jean-Baptiste Giard remarks that this illustrates 'la pénurie constante des moyens

d'échange', the implication being that the coins that appear to be of local manufacture had been produced unofficially to remedy a shortage.[472] But it is not always
easy to be sure of the status of an *aes* coin. There are many examples of the major
*aes* issues of Augustus and Tiberius which appear, from finds, to have been in
ordinary circulation but which exhibit divergences from those belonging to what
one may call in each case the main group. These divergences have led to their
being sometimes classed as 'barbarous' or as imitations, but some numismatists
now hold that most of these divergent coins were produced officially at subsidiary
mints. If so, their existence would constitute evidence for steps taken officially to
increase the supply.

On the other hand, some coins are so aberrant, in lettering, for instance, or in
weight, that we can not suppose them to have been produced officially.[473] Their
existence may point to a shortage which the authorities failed to remedy.[474] But
one must bear in mind that production of unofficial imitations of official *aes* coins
could have yielded a profit, if their makers could successfully put them into
circulation, like the production of counterfeit 50p pieces. If the official *aes* coins
were fiduciary or token coins, as has been commonly supposed, production of
copies could have been profitable even if they were of similar composition and of
full weight,[475] so that their existence does not necessarily point directly to a failure
in supply.

Such is what the published evidence permits one to say about the use of small
change in Gaul, and the increasing demand for Roman *aes* which it engendered.
Investigation could with advantage be carried further, but, although it would be
easy to add miscellaneous information about Gallic finds, any attempt at a more
systematic study would require prolonged study of collections, since published
information on finds in France is very scattered and patchy.[476]

As in Gaul, so also in the south of Noricum conditions favouring the use of
money, even small change, survived the collapse of La Tène civilisation. Here,
where the Magdalensberg had developed into an important trading centre,[477]
small Celtic-type silver coins, worth about one-sixth of a *denarius*, had been
produced since about 70–60 B.C.,[478] and production evidently continued down into
the reign of Augustus, but it then ceased, for one reason or another, and although
they were still circulating under Tiberius their place had to be, and was, gradually
taken by Roman *aes*.[479]

Here, then, we have two areas which exemplify, in relation to *aes*, what was
said above about the extension of the area in which Roman gold and silver were
needed in the time of Augustus and Tiberius.

Meanwhile in many other parts of the Empire the production of coinages of base
metal continued through the reign of Tiberius, when the production of silver,
except by the Roman government, had virtually ceased.

It has been argued that these local *aes* coinages are of no economic importance.
In the words of Professor Louis Robert, 'il n'est guère possible de se cantonner
dans une recherche économique avec un tel matériel'.[480] 'Non seulement parce
qu'il n'est pas assez abondant, quand on le répartit en tranches chronologiques,
mais parce qu'il s'agit de bronze', and 'a l'époque impériale . . . ces émissions de
cité n'ont pas de valeur "économique".' 'Ce bronze ne représente pas un valeur de
marchandises en contrepartie, comme une trésor de tétradrachmes. Il n'atteste
point un échange de marchandises.'[481] Now, it is true that some of the civic issues

that were put out during this period, commemorating some benefit bestowed by Rome, were too small and isolated to have, by themselves, any measurable monetary significance.[482] But if one considers the whole amount of such money that was in circulation, including the larger issues, and older coins still circulating, and if one bears in mind that it was the money used in everyday life in the purchase and sale of goods at retail level,[483] one is surely compelled to recognise that this civic *aes* had a real monetary significance in a world in which the great majority of enterprises and transactions were small, and in which (in contrast with the modern world) currency of gold, silver or bronze was by far the most important form of money.[484] One may also point to the presence of marks of value on some coins, evidence that they were intended for use.

Generally speaking, such coins did not travel far from their homes,[485] though finds show 'that coins do move from one town to another frequently enough, so that this must have been considered normal'.[486] But among the more productive mints there were a few whose issues circulated quite widely within their own regions in the first century B.C. (and in some cases longer): as widely as most, and more widely than many, of the vast number of silver issues of earlier periods.[487] In the west, for instance, there were coins of Gades, Tarraco, Emporiae and Ebusus, the *aes* of Massalia, and subsequently the *asses* of the Gallic *coloniae*, the small potin pieces attributed to the Leuci; in the east, the issues of Athens, Antioch, Amisos (spread abroad largely, no doubt, by the activities of Mithridates VI), Rhodes and Pergamon.[488] These local coinages have hitherto been studied mainly for the sake of the light thrown by their types on art or religion, or as evidence for political events, institutions and ideas, and there is still an enormous amount of work to be done, especially in collecting and analyzing find-evidence, before one can speak with confidence in more than very general terms about their economic role, as money. However, one must make the best use one can of such evidence as one can find relating to these coinages in attempting to assess the significance of Rome's official issues of *aes*.

For the eastern provinces, what reports of coin finds in major excavations and of isolated finds already suffice to show quite clearly is that, under the Republic and down through the reigns of Augustus and Tiberius, the Greek and Phoenician city states continued to provide the great bulk of the small change in circulation,[489] except in Crete, Cyrene, Cyprus and Judaea.[490] Only at Antioch, where there was certainly a mint for 'official' *aes*, and at Curium, where there may have been one near by, has 'official' *aes* of Augustus or Tiberius been found in considerable quantities on excavated sites.[491] As an example of surface finds, one may mention those made at Tell Rifa'at, 35 km north of Aleppo: of the second and first centuries B.C., there were ten or eleven Greek *aes* coins (and one tetradrachm), but the oldest Roman coin was of Nerva: 'it is a reasonable assumption that, as surface finds, they represent a random sample of the coins available at any given time.'[492] Even next door to Italy, in northern Epirus, a Roman protectorate since the third century B.C., Roman *aes* played a relatively modest part down through the time of Tiberius.[493]

If one turns to the south-western part of the Empire—Corsica, Sardinia, Sicily, Africa, Mauretania and the Spanish provinces—the available evidence suggests that here also there was no substantial increase in the circulation of Roman *aes* among the native population during the reigns of Augustus and Tiberius.

In Africa, after the destruction of Carthage, there was no local minting for over a century within the region that was made into a province. So already under the Republic the stock of local currency must have been becoming depleted, but I have encountered no find-evidence that makes it possible to tell whether coins of small denominations were being extensively used in this area (certainly one of the most highly developed in the western Mediterranean) before the conquest, and, if so, whether their gradual exhaustion resulted in the introduction of Roman *aes*, as well as Roman silver, into the area, or whether it led rather to an increased use of the *aes* coinage of the Numidian kings, which was being produced in abundance from the reign of Massinissa onwards.[494] The use of this Numidian *aes* is more probable, in view of the fact that the need would have become acute at a time at which the Romans themselves had suspended the minting of *aes*. The Numidian royal coinage ceased in 46 B.C., but in the following years and under Augustus and Tiberius a number of towns struck *aes*, both in the old province of Africa and in what had been Numidia, and analogy with the evidence from Mauretania suggests that their issues will have satisfied regional demand.

In Mauretania the kings continued to strike both silver and *aes* until A.D. 40, and *aes* coins were produced also by a number of the towns. It has been said that this coinage did not answer any real economic needs and was rather an expression of the desire of the kings and the towns to assert themselves.[495] Certainly the region was more backward than Africa or Numidia, but the find-evidence[496] suggests both that there was some demand in the towns for small change and that it was largely satisfied by local *aes* issues until the time of Claudius, especially the royal issues and those of Lixus and Semes.[497] It is anyhow abundantly clear that it was not until the time of Claudius that Roman *aes* began to be used at all extensively.

Corsica and Sardinia had long depended on the Romans for their supply of money. In Sicily civic production had largely ceased by the first century B.C.,[498] so that already under the late Republic the Sicilians must have become for the most part dependent on the Romans for replenishment of their supply of small change, and finds show that in fact a considerable quantity of republican *aes* found its way to Sicily from the third century onwards.[499] During the first half of the first century B.C., when minting of *aes* in Italy ceased, the Roman government, for reasons at which we can only guess, made direct provision for a time for Sicily's needs: quartuncial *aes* coins, probably intended as *asses*, were struck by Roman quaestors in Sicily, chiefly at Panormos, in large enough quantities to make a considerable contribution to the circulating medium.[500] Under Augustus and Tiberius there was some revival of civic coinage. In Grant's view 'it was for a record rather than for a currency that such rare issues were intended', while imports from Italy of the revived Roman *aes* coinage constituted 'the *aes* coinage which supplied economic needs in Sicily',[501] but recent excavation finds at Palermo suggest that, in a few cases at least, the civic issues were of some monetary significance;[502] which would mean that there was somewhat less reliance on the Roman authorities for the provision of small change.

In the Spanish provinces there was a fair amount of republican *aes* in circulation already in the first century B.C.[503] This was no doubt the result of the continuing presence of considerable numbers of Roman soldiers. However, finds indicate that Spanish *aes* predominated even in the neighbourhood of a Roman camp, and that in general Roman *aes* was a much less important factor in the situation in Spain under the Republic than it was in Sicily.[504] Although there is much uncertainty about the dating of the *aes* issued by Spanish communities, it seems likely that production, which began in the second century B.C., continued at some mints on a considerable scale down into the time of the Sertorian war, at others into the time of the civil wars, and at a few mints perhaps even through the civil wars down into the reign of Augustus. All in all, there was probably more monetary continuity than one might expect, considering the disruption of civil wars.[505] *Aes* from southern mints travelled to north Africa, from northern mints into Gaul.[506] Certainly there were large quantities of Spanish *aes* of the republican epoch still in circulation in the time of Augustus: this is shown by the finds on the site of the town of Numantia, re-established under Augustus.[507] But by that time there may well have been a shortage, even if a less acute shortage than in Italy. However, under Augustus and Tiberius *aes* was struck in important quantities by local communities.[508]

Correspondingly, the amount of official Roman *aes* that came to Spain during the reigns of Augustus and Tiberius was probably quite small in relation to local production, less, perhaps, than in the second and early first centuries B.C., to judge from finds. Most of what came was probably brought from Gaul by or for Roman soldiers (along with some Nemausus *aes*), supplementing what had been struck for them officially at Emerita and perhaps elsewhere during the Augustan campaigns in the north-west in the twenties B.C. But production at the mints of some of the Spanish towns, if not planned by the Roman government,[509] may at least have been intended by the local authorities concerned to meet the needs of Roman soldiers, after the cessation of minting of official *aes* at Emerita, for many of these towns were now *coloniae* or *municipia*. (It is perhaps significant that some two dozen of these 'Spanish imperials' have turned up on the Rhine frontier.) It is with coins of Claudius that one can discern a marked increase in the circulation of official *aes* in Spain, after local coinages had ceased in about A.D. 40.[510]

Looking at the Empire as a whole, one receives the impression that there may have been no diminution in the total volume of production of *aes* by local communities down through the first half of Augustus' reign at least, since the cessation of some issues was offset by the initiation of others, and some of the communities that struck coins for the first time between 50 B.C. and 2 B.C., or after a long lapse, produced issues which, although commemorative in purpose, were evidently large enough, to judge from surviving examples, or numerous enough to constitute a significant contribution to the currency of the period.[511] 'No one can consider the halves and the abundant quarters' of Ilion, with a portrait of Augustus, 'without realizing that they were intended to form an important element in the currency of the district, with higher denominations, from *sestertius* down, supplied by more important Asiatic mints . . . [They] were money first and commemorative pieces only incidentally.'[512] Likewise in Spain, whereas a few mints that had been productive earlier in the first century B.C., such as Ilerda, seem to have lapsed into inactivity under Augustus, a few others, such as Calagurris, became far more productive than they had been.[513]

However, I have the impression that in the forty years or so after 2 B.C. markedly fewer civic issues were produced than in the fifty years or so before. If this is so, it may have been simply because there were fewer occasions to commemorate, or there was less eagerness to find occasions to commemorate and less encouragement from above to do so. But even issues the motive for which was purely or primarily commemorative made collectively some contribution to the supply of *aes* currency (unless one supposes that all the coins produced were kept as souvenirs), so this falling off must eventually have contributed to some small extent to an increasing demand for official *aes*.[514] Moreover, apart from primarily commemorative issues, some issues ceased which had 'contributed more or less considerably to the bulk of the empire's *aes* coinage',[515] and though their cessation was to some extent counterbalanced by the initiation of other issues of considerable importance, it seems likely that in Augustus' later years and under Tiberius the average annual volume of new *aes* coinage that was being put into circulation by local communities was smaller than it had been.[516] However, it would have taken a good many years, one would think, for the effects of this contraction to become felt. They may not have begun to be felt before the time of Claudius: they may then be reflected not in anyone's comprehension or calculated reaction but in those signs of increased provincial circulation of Claudian official *aes* that we have noted.[517]

This brings us to the question of official planning. 'How far the cities planned to have their issues supplement each other and how much planning was done by Hellenistic kings and Roman emperors are questions which are just beginning to be asked and for which', as Bellinger has said, 'the evidence is as yet very imperfectly recorded.' Were decisions about the beginning and end of base-metal coinages and about size and frequency of issues taken locally *ad hoc* 'without being part of anybody's plan'?[518] To me it does not seem likely that at this period there was any coherent economic planning of non-official coinages by the Roman authorities. What has recently been established, by the investigation of die-links, is that in the third century A.D. the issues of a great many of the cities of Asia Minor were produced at a small number of mints, probably five or six at most for the whole province of Asia,[519] and though the evidence has not yet been fully examined it appears that co-operation of this kind, if on a smaller scale, extended back into early imperial times, and beyond.[520] But it does not follow from this that under Augustus and Tiberius the size or frequency of issues was planned by the Roman government. 'That there was no Roman control of minting is suggested' in the case of Spain, for instance, 'by the sheer profusion of mints—and by their quite un-Roman types'.[521] Even where there are clear indications of political supervision, these do not constitute evidence for economic planning, while in the rare instances in which there is evidence suggesting that certain mints 'were definitely intended to supplement one another', this may have been still the result of local initiative.[522]

I must now turn to considering the contribution made by the Roman authorities to currency circulation through official issues of *aes* under Augustus and Tiberius. It may first be mentioned that between 50 B.C. and 27 B.C. *aes* was struck by a number of Roman generals or their deputies in a variety of places outside Italy. These issues were of considerable political importance, but it is not easy to form a clear idea of their monetary significance.[523] Owing their birth 'too often', if not always, to civil war, they were surely too small, to judge from surviving examples, and too scattered to deserve to be described as 'a complex group designed to satisfy different needs, strategic, administrative and (it may be added) economic',[524] or 'as beginning to cover the Mediterranean world'.[525] Thus, for instance, although Grant speaks of a seemingly tiny Caesarian issue at Amisus as 'a further example of Caesar's unrecognised provision of *aes* currency for the Empire',[526] one may wonder whether Caesar himself was even aware of this example. The rest probably did no more, and were probably not intended by anyone to do more, than go some way towards satisfying the immediate needs which civil war engendered from time to time and from place to place, subsequently making an insignificant contribution (in comparison with republican *aes* still in circulation) to the sum total of small change in the Roman world in the time of Augustus and Tiberius.

Under Augustus a number of mints in the eastern half of the Empire produced official *aes* coins, a large proportion of which can be grouped into two series.[527] The coins of one of these two series all bear on the reverse the bold letters SC, in a laurel wreath, recalling the 'senatorial' coinage at Rome.[528] Those of known provenance[529] emanate mainly from the Asiatic provinces and especially from Syria and Cyprus. Examples of the other series, in which the *sestertii* and the *dupondii* have a similar reverse but with the letters CA, have been found in larger numbers, the bulk of them in an area extending from south-eastern Europe to Syria.[530] These finds suffice to show that coins of this second series did indeed travel more widely and in larger quantity than was normal for *aes* produced by eastern civic mints.[531] However, with respect to its classification as one of 'the main *aes* coinages of Augustus' along with the coinages of Nemausus, Lugdunum and Rome, it must be said that, even if one allows for the comparative scantiness of eastern find-evidence, the series does not seem to have been anything like as prolific as any of these, or to have made anything like as large a contribution to currency circulation in the eastern provinces as these made in the west, or at least in Italy, Gaul and Germany. It is surely significant that so few coins of this series turned up alongside the large quantities, all told, of eastern civic *aes* on the large sites that have been carefully excavated and published: none, it seems, at Athens or Corinth or Troy or Tarsus, five at Priene, two at Sardes, five at Curium, three at Dura, twenty at Antioch, the great crossroads.[532] The wide but not very thick distribution of this series—heaviest, so far, towards the eastern frontier—would surely be explained if it had been produced, as was the Lugdunum series in the west, to meet the needs of Roman soldiers, far fewer of whom were stationed in the east, and perhaps also of Roman administrators—a few consequently travelling with soldiers to the west.[533] This explanation would be wholly consistent with one interpretation of the letters CA, as standing for *Commune Asiae;* it might be that 'the coins were issued in accordance with some special permission granted to the *Commune* similar to that granted a few years later to the provincial mint of Lugdunum under the *Concilium Galliarum*'.[534]

On this view, the SC series would be an even less large, though still important, series, produced at Antioch, and perhaps elsewhere, likewise to satisfy military needs. Since there was evidently not thought to be any suitable local machinery to use as a facade, the expedient adopted was to obtain the Senate's authority for the operation of an *aes* mint or mints, as for the *aes* mint at Rome.[535] While the CA series, including the associated *asses*, seems not to have had a long life, production of this SC series may have continued intermittently through the reign of Augustus, and it was revived under Tiberius (and continued under his successors). It had presumably been found to be the most satisfactory expedient for giving the Syrian legions a supply of small change of Roman character.[536] With the exception of a seemingly small issue in the name of Germanicus, the Tiberian coins of this series all bear the tribunician dating XXXIII, A.D. 31–32; but, if one can judge from the number of examples in collections, this single issue was not much less large than all those of Augustus combined.[537]

In Italy the civilian need for new *aes* coinage must have been extremely pressing at the time of the establishment of the Principate, since none had been produced there by the Roman authorities between the eighties and the thirties.[538] This long suspension of the minting of *aes* has never been altogether satisfactorily explained. Part of the explanation may be that it was now no longer needed in any considerable quantity for paying the army.[539] However, soldiers serving for long periods must often have wanted to draw some of their pay in *aes*, or change some of it into *aes*, to pay for goods or services in small quantities, and so the civil wars, keeping huge numbers of Romans under arms, must in fact have increased the demand for Roman *aes*. Hence the various issues by generals, to which I have referred: and it was most probably for this purpose that Octavian put out two closely related issues of *asses* in the thirties. To judge from finds, these were probably struck in Italy, where they made a considerable contribution to circulation,[540] but they must have fallen far short of satisfying all the needs of Italy.

One need will have been for coins of lower denomination than the *as*. It was argued above that the continued failure of the authorities to produce any such coins was what led people to cut *asses* in half.[541] If that is the correct interpretation of this practice, it will surely have continued in Italy at least until *quadrantes*, which began to be produced again by the Roman mint in about 8 B.C., were circulating in reasonable quantities.[542]

Meanwhile, in about 20 B.C., a mint for *aes* was at last opened again at Rome. It proceeded to produce issues of *sestertii*, *dupondii* and *asses* (including an extremely large issue of *asses* in 6 B.C., or a few years later). These issues clearly went much further towards meeting the pent-up demand than Octavian's issues in the thirties. Before the end of the century the mint was closed, but part of its last and biggest issue of *asses* was perhaps held in reserve for use in Italy during the following years.[543] It was reopened for a couple of years towards the end of Augustus' life, but at that time only two quite small issues of *asses* were produced.

We do not know what expedients were used for putting *aes* coins into civilian circulation in Italy. They might have been supplied to bankers, in exchange for worn *aes* or for silver; perhaps also to officers of the praetorian and urban cohorts and the cohorts of *vigiles*, so that they could issue small sums to men who, like legionary soldiers, probably banked the bulk of their pay.[544] It does not seem likely that officials had otherwise to make any purchases or payments for public purposes within Italy on such a small scale that they would use *aes*, while they could no doubt demand exact payment of sums owing, if these ever included fractions of a *denarius*, without being obliged to offer change (so that for the republican state machine cessation of the minting of *aes* had created no difficulties).

It is tempting to imagine that among Augustan *aes* from the Roman mint 'the remarkable copper coins issued by P. Lurius Agrippa and his colleagues with the obverse type of Victory crowning the head of Augustus', which Mattingly regarded as constituting 'an extraordinary issue of a commemorative character'[545] were used for a *congiarium*, each recipient being perhaps given one of these along with ordinary new pieces; but it is said that the use of *aes* for *congiaria* would have involved 'difficultés matérielles trop grandes',[546] and on the other hand it has been shown exactly how distribution could have been carried out expeditiously if *denarii* had been used.[547] Similar difficulties would have stood in the way of using *aes* for donatives, but it has nevertheless been suggested that one major *aes* issue of this period[548] was produced partly for the payment of donatives and suchlike.[549] However, not much *aes* could have been put directly into circulation in Italy in that way, nor by commemorative distributions in colonies or *municipia*, although these, being at the rate of a *denarius* or two per head[550] could have been made in *aes* without too much difficulty.

We have seen that from about 11 B.C. *aes* had been flowing in abundance from the mint at Lugdunum (and perhaps from subsidiary mints in the western provinces); and that already before that some smaller but not inconsiderable official issues had begun to flow from several mints in the eastern provinces. But the *aes* struck outside Italy was no doubt not intended to meet governmental needs in Italy, and finds suggest that the eastern *aes* found its way to Italy hardly at all, and the western *aes* only in quantities that were quite small in proportion to the volume of production.[551]

Thus the issues of the Roman mint are the *aes* issues that we need chiefly to take into account in considering the amount of currency in circulation in Italy in Augustus' time and in the time of Tiberius.

Assessment of circulation in Italy is complicated by the fact that *aes* struck at the Roman mint during the reign of Augustus, and in particular *asses*, the coins that were struck in the largest quantities, by far, at this mint (as indeed at Lugdunum and whatever other mints may have helped to produce the 'Lugdunum' series), found their way sooner or later out of Italy in large quantities, to circulate among the armies of the west. This comes out clearly in all find reports from frontier districts.[552] Indeed, on the strength of the find-evidence, the view has been expressed that both the *asses* and the larger *aes* coins struck at Rome 'were, without doubt, intended for a far wider area of circulation than Rome and Italy alone' and were almost certainly intended to amplify the volume of small change in the western provinces as a whole'.[553]

One's opinion on this last point will be inextricably bound up with one's views concerning Augustus and concerning Roman monetary policy. Certainly the evidence of finds renders in the highest degree improbable the hypothesis which was once widely held, according to which *aes* from the Roman mint was legal tender only within Italy and was intended not to circulate in the provinces. On the other hand, among finds in Gaul away from the military zone *aes* struck in Gaul does predominate.[554] One must also bear in mind that the evidence from military sites along the German frontier is said to indicate that Augustan *aes* from Rome did not reach the peak of its circulation even at Vindonissa, the camp least remote from Rome, until many years after it was issued.[555] If this is so, and if the time-lag is due, as has been suggested, to the slowness of travel of *aes*, it would seem that it cannot have been part of the purpose of those who decided on these Roman issues in the time of Augustus that they should be put into circulation outside Rome; for, if this had been intended, there would surely have been no serious difficulty about transporting the desired amount of coin forthwith to the region where it was to be put into circulation.[556] (The only alternative would be to suppose that some of the Roman *aes* of Augustus' reign was indeed earmarked for issue outside Rome but that for some reason some of this earmarked money was held back in store and was not transported to Gaul until after *aes* which had been struck at Lugdunum at a later date had already been put into circulation.)

It may, then, be that under Augustus the times at which and the quantities in which *aes* was struck in Rome and issued in Italy were regulated with reference only to Italian and Roman opportunities and needs, however these may have been assessed and whatever the methods of satisfying them may have been; but that some of what was issued in Italy passed out of Italy, and especially to the northern frontiers, through normal channels of circulation[557] Subsequently, however, under Tiberius, when Rome had become the sole source of supply of official *aes* for the west, there must also have been deliberate production for export to the armies.[558]

It follows that there must have been a flow of *aes* currency out of Italy, in one way or another, far exceeding the flow of *aes* currency into Italy from outside. But there are so many unknown factors in the situation that it would be incautious to assume that this continuing outflow of fiduciary currency was necessarily detrimental in any way.[559]

Likewise, if there was as serious a shortage of currency in Italy in A.D. 33 as Frank supposed, it must surely have extended to *aes* coinage, for a shortage of gold and silver would have impelled people to resort to *aes* for transactions for which it would not normally have been used.[560] It would not be surprising if in such circumstances Tiberius had arranged for a new issue of *aes*, especially as this might have been an economical expedient. So long as there was an increase in demand to justify an increase in the amount of currency in circulation, there was no reason why it should not be satisfied by issuing fiduciary coins instead of, or in addition to, value coins; the fact that this helped the government (and/or the issuing authority, in cases where the government delegated or left the task to some other body) is not a point against it. It would have been an unsound expedient only if it had been adopted on so large a scale as to cause a collapse of confidence in the fiduciary coinage. Augustus, it may be said, had incurred this risk; if so, he had evidently got away with it; for there is in our evidence no hint or sign that anyone tried to avoid accepting the *aes* that was issued officially during his reign at the official rate of sixteen *asses* to the *denarius*.[561]

If, then, it could be shown to be likely that an issue of *aes* was made in A.D. 33, this would provide some support for Frank's interpretation of the crisis, the more so if it could also be shown that there had been no issues of *aes* for some years past. It is curious that Frank himself had nothing to say on this subject, for the idea had already occurred to Mattingly. The bulk of the official *aes* coins bearing the portrait and titles of Tiberius or of his son Drusus are 'dated' by the inclusion in the legend of their years of tenure of tribunican power,[562] and Mattingly had argued on the strength of these legends that we are bound to attribute to A.D. 15–16 some *asses* from the Roman mint, and also 'bound to recognise a period of intense coinage' in A.D. 22–23.[563] This period was, he thought, 'followed by a complete lull of twelve years'.[564] Then in A.D. 34–35 there was a resumption of 'dated' issues, continuing into A.D. 36–37. 'It is perhaps worth noting', he wrote, 'that this resumption of coinage follows close on the great financial crisis of A.D. 33.'[565]

In Mattingly's view, the resumption of the minting of *aes* after A.D. 33 was indeed on an enormous scale, for, in addition to the 'dated' *aes* issues of A.D. 34–37, he was inclined to attribute to 'the last period of Tiberius' seven other *aes* issues which carry no indication of date and no reference to Tiberius. Six of these commemorated *Divus Augustus Pater*, the seventh was in honour of Agrippa. The issue in honour of Agrippa was extremely large, while one of the issues honouring Augustus, that which celebrated his *providentia*, was even larger.[566]

It may well be that both these major issues were produced largely for circulation in the western provinces; it has indeed been argued recently that part of both issues was actually produced in Gaul.[567] Finds, however, indicate that, whatever may have been the means by which part of each issue was put into circulation in Italy, they did circulate there far more freely than the *aes* that was struck outside Italy in the time of Augustus in and for the western provinces, especially Gaul and Germany.[568]

If the attribution of these 'undated' issues to the years A.D. 34–37 could be accepted, they would render the 'period of intense coinage' in A.D. 22–23 insignificant by comparison (though Mattingly did not stress this contrast) and would make the 'lull' preceding A.D. 34 all the more remarkable. But the attribution is far from certain. A somewhat different chronology had indeed already been proposed before Mattingly wrote. The crucial difference, so far as our problem is concerned, lies in the suggestion that the two largest issues, the one in honour of Agrippa and the one celebrating Augustus' *providentia*, 'should be assigned on account of their finer style . . . most probably to the years A.D. 23–32'.[569] In the case of the issue honouring Agrippa this alternative dating, based, as it originally was, on judgement of style, has been rejected by most numismatists.

Some, taking into account other evidence of various kinds, have reasserted Mattingly's view; others, while agreeing with him that it was initiated in the last years of Tiberius' reign, have argued that it went on being produced under Gaius, and perhaps under Claudius; others hold that it did not even begin to be produced before the reign of Gaius.[570] On the other hand, there seems to be universal agreement that the 'Providentia' issue was initiated well before A.D. 33, and that is sufficient for the purpose of our argument.[571] If one vast issue of *asses* was being produced and put into circulation before A.D. 33, the initiation of several smaller *aes* issues in A.D. 34–35 becomes much less significant. Even if another vast issue, the issue in honour of Agrippa, was initiated in Tiberius' last years, this would then represent no shift in policy.[572] If it was not initiated until after Tiberius' death, we are left with no evidence at all for increased production of money to relieve the shortage that was felt at Rome in A.D. 33. But whichever view we take of this great issue, it is clear that the only marked break during Tiberius' reign in the minting of *aes* at Rome for circulation in Italy came at the beginning, after the first modest issues of A.D. 15–16, the issues that introduced him as Princeps, and that from A.D. 22 onwards there was minting on quite a large scale of *aes* coins which did in practice circulate in Italy, even if this was not their main function.[573]

CONCLUSION

# THE POLICY
# OF TIBERIUS

SO THERE IS REASON to suspect that Tiberius did follow 'a vigorous policy of currency expansion' in the minting of *aes*, where he was not tied down to spending no more than he received.[574] But this expansion of the volume of *aes* currency may well have affected Italy less than it affected the armies, and, through them, the provinces to the north.[575] In particular, it does not seem likely that he made any special use of *aes* with the direct aim of alleviating the Italian crisis of A.D. 33, for it is not clear how within a brief period he could have made any considerable addition to the supply of *aes* already in circulation there without withdrawing an equivalent amount of silver. One might think of a *congiarium*, or a donative to the praetorian or urban cohorts; but none such is recorded: he had no taste, we are told, for gestures of that kind, for all his munificence in other ways.[576]

If he had indulged more freely in such gestures, or if he had spent more freely on public works in Italy (and had spent less elsewhere), he would have brought about an increase in the total amount of money in circulation in Italy, and thus he could in the end have put more *aes* into circulation through the bankers. Quite possibly, however, his instinct, prompting him to refrain from such a policy, was sound. If, as things were, the amount of gold and silver currency in private hands in Italy had at the least not decreased in his time, and if the amount of small change had increased, it might have done harm rather than good to put into circulation in Italy a large amount of new money, or a large proportion of the state reserve. There is indeed some reason for thinking that the expansion of currency which the Roman government achieved, continuing, as I have argued, through the later years of Augustus' reign and on into the reign of Tiberius, eventually outpaced the growth of demand and brought about a rise of prices, which will have engendered the soldiers' agitation in A.D. 14 for an increase of pay and which was reflected also from the middle years of Tiberius' reign onwards in increased utilisation of *aes* coins larger than the *as*.[577] In these circumstances all that was needed in A.D. 33 was to release enough money to alleviate a shortage that had occurred, if Tacitus is right, for special reasons.

On the other hand, in so far as Tiberius increased the amount of Roman money in circulation outside Italy by producing large new issues of *aes*, he did so simply because he was following the traditional policy of providing what was needed for the army and the administration, and, so far as he could, the newer policy of spending to win the loyalty of Rome's subjects. Such a policy does seem to have worked well in the time of Augustus and Tiberius. But that was partly because at this time, and for some time afterwards, there was a possibility of expansion and intensification of trade, especially after an age of troubles, and because for this and other reasons there was scope for a wider use of money, within the limits of the existing techniques and economic structures of the Roman world. Moreover, in the time of Tiberius the total output of local currencies was, I have suggested, probably somewhat smaller than it had been in the first half of Augustus' reign.

In the longer run, the continued pursuit, for the same reasons, of a policy of currency expansion proved detrimental to the monetary system and to the economy, for it was dictated by the existence of a larger body of non-productive consumers than a society with primitive technical equipment could sustain. *This* was the fundamental factor, not excessive Italian spending on consumer goods from outlying parts of the Empire or from beyond the frontiers. Augustus, for his part, could probably not have arranged things in any fundamentally different way, short of presiding over the dissolution of the Empire; he had to pay for his success. The deeper causes of the slow progress to breakdown lay in all the steps that had been taken away from reliance on a peasant militia and on the active good will of free cities; lay, that is to say, in the irrepressible Roman will to dominate.

For generations the consequences had been concealed, or rather postponed, by Rome's use of the accumulated wealth of the Mediterranean world, wealth created by Greeks and Phoenicians and their pupils, wealth which successive generations of Romans could plunder.[578] Tiberius, it could be said, was the first man to have to try to make the system work in a 'normal' manner. That was the economic counterpart to his grievous political heritage.

It is now fashionable to allow Tiberius many merits: and I have been following the fashion, for I have argued that we may properly absolve him from blame in respect of the monetary policy that he followed. But we must not be led to the opposite extreme of attributing to him the insights, such as they are, of present day economists, bankers and ministers of finance.[579] Had he enjoyed such insights, he might well have been even more depressed than he was by the decay of Roman *virtus* and by the spread of passivity and servility.

# ABBREVIATIONS

*AEA—Archivo español de arquelogía*
*AIIN—Annali del istituto italiano di numismatica*
ANS—American Numismatic Society
*AJA—American Journal of Archaeology*
*AJP—American Journal of Philology*
*BCH—Bulletin de Correspondance Hellénique*
Bellinger, *Alexander*—Alfred R. Bellinger, *Essays on the Coinage of Alexander the Great* (1963)
Bellinger, *Dura* VI—Alfred R. Bellinger, *Dura-Europos* VI: *The Coins* (1949)
Bellinger, *Troy: The Coins*—Alfred R. Bellinger, *Troy:* Supplementary Monograph 2, *The Coins* (1961)
*BMC—British Museum Catalogue of Greek Coins*
*BMCRE* I—*British Museum Catalogue of Coins of the Roman Empire* I, *Augustus to Vitellius*, by Harold Mattingly (1923)
*CAH*—The *Cambridge Ancient History*
Chantraine, *Novaesium* III—Heinrich Chantraine, *Novaesium* III: *Die antiken Fundmünzen* (1968)
Cic., *ad Att.*—Cicero, *Epistulae ad Atticum*
Cic., *ad fam.*—Cicero, *Epistulae ad familiares*
*CRR—The Coinage of the Roman Republic* by Edward A. Sydenham (1952)
*Dura* VI: see Bellinger, *Dura* VI
*ESAR—An Economic Survey of Ancient Rome*, edited by Tenney Frank (1933–40)
*FMRD—Die Fundmünzen der römischen Zeit in Deutschland*, edited by Hans Gebhart and Konrad Kraft (1960– )
*FMRL—Monnaies antiques découvertes au Grand-Duché de Luxembourg*, edited by Raymond Weiller (1972)
*GCH—An Inventory of Greek Coin Hoards*, edited by Margaret Thompson, Otto Mørkholm and Colin M. Kraay (1973)
Grant, *APT*—Michael Grant, *Aspects of the Principate of Tiberius* (1950)
Grant, *FITA*—Michael Grant, *From Imperium to Auctoritas* (1946)
Grant, *SMACA*—Michael Grant, *The Six Main Aes Coinages of Augustus* (1953)
*Izv. BAI—Izvestiia na Bulgarsko Arkheologicheskiia Institut*
*JbNumG—Jahrbuch für Numismatik und Geldgeschichte*
*JHS—Journal of Hellenic Studies*
*JRS—Journal of Roman Studies*
Kraay, *Vindonissa*—Colin M. Kraay, *Die Münzfunde von Vindonissa* (1962)
*Mél. d'Arch. et d'Hist de l'Éc. Fr. de Rome—Mélanges d'Archéologie et d'Histoire de l'École Française de Rome*
*NC—Numismatic Chronicle*
*Novaesium* III—see Chantraine, *Novaesium* III
*N.Sc.—Notizie degli scavi di antichità*
*Num.hisp.—Numario hispanico*
*Num.Közl.—Numizmatikai Közlöny*
*NZ—Numismatische Zeitschrift*
Pliny, *NH*—Pliny, *Naturalis Historia*
*RE—Real-Encyclopädie der klassischen Altertumswissenschaft*, edited by A. Pauly, G. Wissowa, W. Kroll (1893– )
*Rev.num.—Revue numismatique*

*RIC* I—*The Roman Imperial Coinage* I, *Augustus to Vitellius,* by Harold Mattingly and Edward A. Sydenham (1923)

Rostovtzeff, *SEHRE*²—M. I. Rostovtzeff, *Social and Economic History of the Roman Empire* (second edition, 1957)

*RRCH*—*Roman Republican Coin Hoards,* by Michael H. Crawford (1969)

*SCN*—*Studii și circetări de numismatică*

*SCIV*—*Studii și circetări de istorie veche*

Suet., *Div.Aug.*—Suetonius, *Divus Augustus*

Suet., *Tib.*—Suetonius, *Tiberius*

Sutherland, *CRIP*—C. H. V. Sutherland, *Coinage in Roman Imperial Policy* (1951)

Tac., *Ann.*—Tacitus, *Annales*

Tac., *Germ.*—Tacitus, *Germania*

*Troy: The Coins*—*see* Bellinger, *Troy: The Coins*

*VDI*—*Vestnik drevnej istorii*

*Vindonissa*—*see* Kraay, *Vindonissa*

*ZfN*—*Zeitschrift für Numismatik*

The numbers following the abbreviations *BMCRE* I, *CRR, FMRD, FMRL, GCH, RIC* I, *RRCH* are the numbers of the coins or finds, unless otherwise indicated. The abbreviation *FMRD* without a volume number refers to the volumes I 1, 2, 5, 7; II 1, 2, 3, 4; III; IV 1, 2, 3.1 collectively.

# NOTES

## Preliminary note: Roman and Greek money

4 *quadrantes* = 1 *as*
2 *semisses* = 1 *as*
1 *dupondius* = 2 *asses*
1 *sestertius* = 4 *asses*
16 *asses* = 1 *denarius*
2 *quinarii* = 1 *denarius*
25 *denarii* = 1 *aureus*

The metal first used by the Romans for money was bronze, and their original currency unit was the *as*. The first *asses* were of cast bronze and weighed one Roman pound each, about 325 g. Subsequently the weight of the *as* was repeatedly reduced, and already in the third century it became a struck coin. From *c.* 20 B.C. *asses* struck by the Roman government were token coins of about 11·35 g. Those produced at Rome and in Gaul were of copper, but other alloys, with varying copper content, were used at other mints and for other denominations. The term *aes* is used to cover all such alloys.

The unit used by the Romans for expressing sums of money was the *sestertius*, abbreviated HS.

The *sestertius*, *dupondius*, *semis* and *quadrans* were struck in much smaller quantities than the *as*, though *aes* coins of all these denominations were struck by the Roman authorities from time to time during the Julio-Claudian period, from Augustus' reign to Nero's.

During the third century B.C. the Roman government began to produce silver money in addition to bronze. Before the end of the century the *denarius*, of about 3·4 g, became the chief silver coin. By the time of Augustus the only other silver denomination struck was the *quinarius*, which was produced in much smaller quantities.

After the middle of the first century B.C. gold coins, *aurei*, of about 6·8 g, began to be minted regularly.

Almost everywhere in the Greek world, and among other peoples who had learnt the use of coined money from the Greeks, the basis of currency was the silver drachma. The drachma was divided into six obols. Fractions of the drachma were, by the first century B.C., normally struck in bronze. Some states struck also, or only, two-drachma silver pieces, didrachms; some struck also, or only, four-drachma pieces, tetradrachms —mainly those states whose currency was commonly used in long-distance trade.

There were several different standards for the drachma. By the first century B.C. the most widely used was the Attic, with a drachma of about 4·3 g. The Rhodian standard came near to this, but the 'cistophoric' tetradrachms struck by various city states in western Asia Minor were based on a drachma of about 3·0 g, while in the Phoenician city states the drachma was of about 3·6 g.

For several fairly obvious reasons, estimations of equivalence are bound to be unsatisfactory, but comparison of the *denarius* or the drachma with two pounds sterling or four United States dollars gives some idea of the purchasing power of money in the time of Tiberius. Estimates which were much too low, even when one allows for inflation in recent years, used to be in favour; for instance, Sir Paul Harvey, in the *Oxford Companion to Classical Literature* (1937) stated (278) that a *denarius* was 'equivalent to about 8*d*'. On the other hand, one very recent estimate is much higher: M. I. Finley, in *The Ancient Economy* (1973), referring (104) to the pay of a Roman soldier, equates one *denarius* with ten dollars.

## Chapter I: notes 1–108

1　Tacitus, *Annals* 6.16–17: *Interea magna vis accusatorum in eos inrupit, qui pecunias faenore auctitabant adversum legem dictatoris Caesaris, qua de modo credendi possidendique intra Italiam cavetur, omissam olim, quia privato usui bonum publicum postponitur . . . sed tum Gracchus praetor, cui ea quaestio evenerat, multitudine periclitantium subactus rettulit ad senatum, trepidique patres (neque enim quisquam tali culpa vacuus) veniam a principe petivere; et concedente annus in posterum sexque menses dati, quis secundum iussa legis rationes familiares quisque componerent.*

*Hinc inopia rei nummariae, commoto simul omnium aere alieno, et quia tot damnatis bonisque eorum divenditis signatum argentum fisco vel aerario attinebatur. ad hoc senatus praescripserat, duas quisque faenoris partes in agris per Italiam conlocaret. sed creditores in solidum appellabant, nec decorum appellatis minuere fidem. ita primo concursatio et preces, dein strepere praetoris tribunal, eaque quae remedio quaesita, venditio et emptio, in contrarium mutari, quia faeneratores omnem pecuniam mercandis agris condiderant. copiam vendendi secuta vilitate, quanto quis obaeratior, aegrius distrahebant, multique fortunis provolvebantur; eversio rei familiaris dignitatem ac famam praeceps dabat, donec tulit opem Caesar disposito per mensas miliens sestertio factaque mutuandi copia sine usuris per triennium, si debitor populo in duplum praediis cavisset. sic refecta fides, et paulatim privati quoque creditores reperti. neque emptio agrorum exercita ad formam senatus consulti, acribus, ut ferme talia, initiis, incurioso fine.*

2　Tacitus' words do not seem to have received close consideration since the publication of Furneaux's commentary (vol. I² (1896)). Koestermann (*Cornelius Tacitus: Annalen*, Band II (1965)) adds nothing of importance.

3　It is clear from the whole context that Tacitus refers to convictions on other charges, not on the charge of illegal lending. Whether the *fiscus* was entitled to receive any of the proceeds of sales of confiscated property is a question that need not concern us. The meanings of the term *fiscus* and the relation of the *aerarium* to the *fiscus*, in the sense in which Tacitus uses the word here, denoting, in the words of A. H. M. Jones (*JRS* 40 (1950), 25), 'the whole financial administration controlled by the emperor', have recently been examined afresh in a careful study by P. A. Brunt (*JRS* 56 (1966), 75–91); I accept his contentions, so far as they concern the subject matter of this study, except that I am not convinced that under the Principate 'the term "fiscus" . . . without qualification . . . originally . . . referred to the private wealth of the Emperor', despite the fact that Seneca so uses the term (*de beneficiis* 7. 6. 3, cited by Brunt, 76). Cicero's use of the term (II *in Verrem* 3. 197, cited by Brunt, *ibid*.), surely shows that it could as well refer to the funds that the emperor had under his control as a public servant—really a conglomerate of *fisci*, in Cicero's sense—e.g. the *fiscus Gallicus provinciae Lugdunensis* (Dessau, *Inscriptiones Latinae Selectae*, 1540): which is why Suetonius (*Div. Aug.* 101) speaks of Augustus leaving money at his death *in fiscis*; cf. G. Ürögdi, *Acta Antiqua* 16 (1968), 247 ff. Naturally enough, the two terms, like the two things, gradually became fused. As Brunt says (91), citing *Ann.* 6. 2, 'already to Tacitus the distinction was unimportant', but in Tiberius' time it had surely not yet 'ceased to be clear which funds were public and which were private'; nor indeed does Brunt suggest this; as he says, the confusion grew 'after Augustus and by a process whose history can never be written'.

4　Cassius Dio, 58. 21. 1–5: ἐπεὶ μέντοι . . . καὶ ὁ Νέρονας μηκέτι τὴν συνουσίαν αὐτοῦ φέρων ἀπεκαρτέρησε διά τε τἆλλα καὶ μάλισθ' ὅτι τοὺς νόμους τοὺς περὶ τῶν συμβολαίων ὑπὸ τοῦ Καίσαρος τεθέντας, ἐξ ὧν καὶ ἀπιστία καὶ ταραχὴ πολλὴ γενήσεσθαι ἔμελλεν, ἀνενεώσατο, . . . τό τε πρᾶγμα τὸ κατὰ τὰ δανείσματα ἐμετρίασε, καὶ δισχιλίας καὶ πεντακοσίας μυριάδας τῷ δημοσίῳ ἔδωκεν ὥστ' αὐτὰς ὑπ' ἀνδρῶν βουλευτῶν ἀτοκεὶ τοῖς δεομένοις ἐς τρία ἔτη ἐκδανεισθῆναι, τούς τε ἐπιβοητοτάτους τῶν τὰς κατηγορίας ποιουμένων ἀποθανεῖν ἐν μιᾷ ἡμέρᾳ ἐκέλευσε.

5  Suetonius, *Tiberius* 48. 1: *Publice munificentiam bis omnino exhibuit, proposito milies sestertium gratuito in trienni tempus et rursus quibusdam dominis insularum, quae in monte Caelio deflagrarant, pretio restituto. quorum alterum magna difficultate nummaria populo auxilium flagitante coactus est facere, cum per senatus consultum sanxisset, ut faeneratores duas patrimonii partes in solo collocarent, debitores totidem aeris alieni statim solverent, nec res expediretur; alterum ad mitigandam temporum atrocitatem* . . .

6  See the full and careful discussion by M. W. Frederiksen ('Caesar, Cicero and the problem of debt', *JRS* 56 (1966), especially pp. 132–5). Frederiksen argues that it was probably passed late in 46 B.C. or in 45 B.C., and that it also cannot be identified with the law to which C. Matius refers in a letter to Cicero (*ad fam.* 11. 28. 2), as has been suggested by some, most recently E. Koestermann in his commentary on the *Annals* II. 277, since 'it is hard to see how Pompeians would avoid *infamia* because of it' (Frederiksen, *ibid.*, 138, n. 76).

7  So Mommsen, *Römische Geschichte* III⁸, 537–8.

8  This was the view of Tenney Frank (see below, n.12). It has been stated most recently by Frederiksen, *JRS* 56 (1966), 134. For *faenus* meaning 'interest', see *Germania* 26. 1 (where Tacitus expresses his dislike of this mode of adding to one's wealth), cf. 19. 14, and cf. *faenero* in Pliny, *Epistulae* 3. 19. 8.

9  This excursus, which I have omitted, follows *postponitur*, 'welfare'. There is no other evidence for Caesarian legislation on the rate of interest, although it is possible, as Mommsen (*loc. cit.*, n.7) suggested, that Caesar re-enacted the senatorial decree of 51/50 B.C. (Cic. *ad Att.* 5. 21. 11–13), perhaps making it clearly applicable to the provinces also.

10  Cassius Dio 41. 38: ἐπειδή τε συχνοὶ πολλά τε χρήματα ἔχειν καὶ πάντα αὐτὰ ἀποκρύπτειν ἐλέγοντο, ἀπηγόρευσε μηδένα πλεῖον πεντακισχιλίων καὶ μυρίων δραχμῶν ἐν ἀργυρίῳ ἢ καὶ χρυσίῳ κεκτῆσθαι, οὐχ ὡς καὶ αὐτὸς τὸν νόμον τοῦτον τιθείς, ἀλλ' ὡς καὶ πρότερόν ποτε ἐσενεχθέντα ἀνανεούμενος.

'As it was being said that there were many wealthy people who were concealing the whole of their wealth, he made it illegal for anyone to hold more than fifteen thousand drachmas [i.e. sixty thousand sesterces: Dio here equates drachma and *denarius*] in silver or in gold, claiming that he was not himself the author of this law but was reviving a law that had been enacted at some time in the past.'

11  Frederiksen, *JRS* 56 (1966), 134 and n.39. The incorporation of this rule in the law is not as self-evident as Furneaux, in his commentary on the *Annals*, followed by Koestermann, asserts.

12  'The financial crisis of 33 A.D.', *AJP* 56 (1935), 336–41. This view of the causes and character of the crisis was later incorporated in Frank's volume on *Rome and Italy of the Empire* in *ESAR* v, 32–5. It has since stood unchallenged. It is, for example, accepted as basic by Paul Petit (*Nouvelle Clio: L'histoire et ses problèmes*, 9; *La Paix romaine* (1957), 295–6), and A. J. Christopherson (*Historia* 17 (1968), 355), in an article on the administration of Gaul. (But see Michael Crawford's expression of disbelief (*JRS* 60 (1970), 46) and L. C. West's general criticism of Frank's treatment of currency, ANS *Museum Notes* 6 (1954), 1–10.) Koestermann, in his commentary on the passage, makes no mention of Frank's article or of his treatment of the matter in *ESAR*, though he refers to a trivial note by Karl Hulley, comparing Tiberius with President Hoover (*Classical Journal* 27 (1932), 525–6), and to the books on Tiberius by Ernest Kornemann (1960), who (204–5) gives little more than a paraphrase of Tacitus' account, and by F. B. Marsh (1931), who (206) says almost

nothing, and the book on Tacitus by Ettore Paratore: on which see below, n.78. S. Mazzarino, *Trattato di Storia Romana* II (1956), 96–7 makes no reference to Frank and offers a rather different interpretation of the crisis.

Among others to whom one might look for comment on these events and on Frank's discussion of them, C. H. V. Sutherland (*CRIP*, 103) adds nothing to Tacitus' account, which he paraphrases in modern terms; H. Mattingly (*Roman Coins*[2] (1960), 176–9) seems to accept Tacitus' account as satisfactory, but remarks judiciously that 'the action taken by Tiberius . . . demands a closer investigation'. C. Kraay (*Vindonissa*, 16) confines himself to saying that Tacitus' account of the financial crisis shows that the supply of currency was inadequate, at least in Italy. M. I. Finley (*The Ancient Economy* (1973), 143, 208 n.46), discussing 'the shortage of coin, a chronic problem' in the ancient world, remarks that 'a proper analysis . . . of this rather mysterious outbreak . . . remains to be made'.

**13**  *AJP* 56 (1935), 340. Frank analyses the evidence for confiscations in *ESAR* v, 38 n.9.

**14**  *AJP* 56 (1935), 337.

**15**  *Roman Coins*[2], 181; cf. the comment of Georges le Rider, *Études Archéologiques* (École Pratique des Hautes Études, VI[e] Section, *Archéologie et Civilisation* I (1963)), 179: 'Certaines d'entre elles nous arrivent si usées qu'il est clair que, contrairement aux principes de l'économie moderne, les lois relatives au frai des monnaies n'existaient pas . . . chez les Romains.'

**16**  For instance, an individual saver might have deliberately selected, over a period, coins less worn than most of those in circulation, if enough coins passed through his hands, but an official would have in his chest, or a trader in his float, whatever happened to have been given him recently. On the ambiguity of hoards, resulting from this and many other factors, see F. Mateu y Llopis, *Numisma* 2.3 (1952), 9 ff; H. Gebhart and K. Kraft, *JbNumG* 7 (1956), 39–40, 45, 65; M. Crawford, *JRS* 59 (1969), 290 f; F. S. Kleiner, ANS *Museum Notes* 19 (1974), 19, 22–3. Attempts have been made to distinguish between hoards of different kinds: see B. Thordeman, *NC*[6] 8 (1948), 200 n.22; M. Thirion, *Les Trésors monétaires gaulois et romains trouvés en Belgique* (1967), 10; T. Fischer, *Schweizer Münzblätter* 18. 69 (1968), 9 ff.; but although conjecture is tempting in some cases (see e.g. below, n.18) such criteria are very difficult to apply comprehensively.

**17**  I. A. Richmond, *Transactions of the Cumberland and Westmorland Arch. & Ant. Soc.* NS 54 (1955), 56–60.

**18**  R. A. G. Carson, discussing the Bredgar hoard of *aurei* (see Table I), appears not to accept this: 'If the find represented some part of official funds, the hoard would have consisted only of coins of recent mintage' (*NC*[6] 19 (1959), 21). But on his plausible hypothesis, that it represents the personal savings, accumulated out of pay, of a centurion, or a higher officer, involved in the invasion of Britain in A.D. 43, how are we to account for the man's acquisition of *aurei* over seventy years old except by supposing that they had been issued to him out of official funds ? A similar hoard of fifty *aurei*, found at Utrecht on the site of a camp burnt down in A.D. 69, of which a similar explanation has been proposed (*Jaarboek voor Munt- en Penningkunde* 47 (1960), 1–6) includes analogously an *aureus* of Augustus and five *aurei* of Tiberius.

**19**  Cic. *ad Att.* 2. 6. 2, cf. 2. 16. 4. (For *cistophori*, see below, pp. 21, 24.) What I have suggested in the text seems to me more probable than the suggestion of Shackleton Bailey in his commentary on 2. 6. 2, '*Pompeiano* refers either to coins struck by Pompey in the East, or, more likely, to those he had deposited in the Roman treasury': cf. *ad fam.* 2. 17. 4. Alexander the Great made some use, at least, of existing coins that fell into his hands (Bellinger, *Alexander*, 49–50, 54, 68, 72, 76), though probably a large proportion of the wealth that he captured was in the form of bullion.

**20**  Willers, *NZ* 31 (1899), 313.

**21** Or merely as trinkets, as Suetonius, *Div. Aug.* 75, seems to suggest: *Saturnalibus, et si quando alias libuisset, modo munera dividebat, vestem et aurum et argentum, modo nummos omnis notae, etiam veteres regios ac peregrinos*, 'At the Saturnalia, and on any other occasion when he felt so inclined, he distributed gifts, sometimes clothing and gold and silver, sometimes coins of all descriptions, even old coins of kings and foreign states.' To someone writing a century afterwards, when most people in the Empire would never see non-Roman coins of precious metal, apart from such as had been kept as souvenirs or ornaments, the giving of foreign coins by the Emperor as presents seemed whimsical, but it would have been perfectly natural for Augustus to give away some of the many foreign coins that must have come into his private possession, in full knowledge of their value, precisely as he gave, as more important presents, some of the lands that he had acquired.

It is equally probable that some of the foreign coins that came into his official *fiscus* or into the *aerarium* were used, where appropriate, for official disbursements.

**22** P. Grierson, *JRS* 50 (1960), 267. An ancient example can also be cited: 'In Delphi, reminting of the Amphictyonic contributions towards rebuilding the temple in 336 B.C. and the years immediately following entailed a loss of perhaps 14 per cent, because so many of the old coins were worn and for other reasons' (M. I. Finley, *Deuxième Conférence Internationale d'Histoire Économique*, 1962, I (1965), 22, summarising the conclusions of E. J. P. Raven, *NC*[6] 10 (1950), 1–22). However, in melting down Greek coins the Romans would have been compensated by their habitual undervaluation of these in relation to *denarii*.

**23** Cf. Cic., *ad fam.* 2. 17. 4, on *vecturae periculum*, 'the risks of transport'.

**24** It is possible that some of the issues that are ascribed to Lugdunum were produced in part at branch mints, as Michael Grant has suggested (*SMACA*, 69, 162; *Roman Imperial Money* (1954), 78, 133): cf. H. Mattingly, *Roman Coins*[2], 102–5: but this is of no great importance in the present context.

**25** Thus the Roman government will have profited by recalling the surviving republican *denarii* in A.D. 107, for in a Trajanic hoard from Britain in which one third of the *denarii* were republican the republican coins had lost not more than 10–14 per cent of what should have been their original weight (C. M. Kraay, *NC*[6] 20 (1960), 271–3); and Nero had in the meantime reduced the official weight of the *aureus* and thus of the *denarius* by 14 per cent (Pliny, *NH* 33. 3. 47: confirmed by the coins). (Moreover the new *denarii* were struck at a lower standard of fineness (average about 80 per cent) than had been maintained under the Republic (average about 95 per cent), if some samples recently analysed can be regarded as representative (Hans-Jörg Kellner and Walter Specht, *JbNumG* 11 (1961), 43–52; but cf. Lawrence H. Cope, *NC*[7] 7 (1967), 107 ff.).) The resulting profit will have sufficed to outweigh the loss involved in accepting among the withdrawn republican *denarii* a proportion of plated coins.

**26** Under Augustus and Tiberius the weight and the silver content of the *denarius* do not appear to have been significantly reduced: see e.g. *BMCRE* I, xliv, lii. (For fineness Mattingly was relying on analyses by what are now considered inadequate methods (J. Hammer, *ZfN* 25 (1908) 1 ff.), but it does not seem to be thought that these are seriously misleading in respect of republican, Augustan and Tiberian *denarii* (Cope, *op. cit.* (n.25), 107 ff.).) But, as site finds in the Rhine–Upper Danube frontier region show, the *denarii* that were in circulation included a proportion of coins of base metal thinly plated with silver, the proportion rising from republican through Caesarian, Augustan and Tiberian issues, as the table below illustrates (though obviously one cannot assume that the proportion found is anything like an accurate reflection of the proportion that was in circulation). It seems most likely that they were the work of counterfeiters: 'if the state had engaged in forgery, the attempt to suppress it when practised by others would have been most unlikely to succeed and thus virtually pointless' (Crawford, *NC*[7] 8 (1968), 58). But even if one supposes that some or all of these plated coins were produced officially, as many numismatists have argued or assumed (Chantraine, *Novaesium* III, 37; Kraay, *Vindonissa*, 17; Mattingly, *CRR*, p. 224, *Roman Coins*², 132, cf. 187; but he would exclude Augustus and Tiberius from blame), the authorities would have had no motive for withdrawing good older coins when they put new plated coins into circulation.

Ratio of plated to good *denarii*

|  | Republican period | | | Imperial period | |
|---|---|---|---|---|---|
|  | Caesar, Gaul | Antony, legionary | Others | Augustus[a] | Tiberius |
| *FMRD* (excluding hoards) | 4:18 | 2:110 | 17:276 | 13:86 | 5:23 |
| *FMRL* | 1:3 | 0:4 | 4:27 | 5:13 | 1:3 |
| Sels'sche Ziegeleien | 1:4 | 1:7 | 5:28 | 6:4 | 1:4 |
| Neuss (1887–1904 excavation | – | 0:4 | 0:10 | 1:2 | 1:2 |
| Neuss (1955–1962 excavation) | – | 2:3 | 3:12 | 9:1 | · 5/6:2/1 |
| Oberaden | – | 0:1 | 0:5 | 0:3 | – |
| Hofheim | – | 0:1 | 0:5 | – | 1:0 |
| Vindonissa | 1:3 | 1:18 | 5:66 | 16:22 | 4:7 |
| Magdalensberg | 0:2 | 0:1 | 3:26 | 1:4 | 0:2 |
| Proportion of plated *denarii* in total (%) | 19 | 4 | 7½ | 27½ | 29½–31 |

[a] Including coins with legend IMP CAESAR or CAESAR DIVI FILIUS commonly classed with the coins of Augustus

(References: Sels'sche Ziegeleien: *Bonner Jahrbücher* 111–12 (1904), 419–53, cf. *JbNumG* 6 (1956), 54 n.74; Neuss, 1887–1904 excavations: *Bonner Jahrbücher* 111–12 (1904), 243–89; Neuss, 1955–62 excavations: *Novaesium* III; Oberaden: *FMRD* VI, 5 (1972); Hofheim: *Annalen des Vereins für nassauische Altertumskunde* 40 (1912), 98–117 (unsatisfactory, but the volume of *FMRD* containing a revised list has not yet been published); Vindonissa: Kraay, *Vindonissa*; Magdalensberg: see below, n.425.

**27**    This was the sole justification of much of the striking of coins in the Greco-Roman world. Bellinger (*Troy: The Coins*, 101) referring to a tetradrachm of Alexandria Troas that had been restruck on a coin of Thasos, comments: 'Since there is no reason to suppose that the Thasian coins were not valid in Asia, local pride is still a factor . . . for it is unlikely that the expense of restriking would be compensated by any practical advantage': cf. *ibid.*, 21–3.

**28**    The comments of Suetonius (*Div. Aug.* 41. 2), *invecta urbi Alexandrino triumpho regia gaza tantam copiam nummariae rei effecit*, 'When the royal treasure was transported to Rome for the Alexandrian triumph, it created such a glut of currency . . .' and of Dio (51. 21. 5), τοσοῦτον γὰρ τὸ πλῆθος τῶν χρημάτων διὰ πάσης τῆς πόλεως ἐχώρησεν, 'for such a mass of money went into circulation all over Rome', are so worded as to imply that they supposed, rightly or wrongly, that the Egyptian treasure included money that was put into circulation as soon as it reached Rome. The experience of Henry VIII indicates a possible motive: 'To organize a smooth flow of metal through the Mint was not at all simple; the money was liable to be held up, awaiting recoinage, just when it was wanted to be spent' (Sir John Hicks, *A Theory of Economic History* (1969), 89, citing J. D. Gould, *The Great Debasement* (1969)).

**29** Cf. Bellinger, *Alexander*, 50, 54–5, on Alexander and Persian coins; and Cassius Dio 65. 6. 1, on Vitellius.

**30** The *denarii* that have survived in far greater numbers than those of any of the other varieties produced under the Republic or the early Empire are the so-called legionary *denarii* that were struck for Antony. But their survival in such vast numbers probably indicates not simply that they were produced on a very large scale but that, being rather light, and their fineness being suspect, they were excluded when coins were melted down. (Mr Michael Crawford informs me that 'analyses show that legionary *denarii* are debased'.) But if they were deliberately left in circulation for these reasons, it follows that Augustus or his agents were more concerned to avoid unnecessary expense than to eliminate memorials of Antony. Doubt is thus cast on Sutherland's suggestion (*The Cistophori of Augustus* (1970), 105–6) that 'the recall of his great cistophoric coinage was undertaken with unusual energy and thoroughness as a literal means of helping to expunge a shameful chapter', and that it was by this means that Augustus obtained much of the silver for his own cistophoric coinage.

**31** *AJP* 56 (1935), 337; *ESAR* v, 18: cf. T. R. S. Broughton, *ESAR* IV, 557.

**32** See n.28: cf. Dio 51. 17. 6–7.

**33** Louis C. West and Allan Chester Johnson (*Currency in Roman and Byzantine Egypt* (1944), 5–6) repeat the statement of J. G. Milne (*Catalogue of Alexandrian Coins in the Ashmolean Museum* (1933), xxvi) that the silver which Augustus found in circulation was about 20 per cent fine, but observe that 'this statement seems to rest on Poole, *Catalogue of Greek Coins in the British Museum: The Ptolemies* (1883), lxxx, where the statement is made that the late Ptolemaic issues of silver resemble the potin of Tiberius. There seem to be no analyses of the Ptolemaic silver.'

**34** By making Egypt into a closed monetary area, Augustus avoided the expense of reintroducing true silver currency into a land that had been effectively on a copper standard since the end of the third century (cf. T. Reekmans, *Chronique d'Égypte* 48 (1949), 324 ff.); so all the silver that had been in Egyptian hands was released to satisfy needs elsewhere.

**35** Orosius 6. 19: *Caesar Alexandria, urbe omnium longe opulentissima et maxima, victor potitus est. Nam et Roma in tantum opibus eius aucta est, ut propter abundantiam pecuniarum duplicia, quam usque ad id fuerant, possessionum aliarumque rerum venalium pretia statuerentur*, 'By his victory Caesar gained possession of Alexandria, by far the wealthiest and greatest of cities. For Rome was so enriched by its wealth that the prices of landholdings and of other things on sale were set at double the previous level as a result of the abundant supply of money.'

**36** Billeter (*Geschichte des Zinsfusses im griechisch-römischen Altertum* (1898), 166 n.1) plausibly argued that *duplicia* 'double' and *aliarumque rerum venalium*, 'other things for sale', represent later embellishments of the account which Suetonius (*Div. Aug.* 41) and Dio Cassius (51. 21) give us. (Dio's 12 per cent must have been a wartime figure: the normal rate, before the civil wars, had been more like 4–6 per cent.)

**37** J. Guey's discussion of this question is most valuable (*Mélanges Carcopino* (1966), especially 466–75).

**38** This increase in demand is discussed in Chapter II. Mattingly held that under the Republic supply had outpaced demand (*Roman Coins²*, 86).

**39** Florus 2. 33, Dio 54. 21.

**40**  *AJP* 56 (1935), 338. Sutherland (*CRIP* 48) speaks ambiguously of a 'considerable quantity' (cf. *ibid.*, 188, 'very considerable'): but find-evidence (see Table I) suggests that although the issues were numerous the total output was small in comparison with that of the other Augustan mints. Buttrey, *AJA* 76 (1972), 43, calls them 'modest issues'.

**41**  *AJP* 56 (1935), 338–9: there are similar statements in *ESAR* v, 20.

**42**  This statement is based on an extremely hazardous and dubious calculation, involving comparison of a passage in Orosius (6. 15. 5) with a passage in Pliny (*NH* 33. 56), both emended by Frank to fit his thesis: see *ESAR* I, 338.

**43**  *AJP* 56 (1935), 339.

**44**  To begin with, we do not know exactly what Frank meant by an 'issue', but if we treat as an 'issue', in most cases, the coins subsumed by Sydenham under a single number in *CRR*, analysis of some publications of finds, firstly in the German frontier region and secondly in Italy and Sicily, reveals wide variations in the representation of individual issues, variations which are largely in keeping with the classification by degrees of rarity which Sydenham established (but which had not been published when Frank wrote). At the one extreme, there are altogether seven or more examples of each of twelve issues; these twelve comprise seven (*CRR*, 578, 646, 684, 698, 700, 724, 732) of the seventeen classed by Sydenham as 'extremely common') together with five issues (*CRR*, 588, 702, 705, 723, 742) which he classed as 'very common'. At the other extreme, some thirty-five issues (none classed by Sydenham as common), out of a total of about one hundred and five, are not represented at all in these two samples. Finally, two (*CRR*, 578, 588) of the twelve most heavily represented issues were made in the nineties, the period which was evidently, overall, much less productive. (One of these, *CRR*, 588, is an issue of *quinarii*; another issue of *quinarii*, *CRR*, 597, made in the nineties, would no doubt also have figured among the most heavily represented issues were it not that the hoards from Italy and Sicily included in the analysis contain, like so many other hoards, no *quinarii* at all.)

These examples may suffice to show how misleading Frank's statements were so far as the republican period is concerned. (Mr Michael Crawford informs me that table L in his forthcoming *Roman Republican Coinage* will substantiate this.) One may add that, if we accept Sydenham's dates, output was lower again in the seventies, sixties and fifties B.C. than it had been in the eighties (cf. Kraay, *Vindonissa*, 15), but whereas in the seventies and fifties the number of separate issues is in proportion, there was a disproportionately large number of issues in the sixties.

**45**  *RIC* I Augustus, 18; *BMCRE* I Augustus, 647 ff.

**46**  See Table I for some examples.

**47**  These *quinarii* have turned up in the German frontier regions in so much larger quantities than any of the numerous issues of *denarii* that were struck for Octavian from *c*. 34 B.C. to 27 B.C. that one might be tempted to doubt the usually presumed eastern origin of the *quinarii*. (At Neuss, in the 1955–62 excavations, three against one of these *denarii*, at Sels'sche Ziegeleien four against two, at Vindonissa six against three, at Haltern, excluding hoards, six against three (*FMRD* VI, 4), in *FMRD*, excluding hoards, nine against eight, in *FMRL* four against four, at Augusta Raurica, one against none (Herbert Cahn, *Provincialia*, *Festschrift für Rudolf Laur-Belart* (1968), 58, 66). So also in finds in the River Liri in Southern Italy: three against one ( ?): *NC*[7] 10 (1970), 95.) However, the reverse type would have meant nothing to most people in the west, and coins struck in the east could be expected to travel to the west, either as part of the savings of returning soldiers, or in official chests, in so far as Asia yielded revenue in excess of expenditure: while the commonness of this particular issue in the west may give us an exaggerated notion of its relative size, for if there was a greater demand for *quinarii* in the west than in the east (where small change was more abundant) the authorities might have sent a large proportion of this issue to the west. One possible reason for this demand is that native Gallic silver coins had approximated in weight to *quinarii* rather than to *denarii* (see J. B. Colbert de Beaulieu, *JbNumG* 16 (1966), 52–8). A consequent preference for *quinarii* is reflected in a number of Gallic hoards (J.-B. Giard, *Rev.num*[6] 9 (1967), 122–3, 131 n.1); cf. a curious hoard of plated *quinarii* found at Lausanne in 1945, 'presumably a forger's stock' (Crawford, *RRCH*, 482), comprising sixteen of this issue along with nineteen republican *quinarii* (seven of *CRR*, 588, twelve of *CRR*, 703) and ten abnormal *quinarii*, with legend CAESAR as on Julius Caesar's Gallic *denarii*, all struck from the same pair of dies, no doubt, therefore, locally (Niklaus Dürr, *Schweizer Münzblätter* 6 (1956), 7–9).

**48**  *Aes* is discussed in Chapter IV.

**49**  *RIC* I Augustus, 350, *BMCRE* I Augustus, 519 ff.

**50**  The great size of this issue has often been pointed out, but figures speak more clearly than words. Among finds, other than hoards, recorded in *FMRD* there are about eighty-six Augustan *denarii*; thirty-six are of this issue. From Vindonissa Kraay lists thirty-eight Augustan *denarii*; twenty-four are of this issue; of twenty-nine identified Augustan *denarii* found, outside hoards, at Haltern sixteen are of this issue (*FMRD* VI, 4), from the 1955–62 excavations at Neuss, the figures are ten and four. It is, not surprisingly, somewhat less conspicuous in finds away from the Rhine–Danube frontier area, at least in hoards, which constitute the bulk of accurately recorded finds of silver and gold coins in other areas, but the Aquileia and Vicopisano hoards shows what an important share it had in currency circulation even south of the Alps before the end of Augustus' reign (see Table I). The range of condition of examples in the Bredgar hoard indicates that production continued over many years, until late in Augustus' reign (R. A. G. Carson, *NC*[6] 19 (1959), 20). It has been stated that an exceptionally high proportion of the coins of this issue are plated, but this seems to be either a legend, believed on the authority of Eckhel (*Doctrina Numorum Veterum* (1796) VI, 171) and Mommsen (*Geschichte des römischen Münzwesens* (1860), 726, 760; cf. below, n.395) or an illusion, engendered by the great size of the issue, and the correspondingly large number of plated examples. Of the twenty-four from Vindonissa, eight are plated—but so are eight of the fourteen *denarii* of other Augustan issues; four of the thirty-six-odd of this issue in non-hoard finds in *FMRD* are plated, but so are eight out of fifty of other Augustan issues.

**51**  *RIC* I 3, *BMCRE* I, 34 ff. Variations in the details of the chair on the reverse, coupled with different renderings of Tiberius' portrait, which can be compared with 'dated' coins, permit a threefold division of this issue (*BMCRE* I, p. cxxx) but publications and photographs often do not suffice to make it clear which of the three varieties distinguished by *BMCRE* a particular example represents.

**52**  I have the impression that examples of this issue are found in relatively large numbers throughout the Empire, not merely in the Rhine–Danube frontier zone, and that *aurei* of this issue are also commoner than of any previous issue, but it is difficult to furnish any proof of this, since non-hoard evidence is scarce, hoards deposited during the largely peaceful half-century after Augustus' death are scarce, and Julio-Claudian coins are scarce in later hoards. I have noted four examples of the *denarius* in reports of isolated finds and excavation finds in Spain, and three of the great Augustan issue (see n.33), but no examples of any other Tiberian issue and only three examples of all other Augustan silver. In a hoard found at Krefeld, all the approximately three hundred imperial coins are said to have been examples either of this issue or of *RIC* Augustus, 350 (*Bonner Jahrbücher* 41 (1861), 184); for other hoard evidence from within the Empire, see Table I. (I discuss the curious evidence from India in Chapter III in the context of export of Roman currency.) Many plated examples of this issue are found, but again not an exceptionally large proportion.

**53** Mattingly, *BMCRE* I, p. cxxx; Sutherland, *CRIP*, 84–5.

**54** See A. H. M. Jones in *Essays in Roman Coinage presented to Harold Mattingly* (1956), 23; Michael Grant, *ibid.*, 112. For the period from Actium to the accession of Vespasian there is not even the rough but readily accessible guide to the size of issues provided by Sydenham (*CRR*) for the Republic and by Mattingly (*RIC*) for subsequent reigns.

**55** 'There is absolutely no evidence to suggest that all dies were always used to their maximum capacity, nor that the magic number of 10,000 coins per die has any relation to reality. . . . There are usually far too many variables to allow statistics to do more than a general quantitative analysis' (M. Jessop Price, *JHS* 94 (1974), 255 f.). However, it seems reasonable to suppose that in the case of Roman issues of silver under Augustus and Tiberius minting techniques were sufficiently uniform to make the average values of $x$ and $y$ fairly constant, so that the relative size of these issues can be assessed: cf. G. le Rider, *op. cit.* (n.15), 178 n.3, 181 f.

**56** *The Cistophori of Augustus* (1970), 105–9, following a method devised by D. M. Metcalf: see *JbNumG* 9 (1958), 187 ff. Lodovico Brunetti, *Aspetti statistici della metanumismatica* (1963), following a different method, has estimated that Tiberius' issue of Alexandrian tetradrachms comprised some 610,000 coins; but see the critique by Hansheiner Eichhorn, *Hamburger Beiträge zur Numismatik* 6. 20 (1966), who believes that great variations in the life of dies between issues as diverse as those analysed by Brunetti vitiate resulting estimates of total output: cf. Price, *loc. cit.* (n.55).

**57** Julien Guey, *XIe Congrès International des Sciences Historiques*, Stockholm 1960, *Rapports* II, 55–6.

**58** Attempts have nevertheless been made to estimate the likely survival rate of ancient gold and silver coins, partly on the basis of the knowledge that we possess concerning the actual size of certain issues, e.g. the Athenian gold coinage of 407–406 B.C. A rate of one in four thousand or five thousand has been suggested (E. S. G. Robinson, ANS *Museum Notes* 9 (1960), 9 ff; Bellinger, *Alexander*, 74; H. A. Cahn, *Knidos: Die Münzen des 6. und 5. Jahrhunderts v. Chr.* (1970), 144). It is interesting to note that if this were correct the 670 examples of Augustan *cistophori* inspected by Sutherland, which probably constitute a large proportion of the total number surviving, would represent issues comprising between 2,700,000 and 3,400,000 coins. But Margaret Thompson's estimates of the survival rate of 'new style' Athenian silver coins are quite different, ranging from 1 :2,625 to 1 :395; she concludes that there is no such thing as a general survival rate (*The New Style Silver Coinage of Athens* (1963), 709).

**59** For the relative importance of *aes* coinage and precious-metal coinage, see Chapter IV. On *aes* statistics, see in particular n.575.

**60** *AJP* 56 (1935), 339.

**61** Concordia: so Konrad Kraft, *Zur Münzprägung des Augustus*, Sb. Frankfurt 7 (1968) 5, 242–51. This interpretation does satisfactorily explain Tiberius' long retention of the type.

**62** Taking into account the seemingly increased production of *aurei*: cf. Table I. (Allowance must be made for the fact that six hoards are included with no coins later than 10 B.C.)

**63** For substantiation of this estimate, see Table I. Note that seventeen of the hoards, together containing two-thirds of the *denarii* and over half of the *aurei* listed, contained no post-Augustan coins, and that the content of hoards and finds that did may somewhat under-represent Tiberian in relation to Augustan output, since Tiberian *denarii*, some of which had been circulating for less than thirty years at the time of Nero's currency reform, would be on average somewhat less worn, and therefore more attractive for melting down, than those of Augustus, some of which had been circulating for nearly a century.

**64**  Suet., *Div.Aug.* 101.

**65**  Suet., *Gaius* 37.

**66**  *ESAR* v, 37.

**67**  If he were speaking of what Tiberius left under his will to Gaius (or rather to him and Tiberius Gemellus: *Tib.* 76, *Gaius*, 14), it would follow that Tiberius must have done very well for himself out of being Princeps: but Tacitus acknowledges that he was quite resolute in resisting the appeal of money (*satis firmus adversum pecuniam*) (*Ann.* 3. 18).

**68**  This, Augustus' *patrimonium*, was surely still something clearly distinct from the funds which he administered as a public servant and which he left at his death 'in fiscis' (Suet., *Div.Aug.* 101. 4): cf. n.2.

**69**  Cf. Frank's calculations, *ESAR* v, 38. Tiberius' reputation: cf. p. 70 and n.576.

**70**  *ESAR* v, 32.

**71**  Professor T. V. Buttrey has pointed out to me that bullion could have been bought on credit. In that case no money need have left Italy.

**72**  *AJP* 56 (1935), 337.

**73**  It is to be noted that the special causes which had produced really severe shortages of currency in the eighties and forties of the first century B.C. (and a minor shortage in the late sixties)—especially the fear of lenders that debts might be cancelled or scaled down by the government, which was what led them to call in their loans at those times; the desire of the wealthy, at times of great danger to visible property, to increase the proportion of their wealth that was in the form of money, which could be hidden; and, in 49, the suddenly increased need of the potentates for money to pay their soldiers—were not present in A.D. 33: see M. W. Frederiksen, *JRS* 56 (1966), 132–3. (It has, however, been suggested to me by Dr John Briscoe that in A.D. 33 there might again have been fear of confiscation, leading people to try to hide at least a portion of their wealth.) Frederiksen refers also to the difficulties that arose in the Second Punic War, but at that time the authorities did not merely lack coin, they simply had not sufficient wealth that they could lay hands on: a different matter. Probably this was so in the eighties also, but it was not so in the forties, so far as the potentates were concerned. One might ask, why, then, were they short of money? Why did they not strike more coins? Probably because they could not quickly get hold of the metal they needed. 'Caesar sold off Gallic gold at 3,000 sesterces per pound, half its true value' (Frederiksen, *ibid.*, 132)—presumably because at that juncture he needed silver.

**74**  *AJP* 56 (1935), 337. It should be noted that to speak of a 'market for land' is perhaps almost as inappropriate with reference to Italy in the first centuries B.C. and A.D. as with reference to Athens in the fifth and fourth centuries B.C.: see M. I. Finley, *The Ancient Economy* (1973), 116 ff.

**75**  Billeter, *op. cit.* (n.36), 180, summarising his findings for the whole period from Augustus to Justinian: 'Der eigentliche Typus liegt zwischen 4 und 6%, wobei innerhalb dieser Sätze weder eine zeitliche noch örtliche Differenzierung sich nachweisen lässt'; Heichelheim, *Oxford Classical Dictionary*[2], *s.v.* Interest, Rate of: 'during the first century B.C. and probably the first and second centuries A.D. normally *c.* 6–10%'. This corresponds to the return to be expected by an owner of agricultural land, which 'usually tended to be 6%' (Duncan-Jones, *Papers of the British School at Rome* N.S. 20 (1965), 202; cf. 279, 302, No. 1184): though it must be noted that the evidence that he is discussing is mainly from the second century A.D.

**76**  Some time before February of 50 B.C., probably late in 51 B.C., the Senate had decreed a maximum of 12 per cent per annum, with simple interest (Cic., *ad Att.* 5. 21. 11–13).

**77**  Thus, for instance, Horace could plausibly allege (*Sat.* 1. 2. 14) that in some cases money was lent, in Italy, at 60 per cent.

**78** Koestermann, in his commentary, refers here to Friedländer, *Sittengeschichte* I⁹ (1920), 129, who from this period, however, can cite only the well-known example of Seneca. Paratore (*Tacito*, 1951¹, 722, 1962², 495) thinks that Tacitus here reveals sympathy with senators, even as usurers: perhaps not the most natural interpretation of his treatment of the episode.

**79** See pp. 3–4.

**80** A couple of generations later, Trajan did cause a rise in the price of land, particularly in the neighbourhood of Rome, by requiring candidates for office to put one third of their patrimony into land (Pliny, *Epistulae*, 6. 19).

**81** That senators had long been active as moneylenders is emphasised by Brunt (*Deuxième Conférence Internationale d'Histoire Économique*, 1962, I (1965), 126), but members of a class sometimes behave as if an image of themselves formed in the past retained its validity. Even a couple of generations later the younger Pliny shows a slight shamefacedness about moneylending: *sum quidem prope totus in praediis, aliquid tamen faenero*, 'I am almost completely in land, but I do lend some money on interest' (*Epistulae* 3. 19. 8). Cf. M. I. Finley, *The Ancient Economy* (1973), 54–5, and, for the contrast between fantasy and reality, Horace's second Epode.

**82** Tacitus does not make it clear how the senatorial decree is related in time to the other happenings that he narrates, but, if due weight is given to the pluperfect tense of *praescripserat*, it seems likely that it was passed at a time when the calling-in of loans had only just begun, so that the full effect of this on the money supply could not yet have been felt. Tacitus goes on to explain why the decree did not have the desired remedial effect.

**83** Tacitus implies that to a large extent they did, because debtors were unwilling to take advantage of the moratorium, for fear of losing face.

**84** They had probably adopted the same policy in and after 49 B.C., despite Caesar's prohibition of hoarding of money late in that year, until he took further action in 46 B.C.: cf. M. W. Frederiksen, *JRS* 56 (1966), 133–4.

**85** Frank thought that they *obtained* the land by foreclosing on mortgages (so also Heitland, *Agricola* (1921), 288 f.)—but Tacitus says nothing of this—only that some debtors who could not pay had their land seized.

**86** Dio 58. 21, quoted above, n.4.

**87** This interpretation of Dio's account is accepted by Koestermann in his commentary on the *Annals* (II 277), following Furneaux (I², 614).

**88** Tac., *Ann.* 6. 26. 1–3.

**89** Cf. Suet., *Tib.* 33, 59.

**90** Tac., *Ann.* 6. 17. 5, quoted above, n.1. Alternatively, Dio's statement that Tiberius revived Caesar's laws could be taken to refer to the decree which the Senate passed in the hope of relieving the crisis, of which Suetonius (see n.5) does clearly make Tiberius the author. Tacitus' suppression of this would be equally surprising. Dio concludes his remarks on the episode by stating that Tiberius ordered the death of the most notorious of the *accusatores*—which might at first sight seem to suggest that he cannot be taken to mean that Tiberius had instigated them—but this detail may be thought rather to support that interpretation: it could be intended to illustrate the treacherous lengths to which he would carry his concealment of his feelings and aims, his *dissimulatio*: and the casual way in which reference is made to *accusatores* at this point also supports the interpretation that incitement of them was what constituted the revival of the Caesarian laws in Dio's view, or in the view of the authority whom Dio followed, who presumably gave a fuller and more intelligible account. (An alternative possibility is that Dio, or his source, has unintelligently run together two quite separate matters.)

**91** Precedents: see Frederiksen *JRS* 56 (1966), 140 n.86. Cf. Mattingly, *Roman Coins²*, 179: 'probably only one of many cases'. But it is unlikely that any acts of Tiberius, or any major acts of Augustus, of this kind have gone unrecorded.

92 Koestermann, in his commentary, does not accept this, since Tacitus says that borrowers had to offer security to the People, indicating that their debt was to the *aerarium*, not to the *fiscus*. This does seem to show that it was to the *aerarium* that repayment had to be made; but if Tacitus had not thought that Tiberius provided the money in the first place, he would hardly have said that he 'came to the rescue'.

93 Suet., *Tib*. 48: *publice munificentiam bis omnino exhibuit, proposito milies sestertium gratuito in trienni tempus . . .*

94 Brunt, *JRS* 56 (1966), 90. A generation later, Seneca was worth three hundred million sesterces, according to Tacitus (*Ann*. 13. 42), while a sum of ten million sesterces in hard cash was only a small part of Trimalchio's fortune (Petronius, *Satyricon* 54. 3).

95 *AJP* 56 (1935), 340.

96 *ESAR* v, 35.

97 Tac., *Ann*. 6. 19; cf. Dio 58. 22. 2, who also states that the charge was incest, but attributes to Tiberius quite a different motive. The evidence is all the more tenuous inasmuch as the passage in Tacitus, as it stands in the MS., ascribes to Marius the ownership of gold mines only: *post quos Sex. Marius Hispaniarum ditissimus defertur incestasse filiam et saxo Tarpeio deicitur. ac ne dubium haberetur magnitudinem pecuniae malo vertisse, aurariasque eius, quamquam publicarentur, sibimet Tiberius seposuit*, 'Next, Sextus Marius, the richest man in Spain, was denounced on a charge of incest with his daughter and was hurled down from the Tarpeian rock; and to remove any doubt from people's minds that his wealth was the cause of his misfortune, Tiberius kept his . . . and gold mines for himself, although they were declared public property.' And in one of the few other statements about the owner-ship of mines at this period that has come down to us, Strabo (3, p. 148) tells us that most of the Spanish gold mines were already state property at the time at which he was writing. But it is generally agreed that a word is missing either before *aurarias-que* ('. . . and gold mines') or before *que* ('gold and . . . mines'). However, the likeliest emendation is the insertion, not of *argentarias* ('silver': Weissenborn) but of *aerarias* ('copper': Ritter), since the error would then be very nearly one of simple haplography, and since Pliny mentions (*NH* 34. 4) *aes Marianum, quod et Cordubense dicitur*, 'Marian copper, which is also called Corduban'; and the confis-cation of copper mines would be of no assistance to Frank's hypothesis. (It might in fact have been of some use to Tiberius, making it perhaps less expensive for him to expand the total supply of currency: for according to Pliny (*NH* 34. 2) the so-called *mons Marianus* in Spain yielded the alloy of copper and zinc that was used for *sestertii* and *dupondii*). Tacitus says of Marius' mines *sibimet Tiberius seposuit*, 'Tiberius kept them for himself.' If the words are to be taken literally, as Fergus Millar would take them (*JRS* 53 (1963), 29), that would not have helped the mint (unless we also accept Millar's view that what the *fiscus* contained was at this time the emperor's private property, for, if that was so, 'the importance of the emperor's private wealth in the running of the state' must have been so great as to extend inevitably to regular subsidising of the mint). But it is likelier, in the context of Tacitus' portrayal of Tiberius the tyrant, that he meant simply to emphasise that Tiberius brought the mines in question under his personal control (Brunt, *JRS* 56 (1966), 91), although the Senate, in whose province they lay, may have formally decreed the transfer (see Brunt, *ibid*., 81–2).

98 Suet., *Tib*. 49. 1–2: *Procedente mox tempore etiam ad rapinas convertit animum. satis constat . . . plurimis etiam civitatibus et privatis veteres immunitates et ius metal-lorum ac vectigalium adempta . . .*, 'as time went on, he even turned his attention to robbery. It is well established that . . . a large number of communities and individ-uals were deprived of long-established exemptions and rights with respect to mines and revenues.'

99 Assuming that Suetonius' words can be taken to refer to the confiscation of private

property. In themselves they would refer more naturally to the cancellation of concessions that had been granted for the collection of *vectigalia*, revenues, and for the exploitation of *metalla*, mines (cf. Livy 34. 21. 7: in 195 B.C. Cato *vectigalia magna instituit ex ferrariis argentariisque* 'instituted large revenues from iron and silver mines'); but on the other hand the context is a list of robberies (*rapinae*).

**100**    Cf. the remarks of Henri Seyrig, discussing Attalid and Seleucid coinage (*Rev.num.*[6] 5 (1963), 28): 'Encore bien plus sujette à caution paraît être l'idée . . . d' après laquelle il serait nécessaire de posséder des mines d'argent pour émettre des monnaies en abondance. Rien n'est moins probable . . . Lorsqu'on n'avait pas de mines, on achétait le métal . . . .' Cf. Mattingly's speculations (*Roman Coins*[2], 35) concerning Roman republican practice. According to Sutherland (*CRIP*, 13), by the time of Octavian's rise to power the 'supreme governing authority' possessed 'strict economic control of the coinage metals . . . gold, silver and aes'; but it is not clear precisely what he meant by this. Indeed, the whole question of the relationship between mining and coinage at this period remains obscure: 'l'on ignore presque tout de l'importance de l'activité miniere: valeur réelle du métal extrait (or, argent, plomb), rapport avec l'évolution des frappes monétaires' (Paul Petit, *La Paix romaine* (1967), 290; cf. 329).

**101**    *AJP* 56 (1935), 337.

**102**    Tac., *Ann.* 6. 45: *Idem annus gravi igne urbem adfecit, deusta parte circi quae Aventino contigua ipsoque Aventino; quod damnum Caesar ad gloriam vertit exsolutis domuum et insularum pretiis. miliens sestertium in munificentia ea conlocatum,* 'In this same year Rome experienced a serious fire, which devastated the part of the Circus adjacent to the Aventine and the Aventine itself: Caesar turned the damage to his own credit by defraying the cost of the houses and tenement blocks. One hundred million sesterces were spent on this munificence': Suetonius, *Tib.* 48. 1, quoted above, pp. 2 ff., ignores this incident, cf. n.576.

**103**    Cf. above, p. 10.

**104**    *AJP* 56 (1935), 341; cf. *ESAR* v, 35.

**105**    See above, n.25.

**106**    Hans Gebhart and Konrad Kraft, *JbNumG* 7 (1956), 46.

**107**    Emona hoard: latest coin *RIC* I Nero, 19, completely fresh: see Table I. Four Claudian hoards are worth considering:

    (i) Laluque (*Rev.num.*[3] 6 (1880), 533–41): approximately 180 *denarii*; 120 examined; Augustus thirteen, Tiberius forty-five, Gaius three, Claudius (to A.D. 43) two.

    (ii) Niçulitel (*SCIV* 17 (1966), 577–92): approximately 161 *denarii*; Augustus forty-plus (mostly *RIC* I Augustus, 350), Tiberius eighty-plus (mostly *RIC* I Tiberius, 3), Gaius two, Claudius (to A.D. 47) five.

    (iii) Bredgar (*NC*[6] 19 (1959), 17–22): thirty-four *aurei*; Augustus twelve (*RIC* I Augustus, 350: eight), Tiberius seventeen (*RIC* I Tiberius, 3: sixteen), Claudius (to A.D. 42) four.

In a hoard from Dombresson (Blanchet, *Les Trésors de monnaies romaines et les invasions en Gaule* (1900), No. 833: 420 *denarii*; Augustus thirty-eight, Tiberius eighty, Gaius two, Claudius seven, according to Blanchet) it now appears that the correct total is 405 and that Nero too is represented (C. Martin, *Musée Neuchâtelois* 3 (1971), 3–34, summarised in ANS *Numismatic Literature* 92 (1974), No. 286); it is thus comparable with the Emona hoard.

**108**    Kraay's Vindonissa catalogue includes only one *denarius* and one *aureus* of Claudius and one *denarius* of Gaius, against eleven *denarii* of Tiberius and thirty-eight of Augustus; *Novaesium* III has ten *denarii* of Augustus, seven of Tiberius, none of Gaius or Claudius; compare the comment of Willers on Gaian and Claudian coins: 'Denare dieser Kaiser sind schon an sich seltener und kommen in unserem Norden fast gar nicht vor' (*NZ* 31 (1899), 347).

However, one must bear in mind that Gaian and especially Claudian coins are likely to be misleadingly rare in settlement finds, in proportion to Tiberian and especially Augustan coins, for the same reason for which they are rare in hoards deposited after the Neronian reform, though not to the same degree, since some are likely to have been lost before the effects of the reform were felt. The record of finds at Vindonissa suggests also that more republican *denarii* were lost in the camp after A.D. 40 than before. This suggests that more were brought into circulation after A.D. 40, which could have been a result of the inadequacy of 'the insignificant issues of Caligula and Claudius' (Kraay, *Vindonissa*, 16), although it is not clear who would have been holding a supply of republican *denarii* which they put into circulation at that time.

## Chapter II: notes 109–195

**109**  Tenney Frank, *AJP* 56 (1935), 337. It is not clear how much weight Frank wished to attribute to this flight of gold and silver as a cause of the shortage.

**110**  Mattingly's allusions to this factor, *Roman Coins*[2], 176, 183, are similarly ambiguous. Regling, *ZfN* 29 (1912), 237–8, *RE s.v.* Münzwesen (1933), 462, alluded to the flow of precious metal from the *Kernländer*, especially Italy, into the remote corn-producing provinces, especially Egypt, from the beginning of the imperial period, but he went on to give specific examples only of the flow into regions beyond Rome's control: for which see Chapter III.

**111**  See the remarks of P. Oliva, *Das Altertum*, 1962, 39–46. There was a similar explosion of demand in Tuscany in the twelfth century, for partly similar reasons—increased commercial activity, 'amazing expansion'—which enabled Pisan *denarii* to establish themselves alongside those of Lucca: see David Herlihy, ANS *Museum Notes* 6 (1954), 143–68.

**112**  See e.g. Mommsen, *Römisches Staatsrecht* III. I[3], 712, and Lenormant's lucid exposition of the whole doctrine of *Münzrecht* in the Roman world in relation to the numismatic facts, *La Monnaie dans l'antiquité* II (1878), 105–99. But, as Regling acknowledged (*RE, s.v.* Münzwesen, 489), 'unsere Kenntnis über das Prägerecht ist sehr dürftig', and Roman policy in this matter needs to be further investigated; for this purpose, it would be necessary to examine systematically the evidence for the cessation of non-Roman currencies. Mattingly (*Roman Coins*[2], 92–6) gives a brief survey of the monetary consequences of the spread of Roman power; Sutherland (*CRIP*, 10) mentions a few of the special arrangements made by the Roman authorities. The advice to Octavian in 29 B.C. on the treatment of his subjects which Dio (52. 30) puts into the mouth of Maecenas, μήτε δὲ νομίσματα ἢ καὶ σταθμὰ ἢ μέτρα ἰδίᾳ τις αὐτῶν ἐχέτω, ἀλλὰ τοῖς ἡμετέροις καὶ ἐκεῖνοι πάντες χρήσθωσαν, 'let none of them have currency or weights or measures of their own; instead let all of them use ours', is not to be regarded as evidence for that period. What it does show is that to Dio it did not appear evident that the Roman government exercised a monopoly in Augustus' time.

**113**  Aristotle, *Oeconomica* 1345b 20; I Maccabees 15.6.: καὶ ἐπέτρεψά σοι ποιῆσαι κόμμα ἴδιον νόμισμα τῇ χώρᾳ σου.

**114**  Bellinger, *Alexander*, 41; cf. 45 n.44; and the comments by Henri Seyrig, quoted in *Troy: The Coins*, 21 n.90, on seeming Seleucid toleration of civic issues of drachmas.

**115**  A decree of Olbia, a Greek polis on the north coast of the Black Sea, passed in the fourth century B.C. (Dittenberger, *Sylloge Inscriptionum Graecarum*[3], 218) prescribes the use of Olbian coins for all transactions in Olbia. It is often cited as if it were representative ('It pretty well sums up the pattern': Finley, *The Ancient Economy* (1973), 68), but, having no other evidence, we do not really know whether the rule was typical or exceptional.

**116**  As the Athenians had decreed with respect to States within their Empire in the fifth century B.C.; again, no other Greek republic exercising power over other states is known to have instituted such a rule.

**117**  See below, pp. 19 ff., and for base metal, pp. 57 ff., 62 f.

**118**  Cf. the comments of P. R. Franke, *Die antiken Münzen von Epeiros* (1961), 219 f., on Roman motives for tolerance in this matter 'schon aus rein praktischen Erwägungen'.

**119**  In the Aegean area the Mithridatic wars may well have dealt the final blow to a number of mints: see John Kroll, ANS *Museum Notes* 11 (1964), 81–118, on Cos.

**120**  The pride of communities, their will to assert themselves had been the main, if not the sole, *raison d'être* of many of the coinages of the Greek world: see above, n.27, and cf. the remarks of L. Robert, *Monnaies antiques en Troade* (1966), 86–8.

**121**  It may have been either the expense involved or difficulty in getting silver that put an end to the minting of tetradrachms in Noricum (Robert Göbl, *Typologie und Chronologie der keltischen Münzprägung in Noricum* (1973), 63): see below, p. 36. Of the few eastern states that went on producing silver currency on a considerable scale. down into the first century B.C. (see below, p. 21) several had their own supplies of silver: Athens (but the mines were running out: Strabo 9. 1. 23, p. 399), Thasos, the kingdoms of Pontus and Syria. Apollonia and Dyrrhachion may also have had preferential access to supplies, for if one considers the area in which their drachmas chiefly circulated one is tempted to suspect that they had close ties with those who exploited the silver of Damastion, such as May believes the Chalcidic League had for a time in the fourth century B.C. (J. M. F. May, *The Coinage of Damastion* (1939), 38 ff.; cf. 1 ff. on the location of Damastion and on evidence for some travel of silver from that region to the Adriatic). On the difficulties experienced by other states, see Rostovtzeff, *Social and Economic History of the Hellenistic World* (1941), 1289 ff. Note that the rulers of Simon Maccabaeus' line, having been given explicit permission to strike coins (n.116), struck only *aes*, even after they had become fully independent, and strong; this was probably because they had no silver (Arie Kindler, *Proceedings of the International Numismatic Convention, Jerusalem 1963* (1967), 180 ff.). The Romans were, of course, as Rostovtzeff points out, the ultimate beneficiaries of the kings' hoarding of money, which he mentions as one cause of shortage of currency and of precious metals for coining.

**122**  See, for instance, Dittenberger, *Orientis Graecae Inscriptiones Selectae* 629. 54–5. In fairness one should mention that, in some cases at least, the Romans may have undervalued foreign currency only in terms of its face value. While they, having plenty of gold and silver, were producing coins of high quality throughout the period that concerns us, the quality of Seleucid coinage, in the decades before it ceased, and of Parthian coinage seems to have been poorer, and declining (J. Hammer, *ZfN* 26 (1908), 85; E. R. Caley, *Chemical Composition of Parthian Coins* (1955)).

**123**  On exchange commissions of this kind see Raymond Bogaert, *Banques et banquiers dans les cités grecques* (1968), 48–9, 323 ff.; cf. Cicero's reference to the unfairness of Verres' staff in making a deduction for *collybus* from payments by Sicilians: *utuntur omnes uno genere nummorum*, 'they all use coins of one and the same kind', i.e. *denarii*, so there was no excuse for it (II *in Verrem* 3. 181).

**124**  *Deuxième Conférence Internationale d'Histoire Économique*, 1962, I (1965), 23. After the collapse of the Empire, Athenian currency, being firmly established as the chief international trading instrument, continued to command a premium: see Bogaert, *op. cit.* (n.123), 108. Likewise, once *denarii* has assumed that role, they would command a premium without any exercise of pressure.

**125**  *RRCH* records forty-one silver hoards from the Iberian peninsula for the period 211–49 B.C., far more than from any other region except Dacia, whence there are thirty-three. Nineteen of the hoards are mixed; there are also numerous wholly

Iberian silver hoards from the same period. For signs in the hoard evidence of the transition during the second and first centuries B.C. from the use of uncoined silver as money (except on a narrow coastal strip) to the use of coins, see Klaus Raddatz, 'Die Schatzfunde der iberischen Halbinsel', *Madrider Forschungen* 5 (1969), 31–67. Hoards from the western half of the peninsula suggest that *denarii* were fully established in circulation from the Douro to the Tagus by 45 B.C., though not yet circulating freely further north or south (Isabel Pereira, Jean-Pierre Bost, Jean Hiernand, *Fouilles de Conimbriga* III; *Les Monnaies* (1974), 195–201).

**126** See Joaquin de Navascues y de Jucan, *Num.hisp.* 4 (1955), 237–64; G. K. Jenkins, *JbNumG* 11 (1961), 75–155; L. Villaronga Garriga, *Ampurias* 26–7 (1964–5), 165–73; M. H. Crawford, *NC*[7] 9 (1969), 83–4. Eighty Iberian *denarii* in a hoard from Albacete province with 307 Roman, to *RIC* I Augustus 350: Villaronga, *Ampurias* 33–34 (1971–2), 205 ff.

**127** D. F. Allen, *NC*[7] 8 (1968), 40, J.-B. Colbert de Beaulieu, *Survey of Numismatic Research, 1966–1971* (International Numismatic Commission, 1973), 270.

**128** *RRCH*, 216; three *denarii*, with forty-five Gallic silver coins, in a hoard of the early first century found near Blois.

**129** Joseph Déchelette, *Rev.num.*[4] 3 (1899), 129 ff.; summary of the finds in *RRCH*, 567: cf. Font-Garnier (Charente-Inf.): five republican *denarii* (no *aes*) against 108 Gallic coins, then thirty-five *aes* of Tiberius, sixteen 'of Agrippa' (*RIC* I Tiberius, 32), one of Gaius, forty of Claudius (*Mémoires de la Soc. des Antiquaires de l'Ouest* 37 (1873), 527: I owe this reference to Mr Michael Crawford).

**130** Simone Scheers, *Les Monnaies de la Gaule inspirées de celles de la République romaine* (1969), 177, referring to the Rhône valley; cf. *RRCH*, 79, 110, 560; *GCH*, 2378, 2380: a few pieces found alongside far more numerous non-Roman coins; *RRCH*, 290, 304: two hoards from the seventies, one found near Perpignan, containing thirteen *denarii*, with six hundred Gallic silver coins, the other from Peyriac-sur-Mer, containing one hundred *denarii* and seventeen *quinarii*. In *GCH* there are six hoards from Gallia Narbonensis (2376–7, 2384–7) with terminal dates probably lying between 123 B.C. and 30 B.C. which comprise over two thousand coins of Massalia, some two dozen Gallic coins, but no *denarii*. In two other hoards of the second or first century B.C. (2382–3) there are again hundreds of Massalian coins and a few Gallic but no Roman coins.

**131** Among some five hundred identifiable coins of the third, second and first centuries B.C. yielded by excavations at Ensérune, an *oppidum* near Béziers, 146 were Massalian, 178 Gallic, twenty-eight Nemausan, twenty-six from north-east Spain, 140 Roman (of which forty-four were in a hoard of *c.* 30 B.C.) (Jean Jannoray, *Ensérune*, Bibliothèque des Écoles françaises d'Athènes et de Rome 181 (1955), 341–50, 444–7). One can not tell how long after issue the Roman coins arrived, for there is no mention of their condition or of the levels in which they were found, but it seems significant that, as against fifteen *denarii* and *quinarii* not from the hoard, there are six *victoriati*.

**132** Michel Labrousse, *Pallas* 9 (1960), 177–217; 10 (1961), 69–90; *Toulouse antique* (1968), 116 ff.

**133** Cicero, *pro Fonteio* 5. 11.

**134** J.-B. Colbert de Beaulieu, *JbNumG* 16 (1966), 58.

**135** See Colbert de Beaulieu, *op. cit.* (n.134), 45–62; *Survey* (see n.127), 269 ff.; D. F. Allen, *NC*[7] 9 (1969), 33–78; Scheers, *op. cit.* (n.130).

**136** Jannoray, *op. cit.* (n.131), 343; A. Alföldi, *Rev.num.*[6] 11 (1969), 55–61; cf. Colbert de Beaulieu, *Survey* (see n.127), 272.

**137** J.-C. Richard, *JbNumG* 20 (1970), 49 ff., and in *Survey* (see n.127), 252 ff., with bibliography.

**138** See Scheers, *op. cit.* (n.130).

**139**  On the disappearance of gold from circulation, see, for instance, Colbert de Beaulieu, in Forrer, *Keltische Numismatik der Rhein- und Donaulande*[2] II (1969), n.28.

**140**  Colbert de Beaulieu, *loc. cit.* (n.135); cf. Allen, *NC*[7] 8 (1968), 51–3. H. Rolland, *Bulletin de la société française de numismatique*, 1955, 330, refers to thirty-five French hoards containing *denarii* with a terminal date between 58 and 31 B.C., mostly from the centre and south-west.

**141**  From Beauvoisin in Narbonensis, between Vienna and Arausio (Grueber, *Coins of the Roman Republic in the British Museum* (1910), II, 5–7; *RRCH*, 459) and Chantenay, near Bibracte (Grueber, *ibid.*; *RRCH*, 461), these two extending down to *c.* 30 B.C. (as does a small hoard, of six Gallic coins and two *denarii*, found on the Tetelbierg in Belgica: *FMRL*, 339), and from Hussigny-Godbrange, near Metz (*RRCH*, 516), a hoard containing also Roman *aes* and Gallic base-metal coins and extending perhaps a decade further; and in one small Tiberian hoard from Belgium there are still several base-gold VIROS staters (Blanchet, *Les Trésors de monnaies romaines . . . en Gaule* (1900), No. 281; Thirion, *Les Trésors monétaires gaulois et romains trouvés en Belgique* (1967), No. 157).

**142**  For base-metal coinages see below, pp. 57 f.

**143**  Karel Castelin has been attempting to establish a relative chronology, largely on the basis of observations of the gradual decline in the weight and fineness of the gold coins: see *JbNumG* 12 (1962), 199–207; 14 (1964), 116–45; *Rev.num.*[6] 7 (1965), 69–78; *Die Goldprägung der Kelten in den böhmischen Ländern* (1965); *Schweizer Münzblätter* 21 (1971), 33–7; *Schweizer Numismatischer Rundschau* 50 (1971), 92–124; *JbNumG* 23 (1973), 53–76. H.-J. Kellner, 'Zur Goldprägung der Helvetier', in *Provincialia, Festschrift für Rudolf Laur-Belart* (1968), 588–602, has compared with these observations the evidence for dating furnished by Celtic artefacts of late La Tène character associated with coins in some finds. I have followed their findings.

**144**  See Karl Pink, *Einführung in die keltische Münzkunde*, 5, 28, 48–9; Georg Kossack, in Rolf Hachmann, Georg Kossack and Hans Kuhn, *Völker zwischen Germanen und Kelten* (1962), 94–100; Evžen and Jiří Neustupny, *Czechoslovakia Before the Slavs* (1962), 161–9; É. B. Bónis, *Acta Archaeologica Academiae Scientiarum Hungaricae* 23 (1971), 33–9.

**145**  The date of cessation even of some important silver coinages is uncertain: see e.g. the debate on Athens between D. M. Lewis (*NC*[7] 2 (1962), 275–300: *c.* 53 B.C.) and M. Thompson (*ibid.*, 301–33: 86 B.C.). Recent participants include: J. R. Melville Jones, *NC*[7] 13 (1973), 227–9, supporting the early dating; John Kroll, Ἀρχαιολογικόν Δελτίον 27 (1972), 86 ff., and Fred S. Kleiner, ANS *Museum Notes* 19 (1974), 16 f., both supporting the late dating. Kroll, 94, argues for cessation 'just before 40'. Here again expense appears to have been the deciding factor.

**146**  M. J. Price, *NC*[7] 8 (1968), 1–12; D. M. Pippidi, *I Greci nel basso Danubio* (1971), 139, 174; Kleiner, *op. cit.* (n.145), 3–25.

**147**  H. Ceka, *Studia Albanica* 3.1 (1966), 214–23; cf. above, n.122. Ceka argues that minting of silver continued until *c.* 27 B.C. But hoards from the areas in which these drachmas circulated suggest that by that time they were greatly outnumbered by *denarii* (see below, nn.287, 303).

**148**  See the brief surveys of circulation, 200–30 B.C., in *GCH*, pp. 3 (Greece), 57 (Macedon and regions to the north), 95–6 (Thrace and the western Euxine), 154 (Asia Minor), 200–1 (the Levant). Whereas many of the states that had gone on minting silver into the first century had access to supplies of ore (see above, n.121), the Phoenician states had not. But Tyre was encouraged to continue striking its tetradrachms and didrachms in large quantities, and to maintain their exceptionally high quality, thanks to demand from Jews, who, wherever they lived, were required to pay their annual temple dues in Tyrian shekels; so the Tyrians could sell them at a premium adequate to cover the cost of production: see Arie Kindler, *Proceedings of the International Numismatic Convention, Jerusalem 1963* (1967), 180–205; *Eretz Israel* 8 (1967), 318–24; Arye Ben-David, *Jerusalem und Tyros* (1969), 5–31. Further east the silver of the Parthian kings was now the dominant currency: see Georges le Rider, *Suse sous les Séleucides et les Parthes* (1965), 443–5; but this seems to have been declining in quality (above, n.123).

**149** For the movement of traders into Gallia Comata after the conquest see, for example, Caesar, *Bellum Gallicum* 7. 3. 1, 7. 55. 5. For the expansion of trade with Egypt see Strabo 17. 1. 13, p. 798.

**150** On the growth within Gaul of trade involving the use of coined money, cf. Giard, *Rev.num.*[6] 10 (1968), 77–8.

**151** Further study of this process is needed, so far as the scanty evidence permits. Other societies offer analogies: see P. Bohannan, 'The impact of money on an African subsistence economy', *Journal of Economic History* 19 (1959), 491 ff., and generally Karl Polanyi and Daniel B. Fusfeld, in *Trade and Market in the Early Empires* (1957), 243 ff., 350, 356. That coinage supplemented barter in Germany was suggested by H. Willers, *Die Bronzeeimer von Hemmoor* (1901), 194–5. Cf. n.236.

**152** *Roman Coins*[2], 85; cf. 96. This question will be discussed by Michael Crawford in chapter 7 of his book, *Roman Republican Coinage*.

**153** *CRIP*, 65.

**154** Statius, *Silvae* 3. 85–105.

**155** Brunt, *JRS* 56 (1966), 90.

**156** Cf. Sutherland, *CRIP*, 10. One must recognise that in frontier regions coin may have circulated in early days almost wholly inside military establishments, the soldiers spending what they did not save on goods and services provided within the camp—most of these being brought by traders from more developed regions. (It has been said that until the middle of the second century A.D. the main function of traders in the Rhineland was to bring goods thither from Italy and Gaul: H. von Petrikovits, *Das römische Rheinland*, 116.) Modern parallels could be cited. But some goods and services would be bought locally (cf. the establishment by Ateius, the great producer of Arretine ware, of a branch factory on the Rhine); and even what the soldiers saved out of their pay would eventually come into civilian circulation. As Michael Crawford has said (*JRS* 60 (1970), 45), 'The use of coined money in the cities of the Empire . . . was probably an accidental consequence of its existence and not the result of government policy.'

**157** Cf. Louis C. West, ANS *Museum Notes* 6 (1954), 6.

**158** They probably did rise to some extent: see below, p. 70.

**159** *Roman Coins*[2], 178. J.-B. Giard, 'L'Empire romain d'Auguste à 284 après J.-C.', in *Survey* (see n.127), remarks that this 'témoigne de l'importance que les gens des petites villes et, sans doute, des campagnes attachaient à cet instrument de crédit', but, so far as the early imperial period is concerned, he is probably alluding to imitations of *aes* rather than of silver coins.

**160** Cf. Sutherland, *CRIP*, 190: imitations were 'produced generally beyond the frontiers of the Empire'.

**161** For the Macedonian coinage in question see Bellinger, *Mattingly Studies* (see n.54), 138–9. The revived, spread-flan tetradrachms of Thasos were interpreted already by Th. Reinach, *Mémoires de l'Académie des Inscriptions et Belles-Lettres* 38 (1911), 360, as a kind of Roman provincial coinage. Production may have begun quite soon after Thasos finally fell under Roman protection, *c.* 180 B.C. (M. Thompson, ANS *Museum Notes* 12 (1966), 61; G. le Rider, in *Guide de Thasos*, École française d'Athènes (1968), 185 ff.), but 'the crude and degenerate specimens which comprise the bulk of the coinage are the characteristic output of a mint operating in the late second and early first centuries' (Thompson, ANS *Museum Notes* 11 (1964), 79), and the evidence of die-links and overstrikes points to most of them having been produced in the early years of the first century (Gina Katzarova, *Izv.BAI* 27 (1964), 131–50, with English summary, 150–2). Some bear a monogram which has been taken to be that of Q. Bruttius Sura, who was *legatus* in Macedonia between 93 and 87 B.C. under the praetor C. Sentius Saturninus; and as the name Suura, with the title LEG(atus) PRO Q(uaestore), appears also on the last issue of Romano-Macedonian tetradrachms, it may be that for some reason Sura arranged for the mint of Thasos to take over the production of tetradrachms: Katzarova suggests that subsequently many were struck for Sulla.

Hardly any of these tetradrachms seem to have been found outside the Balkan–Danubian–Carpathian region: see the list by C. Dunant and J. Pouilloux of all finds of Thasian tetradrachms known to them (*Recherches sur l'histoire et les cultes de Thasos* II (1958)): *GCH*, 234 (Thessaly, 'before 168') is the only hoard in *GCH* from outside that region to include them. Just as coins of Dyrrhachion and Apollonia Illyrici are hardly ever found in Thrace (in one hoard: *GCH*, 976), so those of Thasos are, it seems, seldom found in Illyricum (in 1896 the Sarajevo museum had five or six, found in Albania (Partsch, *op. cit.* (n.285), 113 ff.); and Dunant and Pouilloux mention vague reports of finds in Dardania, to the north of Macedonia).

**162**   See below, p. 39.

**163**   Sutherland, *The Cistophori of Augustus* (1970), 103.

**164**   Woodward, *Mattingly Studies* (see n.54), 152.

**165**   Sutherland, *op. cit.* (n.163), 90.

**166**   The pseudo-Seleucid coinage was first detected by E. T. Newell (*NC*[4] 19 (1919), 69 ff.), who showed that the coins in question were not issued in Philip's lifetime, and argued that their issue extended from 48–47 B.C. down into the reign of Augustus. Bellinger has since shown that some were probably issued already in the fifties, under the auspices of Aulus Gabinius (57 B.C.), M. Crassus and C. Cassius (*NC*[6] 4 (1944), 59–61; *Dura* VI, 201–2; *Studies in Roman Economic and Social History in Honour of Allan Chester Johnson* (1951), 64–5; ANS *Museum Notes* 5 (1952), 53–63). He has argued that if they were struck before *libertas* was bestowed on Antioch, they cannot be regarded as a civic issue but must constitute a Roman provincial issue, like the explicitly Roman tetradrachms of Antioch, initiated by Augustus in 6 B.C. In the few hoards closed after 57 B.C. from the region in which Seleucid coins chiefly circulated that are listed in *GCH*, the pseudo-Philip coins are generally much less prominent than their prototypes (1578, Syria, *c.* 50 B.C., twenty-one against one; 1583, Syria, *c.* 30 B.C., none against four; 1744, Armenia after 30 B.C., four against 134; 1746, Armenia, 30–25 B.C., none against seventeen; 1786, Characene, soon after 45 B.C., none against 227), but *GCH* excludes most hoards closed after 30 B.C., that is to say, in the period in which the circulation of pseudo-Philip coins is likely to have reached its peak. For finds from this later period, see below, p. 46 and n.352.

For the Romano-Syrian tetradrachms, see W. Wruck, *Die syrische Provinzial-prägung von Augustus bis Traian* (1931), 12–63; C. M. Kraay, *Rev.num.*[6] 7 (1965), 58–60. One of these coins, struck in 6 B.C., was of good weight, 14·87 g, but was found on analysis to contain only 61·5 per cent silver. Subsequently, under Augustus and Gaius, there was a further decline, to 37 per cent (Ben-David, *op. cit.* (n.148), 8–9, 14–15).

**167**   E. A. Sydenham, *The Coinage of Caesarea in Cappadocia* (1933), 3 ff., 30 ff.

**168**   Mattingly, *BMCRE* I, cxli; cf. *Roman Coins*[2], 196 where he himself points out that 'in the case of the provincial silver military considerations seem to have played a very large part in determining the extent of the issues', giving as an example 'the extensive issues of Cappadocia for Nero's Parthian War'.

**169**   Donald Magie, *Roman Rule in Asia Minor* (1950), 375, 493, 1239 n.47. Cf. Alexander's establishment at Tarsus, no doubt for the same reason, of the first royal Macedonian mint in Asia: Bellinger, *Alexander*, 49.

**170** Their silver content fluctuated between 73 per cent and 25 per cent (Ben-David, *op. cit.* (n.148) 40). The tetradrachms of Antioch and the didrachms of Caesarea occur hardly at all in recorded finds to the west of their place of origin. Finds of coins in the region in which the circulation of the coins of Antioch could be expected (and from which most known examples doubtless originally emanated) are very seldom accurately recorded. Dura yielded only three, all of Trajan (*Dura* VI, 200). We do, however, know of one major find, a Hadrianic hoard from Palestine (Noe, *Bibliography of Greek Coin Hoards*[2] (1937), No. 381) which included 177 *denarii*, sixty-six Caesarean didrachms and twenty-eight Antiochene tetradrachms. One region to which coins of Caesarea made their way was Transcaucasia, where many coin finds have been recorded: from these records one derives the impression that pre-Neronian issues made little contribution (see below, nn.357–60).

**171** 'At Antioch the Romans took over a going concern and used it for their own needs': Bellinger, *AJA* 51 (1947), 339; cf. *Alexander*, 78.

**172** I. N. Svoronos, *Journal international d'archéologie numismatique* 10 (1906), 191 ff.; 12 (1909), 153 ff.; 13 (1911), 75 ff.; 15 (1913), 39 ff. (six of the republican *denarii* listed are plated; all four of the Augustan *denarii* are *RIC* I, 350). *Denarii* appear also in inventories after 146 B.C.: *Inscr. de Délos*, 1439, 1443, 1449, 1450. Furthermore, it has been argued that, under the name *tetranoma* (see L. Robert, *Hellenica* 8 (1949), 88; *Études de numismatique grecque* (1951), 159, tracing this suggestion back to P. Gardner, *JHS* 3 (1883), 245), they appear, with other Roman silver coins, in several earlier inventories, *Inscr. de Délos*, 407 (c. 190 B.C.), 442 (179 B.C.), 1432 (153–152 B.C.); but those that arrived before 167 clearly came 'als Weihungen von Gläubigen, nicht als Handelsgeld' (Christof Boehringer, *Zur Chronologie mittelhellenistischer Münzserien 220–160 v. Chr.* (1972), 48) (Mr M. Crawford tells me that in his opinion *tetranoma* are 'certainly not Roman'.)

**173** L. T. Shear, *Hesperia* 5 (1936), 123–50, 285–332; M. Thompson, *The Athenian Agora* II (1954) (one of the Augustan *denarii* is *RIC* I, 350, the Tiberian is *RIC* I, 3).

**174** K. M. Edwards, *Corinth* VI (1933); *Hesperia* 6 (1937), 241–56; J. M. Harris, *Hesperia* 10 (1941), 143–55; J. E. Fisher, *Hesperia* 40 (1971), 35–51. The 1941 report lists the Roman coins merely as republican eight, Augustus six, Tiberius one, Agrippa one, Caligula one, and so on, but most probably all the republican and some of the imperial coins are *denarii*. The other reports mention five republican *denarii*.

**175** Thasos: *BCH* 75 (1951), 170; for other coin finds see *BCH* 57 (1933), 73–80 (1949–56); no mention of coins in later reports. Cf. Philia (Thessaly): one Augustan *denarius*: Ἀρχαιολογικὸν Δελτίον 19. 2 (1964), 253–5; Dodona, Elis (see below, n.489): two *denarii*, one *denarius*; Corcyra: two *denarii*: *BCH* 54 (1930), 454; two *quinarii*: Ἀρχαιολογικὸν Δελτίον 20. 2 (1965), 401–6.

**176** Ugolini, *Albania Antica* 2 (1928), 159.

**177** *Troy: The Coins.* The Tiberian *denarius* is *RIC* I, 3.

**178** *Larisa* III (1942), 186 ff. (total finds: eleven silver, thirty-two *aes*).

**179** Leaving aside two hoards, there were, from the second century B.C., one Rhodian drachm and one cistophoric tetradrachm of Ephesos, then, reflecting the early beginning of Rome's active monetary intervention in this province, another of the latter, struck in 57–56 B.C. under the auspices of C. Fabius; then one of the ubiquitous 'elephant' *denarii* of Julius Caesar, five more cistophoric tetradrachms (two of Antony, one of Augustus, and one of Claudius), one *denarius* of Augustus; and finally, occasional *denarii* from Vespasian onwards (H. W. Bell, *Sardis* XI (1916)).

**180** From the second century B.C. again one Rhodian drachm and one *cistophoros* of Ephesos, plus one of Tralleis; from the first century B.C. two republican *denarii* (*CRR*, 919, 1117) and a *cistophorus* of Antony; then two *cistophori* of Augustus and two *denarii* (with Gaius and Lucius as usual), one *denarius* of Vespasian and one of

Nerva: Regling, *Die Münzen von Priene* (1927) (the comment on *denarii* is on
p. 191).

**181** In *GCH*, among hoards found in Greece or western Asia Minor with terminal
dates probably between 150 and 80 B.C., there are three including *denarii* (271, 317,
346), fourteen or fifteen (excluding those from Attica and Delos) that include
Athenian tetradrachms (271, 287, 289, 291, 317, 332, 344, 346 (which could be
Attic), 482, 523, 524, 550, 642, 973, 1336), eight that include *cistophori* (290, 348,
1326, 1327, 1328, 1330, 1336, 1340): add one from Stobi in Macedonia with 488
denarii to *c.* 125 B.C. and one Athenian tetradrachm (*AJA* 76 (1972), 410). Among
hoards with terminal dates probably between 80 and 30 B.C. there are five including
*denarii* (351, 352, 653, 660, 663), two including Athenian tetradrachms (352, 1359),
three including *cistophori* (352, 1358, 1359). Speaking of Greece proper, and of the
period 200–30 B.C. as a whole, the editors state (p. 3) that 'the *denarius* plays no role
in the economy of the region', but the finds suggest that by the end of that period its
role was as large as that of Greek silver.

**182** In the first half of the first century B.C. tetradrachms of Thasos and, a long way
behind, Maroneia, and imitations of these, predominate in Thracian and Moesian
hoards (*GCH*, 960–71), except in the west of Moesia, traversed by routes from the
Adriatic to the Danube, where drachmas of Dyrrhachion and Apollonia are also
prominent (*GCH*, 612–17), and near the Black Sea, where coins of the Greek
coastal states, Byzantion and Mithridates VI are also found (*GCH*, 959, 971–4;
cf. 664). In hoards of the second half of the century *denarii* appear, in most cases as
a majority, with drachmas of Dyrrhachion in western Moesia (*GCH*, 669, 686–8), in
eastern Moesia and Thrace with tetradrachms of Maroneia (679–80) and Thasos
(975–6, 978–80) and imitations of these (664, 977–8). One hoard contains only
*denarii* (*RRCH*, 377) another *denarii* and local imitations only (*RRCH*, 461). (The
evidence from Dacia is considered below, pp. 29 ff.)

**183** To judge from the sparse finds of silver yielded by the excavations at Antioch
(Waage, *Antioch* IV, 2), that city would appear to have been peculiarly plagued with
bad coins: four plated tetradrachms, Philippic or pseudo-Philippic, found together,
then three plated republican *denarii*, and one Augustan *denarius* 'in aes'. But the
prominence of *denarii*, albeit counterfeit, is notable. In recorded hoards of *c.* 100–
30 B.C. found in the Levant (*GCH*, 1569–83, 1607–31) there are still no *denarii*, and
down into the triumviral period, at least, people in Syria continued to reckon in
tetradrachms (Cic., *ad fam.* 12. 13. 4). But Roman ordinances promoted the gradual
adoption of Roman money; Germanicus ruled that all customs dues etc. at Palmyra
should be reckoned πρὸς ἀσσάριον (Dittenberger, *Orientis Graecae Inscriptiones
Selectae*, 629. 154–55); and one of the few recorded hoards of the first century A.D.
from this region, though clearly exceptional in character, does, even so, illustrate
the influx of *denarii* (Kadman, *Israel Numismatic Bulletin* 1 (1962), 9–11; corrected
figures and full discussion in Ben-David, *op. cit.* (n.148), 33–6). Found on Mount
Carmel in 1960, it comprised at least 3,850 Tyrian shekels (tetradrachms) and 1,100
half-shekels, all of the period 40 B.C.–A.D. 52–3, and 275 *denarii*, of which at least
160—all those known to Kadman—were Augustan, of the variety honouring Gaius
and Lucius (*RIC* I Augustus, 350). Kadman suggested that the hoard represents a
shipment of temple-dues (see n.148) and that it had been stopped en route and
buried at the outbreak of the Jewish revolt, but Ben-David argues that it must have
been a merchant's deposit.

**184** Rostovtzeff, *SEHRE*[2], 69.

**185** A. H. M. Jones, *Troisième Conférence Internationale d'Histoire Économique*,
Munich 1965 (1969), 88.

**186** Oertel, *CAH* x, 423.

**187** *SEHRE*[2], 70: cf. Brunt, *loc. cit.* (n.81), 127. Even at this period this was probably
not true of trade with Egypt: 'with a heavy export of luxuries and of staple products

such as wheat, linen, glass and paper, it is probable that the balance went in her favour', according to Johnson (*Egypt and the Roman Empire* (1951), 23; cf. 18). 'Presumably', he continues, 'there was a considerable accumulation of gold, and this went into the hoards of wealthy farmers or industrialists': and later he remarks that 'it is probable that much of the gold' seized by Augustus 'found its way back to Egypt in the early Empire and ceased to exist as currency' (*ibid.*, 29). But an unfavourable balance here might well have been offset by a favourable balance in trade with the west.

**188**  Jones, *op. cit.* (n.185), 103. Finley, *op. cit.* (n.12), 206, insists that the export of wine from Italy was relatively unimportant in relation to the balance of trade.

**189**  Rudi Thomsen, *op. cit.* (n.185), 107.

**190**  Jones, *op. cit.* (n.185), 91–2.

**191**  *Publicani* continued to collect *portoria* (S. J. de Laet, *Portorium* (1944), 363 ff.). The burden of debts, owed, it would seem, to Roman financiers, led to the rebellion of Florus and Sacrovir in Gaul in A.D. 21 (Tac. *Ann.*, 3. 40).

**192**  Decline in Italian business activity in the east: J. Hatzfeld, *Les Trafiquants italiens dans l'orient hellénique* (1919), 148 ff. In this context it may be noted that P. Oliva, *op. cit.* (n.111), in considering the causes of the Neronian currency reform, has drawn attention to another possible cause of increased demand for currency inside Italy, the replacement of slaves in agriculture by rent-paying *coloni*. But there seems to be no reason to suspect that this had occurred in Italy to any considerable extent before A.D. 33; on the contrary, the last century B.C. and the first century A.D. seem to have been the great age of *latifundia* manned by slaves (cf. K. D. White, *Bulletin of the Institute of Classical Studies* 14 (1967), 62 ff.).

**193**  The fact that all the mints for gold and silver were now in the provinces would in itself make no difference one way or the other to the supply of money inside Italy.

**194**  'Rome's corn supply, public works, police and municipal services were paid for by imperial revenues. The salaries of the central administrative officers were spent in Rome, moreover, and as most of the higher imperial administrative officers in the rest of the Empire were domiciled in Italy, their salaries were also largely spent or invested in Italy' (Jones, *op. cit.* (n.185), 91).

**195**  According to Strabo, under Roman administration agriculture had become more productive (17. 1. 3. p. 788) and the revenues had increased (17. 1. 13. p. 798).

## Chapter III: notes 196–416

**196**  Tac., *Ann.* 3. 53: *Quid enim primum prohibere et priscum ad morem recidere adgrediar? villarumne infinita spatia? familiarum numerum et nationes? argenti et auri pondus? aeris tabularumque miracula? promiscas viris et feminis vestes atque illa feminarum propria, quis lapidum causa pecuniae nostrae ad externas aut hostilis gentes transferuntur?*

**197**  Cf. Dio Chrysostom's list (79. 5–6) of the peoples to whom in his time the Romans, in effect, paid tribute by exporting coin: Celts, Indians, Iberians, Arabians, Babylonians (his Celts are presumably the Germans). For the elder Pliny's statements about trade between Rome and the east, see below, pp. 48, 50.

**198**  Thus Oertel suggested (*CAH* x, 423) that 'the outflow of the reserves of precious metal from the Empire may have been one of the main causes' of 'tendencies towards state socialism on oriental lines that were gaining ground *by the middle of the century*', i.e. the first century A.D. (italics mine); cf. E. H. Warmington, *The Commerce between the Roman Empire and India* (1928), 38 ff. Compare Rostovtzeff's view: 'This type of commerce struck the imagination of contemporaries as it strikes that of some modern scholars, and both of them have exaggerated its importance' (*SEHRE*², 66).

**199**  German finds of *aurei* that are perhaps to be accounted for in this way have been listed and mapped by Werner Krapke, *Acta Archaeologica* 14 (1943), 57–8. Over one hundred *denarii*, and a few other coins, found in the eighteenth and nineteenth centuries allegedly 'zerstreut auf den Äckern' round Schloss Barenau (near Osnabrück) were regarded in this light by J. Menadier, *ZfN* 13 (1885), 89–112; H. Willers felt 'das grösste Misstrauen' (*NZ* 31 (1899), 332), but H. Koestermann has recently defended this interpretation (*Historia* 6 (1957), 441–43), and C. M. Wells, *The German Policy of Augustus* (1972), 151), discussing a somewhat similar find of republican and Augustan silver coins at Reckelsum, near Haltern, with 'no trace of buildings or ditches' near by, comments that 'the presence of silver coins without any bronze ones rather suggests loot'.

**200**  The only evidence that might point in this direction comes from the coinage of the Himyarite kings of southern Arabia. During the first century B.C. they, or their predecessors of the Sabaean dynasty, had been striking coins modelled on Athenian 'new style' tetradrachms; they then went on to produce coins with the same reverse type but bearing on the obverse a portrait of Augustus (B. V. Head, *Historia Numorum*[2] (1911), 813; G. F. Hill, *British Museum Catalogue of the Greek Coins of Arabia . . .* (1922), xlv–lxxxiv), and it is said that these bear humiliating inscriptions which might refer to Aelius Gallus' defeat (Boneschi, *Rivista degli studi orientali* 29 (1954), 17–27), and were locally called 'insulters' (Boneschi, *ibid.* 39 (1964), 117–24). This, if correct, suggests the possibility that some of them were produced by melting down captured *denarii*. Cf. below, pp. 47 ff. and nn.364 ff., on Roman trade with and through Arabia and the extent to which Roman gold and silver might have been consumed in this trade.

**201**  For Roman gifts of money to German chiefs, see Tacitus, *Germ.* 15.3, 42. The first recorded example is from the reign of Claudius (Tac., *Ann.* 11.16), but Much in his commentary on the *Germania* (ed. 3, 1967) suggested that Gaius initiated the policy of buying peace.

**202**  Dikomes, a Getan chieftain who fought for Antony, is one instance: see below; p. 41. Arminius, commanding a force of Cherusci, may be another: see below, p. 32.

**203**  Dio 54. 20. 3–6, 54. 36. 2. Raids across the Danube: see below, n.313.

**204**  See above, pp. 19 ff.

**205**  See Rolf Hachmann, Georg Kossack and Hans Kuhn, *Völker zwischen Germanen und Kelten* (1962), especially 13, 36, 96; Karl Schirwitz, *Germania* 30 (1952), 52–3; Hans Schönberger, *ibid.*, 383–8 and *Saalburg Jahrbuch* 11 (1952), 21–130. Unfortunately my work was completed before I saw the study of the relationship between Celts and Germans in the time of Augustus by C. M. Wells, *op. cit.* (n.199), 14–31. Wells describes the inhabitants of the Wetterau and their like as 'in the strict linguistic sense neither true Germans nor true Celts, but a border people who have however assimilated the La Tène culture of their Celtic neighbours' (23). He argues that the Ubii belonged to this category and were not 'true Germans in the usually accepted sense' (29).

**206**  See, for instance, Schirwitz, *op. cit.* (n.205), 54.

**207**  Schirwitz, *ibid.*

**208**  Caesar, *Bellum Gallicum* 1. 39.

**209**  H. J. Eggers, *Der römische Import im freien Germanien, Atlas der Urgeschichte* 1 (1951), chapter 3 and map 3.

**210**  On the cessation of Celtic coinages see above, pp. 19 ff. (gold and silver), and below, pp. 57 ff. (*aes*, etc.). Even if some Celtic chieftains contrived to maintain themselves in some parts of north Germany, as Waldtraut Schrickel suggests (*Jahrbuch des römisch-germanischen Zentralmuseums* 11 (1964), 138–53), there is no reason to think that they struck any coins.

In Britain, on the other hand, Celtic coinages were still being produced during

Tiberius' reign, and there is no reason to suspect any import of Roman currency. On the contrary, there must have been a considerable outflow of gold and silver to the Empire, in payment of tribute and customs duties (Strabo 4. 5. 3, p. 200; S. S. Frere, *Britannia* (1967), 45, 48).

**211** Tac., *Germ.* 5. 3–5: *ob usum commerciorum.*

**212** 'Geradezu kennzeichnend für eine soziale Oberschicht' (Herbert Jankuhn, in Rudolf Much, *Die Germania des Tacitus*[3] (1967), 199–22). It is not clear from the evidence cited by Jankuhn how many of these objects will have reached them from the Roman world in Eggers' Stage B I (see below, n.214), i.e. before the middle of the first century A.D.

**213** Jankuhn, *op. cit.* (n.212) 124–5.

**214** A useful synthesis and cartographic presentation of the evidence is to be found in *Atlas der Urgeschichte*, Band I, *Der römische Import im freien Germanien* (1951), by Hans Jürgen Eggers. Unfortunately, his map (Karte 4) illustrating 'der Import der frühen Kaiserzeit' includes, without further chronological discrimination, all finds of the first one and a half centuries A.D. (his Stage B) and the same is true, for the most part, of his discussion of these finds (chapter 4); a periodisation of the *terra sigillata* finds, for instance, being reserved for a later volume. There is, however, another map (Karte 39) showing only the finds of bronze vessels of a type characteristic of the later Augustan age: for these see n. 262. But see his remarks on the interpretation of find maps in *Einführung in die Vorgeschichte* (1959), pp. 276 ff.

**215** Tac., *Germ.* 5. 5. On the term *bigati* see Appendix B.

**216** This is shown by the composition of numerous hoards found far from free Germany containing both republican and imperial silver. The following fifteen have been selected because the published data make it possible to determine how many of the coins were struck before 49 B.C., and how many of these are *serrati*. Tentative figures for *bigati* have also been given: for the meaning of the term, see below, Appendix B. If Tacitus was referring only to coins bearing a representation of a two-horse chariot, the figures given are rather too high, since cars drawn by various pairs of creatures have been admitted. If *quadriga* types were acceptable, the numbers would be considerably higher. If the horses of the Dioscuri could be described as a *biga*, they would be higher still.

| Hoard | Last emperor represented | Total of *denarii* | of which: struck before 49 | of which: *bigati* | *serrati* |
|---|---|---|---|---|---|
| Medovo | Augustus | 151 | 75 | 6 | 9 |
| Gallignano (Table 1, 3) | Augustus | 441 | 242 | 45 | 16 |
| Olbia (4) | Augustus | 870 | 572 | 75 | 43 |
| Pravoslav (10) | Augustus | 58 | 13 | 0 | 2 |
| Aquileia (12) | Augustus | 560 | 261 | 22 | 39 |
| Krusevo (15) | Augustus | 98 | 40 | 10 | 8 |
| Sicily (18) | Tiberius | 30 | 13 | 2 | 2 |
| Sicily (19) | Tiberius | 33 | 18 | 2 | 3 |
| Magdalensberg | Tiberius | 30 | 18 | 5 | 2 |
| Fotos (20) | Tiberius | 271 | 190 | 30 | 14 |
| Pompeii | Vespasian | 130 | 31 | 3 | 4 |
| Pompeii (31) | Vespasian | 101 | 33 | 5 | 1 |
| Pompeii (32) | Vespasian | 49 | 25 | 11 | 1 |
| Ostia (28) | Vespasian | 35 | 16 | 5 | 1 |
| Budge Row (33) | Vespasian | 74+ | 14 | 1 | 0 |

References, for hoards not included in Table I: Medovo: *Izv.BAI* 27 (1964); Magdalensberg: *Carinthia* 1.151 (1961); Pompeii: *N.Sc.* 1899. Professor Buttrey, in a letter, comments: 'The *serrati* in these hoards represent 5·4 per cent of the *denarii* under Augustus, 5·8 per cent under Tiberius, but only 1·8 per cent under Vespasian—which strikes me as pretty thin pickings, and they going down all the time by a natural attrition.' The figures certainly suggest that if the Germans really had a strong preference for *serrati* in Tacitus' time, they must have acquired it a couple of generations earlier. However, a person may persist in trying to obtain some quite scarce commodity if he is convinced that it is far superior to substitutes.

**217**   It would be generally agreed that very few Britons saw Roman coins before the reign of Claudius; in the north and west, few before the campaigns of Agricola. Yet, according to Professor Anne Robertson, 'the Republican denarius seems to have been a particular favourite in northern Britain and in the less Romanized parts of the province, Wales and Scotland, whose inhabitants were so uncivilized as to prefer old-fashioned silver of a high quality to more recent, but debased issues' (*Mattingly Essays* (see n.54), 272). Whereas fifteen of the thirty-eight Augustan, and four of the eleven Tiberian, *denarii* found at Vindonissa and included in Kraay's catalogue are plated, and likewise one of the three Gallic *denarii* of Julius Caesar (see above, n.26), there are only four plated coins among the fifty-three other republican *denarii* struck prior to his dictatorship. Similarly in *FMRD*, excluding hoards: there the figures are thirteen of eighty-six, five of twenty-one, four of eighteen, fourteen of 229. It may be noted that *bigati* were not really 'safer' than other pre-Caesarian *denarii*: two of the fourteen coins from Vindonissa that could reasonably be described as *bigati* are plated.

**218**   Cassius Dio 56. 18: ἐν γὰρ τῷ αὐτῷ ἐκείνῳ χρόνῳ καὶ ἐν τῇ Κελτικῇ τάδε συνηνέχθη. εἶχον τινα οἱ Ῥωμαῖοι αὐτῆς, οὐκ ἀθρόα ἀλλ᾽ ὡς που καὶ ἔτυχε χειρωθέντα, διὸ οὐδὲ ἐς ἱστορίας μνήμην ἀφίκετο · καὶ στρατιῶται τε αὐτῶν ἐκεῖ ἐχείμαζον καὶ πόλεις συνῳκίζοντο, ἔς τε τὸν κόσμον σφῶν οἱ βάρβαροι μετερρυθμίζοντο καὶ ἀγορὰς ἐνόμιζον · συνόδους τε εἰρηνικὰς ἐποιοῦντο . . . καὶ ἐλάνθανόν σφας ἀλλοιούμενοι · ἐπεὶ δ᾽ ὁ Οὔαρος ὁ Κυιντίλιος τήν τε ἡγεμονίαν τῆς Γερμανίας λαβὼν καὶ τὰ παρ᾽ ἐκείνοις ἐκ τῆς ἀρχῆς διοικῶν ἔσπευσεν αὐτοὺς ἀθροώτερον μεταστῆσαι, καὶ τά τε ἄλλα ὡς καὶ δουλεύουσι σφισιν ἐπέτατε καὶ χρήματα ὡς καὶ παρ᾽ ὑπηκόων ἐσέπρασσεν, οὐκ ἠνέσχοντο . . . The meaning of many of the phrases in this passage has been much debated: the debate is summarised and continued by Dieter Timpe, *Arminius-Studien* (1970), 83 ff. There is no other evidence for the creation of towns in Germany east of the Rhine at this time. Timpe, *op. cit.*, 87, has suggested that Dio may mean that recognition was being given to native *civitates*, as it had been in Gaul, but this seems a strained interpretation of a phrase that is perhaps better taken as a rhetorical exaggeration, or, to put it more charitably, 'eine literarische Veranschaulichung der zivilisatorischen Erschliessung'. He argues (84, 86–7) that Dio intended the term Γερμανία to cover also the subdued areas east of the Rhine, but Dio's words seem to distinguish the province from these areas, as do those of Velleius, even when he is exaggerating what Drusus achieved, 2. 97. 4: *sic perdomuit eam ut in formam paene stipendiariae redigeret provinciae*, 'he tamed it [Dio's Keltiké] so completely that it almost assumed the character of a tributary province'. With Varus' demands, compare the payment of one hundred ox hides which Tacitus says that Drusus compelled the Frisii to render annually, which he calls *tributum* (*Ann.* 4. 27. 1).

**219**   Velleius Paterculus 2. 117–18.

**220**   E. W. Gray, *Classical Review* NS 23 (1973), 62.

**221**   Most recently and thoroughly by Dieter Timpe, *op. cit.* (n.218), chapters 1–2.

**222**   Velleius 2. 118: *adsiduus militiae nostrae prioris comes, iure etiam civitatis Romae eius equestris consequens gradus*. There has been much discussion of the meaning of these words, and whether and how the concluding phrase should be emended. *Romanae* for *Romae* is an almost certain correction, *decus* for *eius* is much more dubious. *Militia prior* probably refers to the fighting in Pannonia, A.D. 6–9, possibly also to the fighting in Germany in A.D. 5–6. My translation is intended merely to bring out the points that Velleius seems to me to have been making, whatever the exact wording should be.

**223** See below, n.544.

**224** Nearly all the Augustan *aurei* listed by Sture Bolin, *Die Funde römischer und byzantinischer Münzen im freien Germanien, 19. Bericht der römisch-germanischen Kommission* (1929), can be accounted for in one of these two ways (cf. n.199 and Wells, *op. cit.* (n.199), 162). There are a few that were unknown to him (e.g. *Germania* 1952, 47–8, Nos. 7 and 21), but such isolated finds are of almost no significance for our purpose, since *aurei* remained long in circulation, and odd examples could easily wander about, as trinkets, even, or especially, among those who did not value them highly.

**225** Most of this area is comprehended in published volumes of *FMRD*: I, I, 5; II 1, 4.

**226** Hachmann and Kossack, *op. cit.* (n.205), e.g. Hachmann, 38.

**227** H. Willers, *NZ* 31 (1899), 329–66 (Bingum; Denekamp, Feins, Onna, Niederlangen); *Neue Untersuchungen über die römische Bronzeindustrie von Capua und von Niedergermanien* (1907), 100–4 (Franzburg bei Hannover; Goldenstedt); W. A. van Es, *De romeinse Muntvondsten uit de drie noordelijke Provincies* (1960) (Feins, Onna, Oude Horne); A. N. Zadoks-Jitta, *Jaarboek voor Munt- en Penningkunde*, 1954, 107 (Bylandse Waard). (What was said above, n.216, about *bigati* applies here also.) Composition of these hoards is shown in the accompanying table.

| Hoard | Number of coins seen | Before 49 B.C. | of which: bigati | serrati | 49– 31 B.C. | of which: legionary | 31 B.C.– A.D. 14 Augustus | A.D. 14–37 Tiberius |
|---|---|---|---|---|---|---|---|---|
| Franzburg | 30 | 19 | 4 | 3 | 6 | 3 | 5 | – |
| Bingum | 18 | 4 | – | – | 4 | 1 | 10[a] | – |
| Goldenstedt | 9 | 5 | – | – | 2 | – | 1 | – |
| Denekamp | 41 | 25 | 4 | 8 | 3 | – | 1 | – |
| Niederlangen | 62 | 61 | 6 | 41 | – | – | 1 | – |
| Bylandse Waard | 61 | 34 | 2 | 4 | 23 | – | 4 | – |
| Onna | 262[b] | 138 | 32 | 7 | 81 | 36 | 20 | 20 |
| Oude Horne | 14[c] | 6 | 2 | 2 | 5 | 1 | 1 | – |
| Feins | 52[d] | 15 | 2 | 1 | 20 | 8 | 13 + 2 frag-ments | 4 + 1 frag-ment |

[a] Including three *aes*: *RIC* I Augustus, 186, 364(2).
[b] Eight unidentified coins.
[c] Including one *aes* and one Juba I *denarius*.
[d] And seven fragmentary *denarii*.

The Reckelsum hoard, of '42 *denarii* down to issue for C. L. CAESARES' is known to me only from *RRCH* (545).

**228** Rostovtzeff, *SEHRE*², 97. Either way, the traders would have been following routes already explored by Roman armies: which is probably true of all the routes from the Empire into Germany, except the route up the Dniester; cf. Eggers, *op. cit.* (n.214), 76. In the north-west they might have made use of the causeway across the marshes built by Drusus, if it remained usable. The Frisians were friendly from 12 B.C. onwards, 'perhaps also the Chauci' (R. Syme, *CAH* x, 376).

**229**  A hoard of twenty-five Roman coins, the latest being of A.D. 74, found in a settlement of the early imperial epoch at Ginderup in north-west Jutland, might indicate that commercial use of Roman coinage had extended that far by the time of Vespasian (H. Jankuhn, in Much, *Die Germania des Tacitus*[3] (1967), 120, citing J. Brøndsted, *Nordische Vorzeit*[3] (1964), 175 ff.). No hoards consisting solely of pre-Neronian coins have been found in the interior of Germany, beyond the Rhine and the Limes.

**230**  Schirwitz, *Germania* 1952, 49, 52.

**231**  See the map by Stade in Putzger, *Historischer Schulatlas*[63] (1954), 39–40. Van Es, *op. cit.* (n.227), is inclined to regard all the German finds of Roman coins down to A.D. 47 as a reflection of Roman military activities.

**232**  *NZ* 1899.

**233**  *Die Bronzeeimer von Hemmoor* (1901), 193. Van Es, *op. cit.* (n.227), having directly studied the Onna and Feins hoards, has suggested A.D. 47 and A.D. 28, respectively, as more likely dates for their burial, but he relates them to military movements in those years.

**234**  *Neue Untersuchungen* (see above, n.227), 103.

**235**  See n.230. Sir Mortimer Wheeler's figure (*Rome Beyond the Imperial Frontiers*, 64)—'only 36 stray copper coins' of the first century A.D. from the whole of free Germany—is much too low. Some *aes* coins found at Bad Nauheim may reflect trading relations in the time of Augustus (Wells, *op. cit.* (n.199), 230).

**236**  Wheeler, *Rome Beyond the Imperial Frontiers* (1955), 63. Find evidence indicates that the state of affairs in Epirus was, or had been, similar (N. G. L. Hammond, *Epirus* (1967), 717–25), with the difference that there local currencies were created 'to ease a local trade which was probably in terms mainly of bartering goods': it seems 'that the export of goods from inland Epirus was in the hands of merchants near the coast and that the materials which were collected for export were purchased not with foreign currency but by barter and sometimes by paying in local currency' (723), whereas in Germany Roman currency had to be used, or none, at least after the collapse of La Tène civilisation. In the evidence from pre-Roman Gaul one can see both stages, a stage at which the coins of Massalia played the same part as *denarii* in Germany in the early imperial period and a stage at which local currencies had emerged to play probably much the same part as in Epirus (Jannoray, *op. cit.* (n.131), 345–50).

**237**  For the Augustan period Rostovtzeff, *SEHRE*[2], 67, expressed the view that 'the articles bought in foreign lands were paid for in the North almost entirely by the export of oil and wine and manufactured goods'.

**238**  So Willers suggested, *Die Bronzeeimer von Hemmoor* (1901), 194–5 (see above, n.151), cf. Sir John Hicks, *A Theory of Economic History* (1969), 64 ff., on the origins of money.

**239**  Stuart Piggott, *Ancient Europe* (1965), 223: cf. R. von Uslar, *Bonner Jahrbücher* 153 (1953), 149: 'genügt heute eine einfache Konfrontation *Kelten-Germanen* nicht mehr': see above, n.205.

**240**  See, for instance, Evžen and Jiří Neustupny, *Czechoslovakia Before the Slavs* (1962), chapter 12.

**241**  The *Rolltierstater*, which was the prototype of the 'rainbow-cup' of Germany and of the *Muschelstater* of the regions to the south of Bohemia: see Karl Pink, *Einführung in die keltische Münzkunde*, 21–3, 37 ff.; Karel Castelin, *Die Goldprägung der Kelten in den böhmischen Ländern* (1965).

**242**  For instance, *phalerae*: cf. D. F. Allen, *NC*[7] 8 (1968), 37–54, on those in a hoard found on Sark, which 'must certainly have been brought to some place in Gaul from the Danube area', and which closely resemble some found in Bulgaria.

**243**  The similar decoration of pottery in Gaul and Bohemia in the first century B.C. has often been commented on, e.g. by de Navarro, *CAH* IX, 539.

**244** For example, the types used by the Boii for silver coinage in the middle of the first century B.C. seem to be derived, in the case of the small silver, from Central Gallic *quinarii*, and, in the case of the large silver, from Iberian-type coins of Gallia Narbonensis and Spain (Pink, *op. cit.* (n.241), 23–7), and the cross on the reverse of much of the Norican small silver may be derived from the wheel on obols of Massalia that circulated widely in western Celtic lands (D. F. Allen, *NC*[7] 13 (1973), 234). Gallic influence can be discerned also in the types of coins struck even further east, in the Munkacs area (Pink, *Die Münzprägung der Ostkelten* I (1939), 85). See also D. F. Allen, *Germania* 49 (1971), 91–110.

**245** Neustupny, *op. cit.* (n.240), 152.

**246** 'There can be no doubt that the normal method of trade was barter' (D. F. Allen, *JbNumG* 18 (1968), 118; cf. Neustupny, *op. cit.* (n.240), 152–3; Andreas Mocsy, *RE* Supplementband IX, *s.v.* Pannonia, 691). A few Gallic coins of the first century B.C. have been found at the Celtic *oppidum* at Stradonice in Bohemia (see below, n.398), a couple of Celtic coins from central Europe have turned up in France (Pink, *op. cit.* (n.241), 19–20, 22–3), and in England there have been at least two such finds, of silver drachmas from Gallia Cisalpina near Penzance, in the tin-mining region (D. F. Allen, *NC*[7] I (1961), 91–106), and of Geto-Dacian tetra-drachms at Portland in Dorset, conceivably a stage on the tin route (id., *JbNumG* 18 (1968), 113–18; cf. Pârvan, *Getica* (1926), 614–15), but by their very rarity such finds tell against rather than for the regular use of coins as an instrument of long-distance trade among the Celts (*pace* G. Alföldy, *Noricum* (1974), 43–4). The lists and maps compiled by Simone Scheers, *Les Monnaies de la Gaule inspirées de celles de la République romaine* (1969), which cover several of the most widely diffused Gallic issues, show clearly how unusual it was for them to travel long distances. There was perhaps some use of coins by those trading between Celtic central Europe and Italy in the first century B.C., for Vindelican 'rainbow cups' reached northern Italy 'in nicht geringer Anzahl', according to K. Castelin, 'Oro Celtico in Italia settentrionale', *Congresso internazionale di numismatica* (Rome, 1961), *Atti* (1965), 185–94; cf. *JbNumG* 13 (1973), 112 n.2b. However, I know of only one find of Celtic coins of any other variety from central Europe in peninsular Italy; a hoard, to which eighty-four coins, variously dispersed, can be assigned with some confidence, of gold third-staters of Pink's *Muschelstater* type (cf. above, n.241), found in 1912 near Cecina in Tuscany, which it is suggested had been used for trade: 'rappresenta quasi certamente il peculio di un mercante di ritorno da quelle lontane regioni o la somma pagata da un Gallo per l'acquisto di merci da riportare in patria' (Franco Panvini-Rosati, *AIIN* 2 (1955), 59–61). For the few finds of Roman republican coins beyond the middle Danube that could be of similar significance, see below, p. 36: from the works there cited it appears that there have been far fewer finds of Greek coins.

**247** Mocsy, *loc. cit.* (n.246). Alföldy (*Noricum*, 42–3) accepts Mocsy's view. He points out that 'the number of names [on the Norican tetradrachms] is much too large for the short period in which the coins were minted (c. 70–40 B.C.)' (but others hold that minting of tetradrachms continued until c. 16–15 B.C.), and he concludes that 'some of them must have been issued simultaneously'. Simultaneous minting of some issues is what investigation of the dies also suggests, but from the likelihood that 'the leaders of the individual tribes recognised the chief of the Carinthian Norici as *rex* and highest authority' it does not follow that they would not have issued coins (cf. Göbl, *op. cit.* (n.121), 54). Alföldy objects further that the name of the Norican king Voccio, who was already in power c. 60 B.C. (Caesar, *Bellum Gallicum*, I. 53. 4) 'does not appear on the coins at all'; Göbl does not accept this, but in any case Voccio could have been responsible for the tetradrachms bearing no name, which are among the earliest 'west Norican' coins.

**248** Castelin, *JbNumG* 18 (1968), 119–25.

**249**  Neustupny, *op. cit.* (n. 240), 161–9; Kossack, *op. cit.* (n.205), 94–100. The scarcity in the south-west and west of free Germany (in the regions represented on the modern map by Westfalen south of the Lippe, most of Hessen, the north and east of Baden, the north of Bavaria and Upper Austria) of finds from the early imperial period, not only of coins (see the maps in *FMRD* I, 2, II, I) but also of other objects, whether German (see the map published and discussed by R. von Uslar, *Germania* 29 (1951), 44–7) or Roman (see Eggers, *op. cit.* (n.209), pp. 24, 35, 36 and map 4), except in close proximity to the frontier, indicates that this whole highland area was only thinly populated. Much of it seems to have been in the hands of the Hermunduri, whose main centre perhaps lay to the north-west of it, in Thuringia, but whose control evidently extended down to the Danube (Tac., *Germ.* 41: his 'Albis' is here perhaps the Elbe's chief tributary, the Saale; cf. Eggers, *op. cit.* (n.209), 36, 76).

**250**  For Roman control of trade across the frontiers, see Tacitus, *Germ.* 41, *Historiae* 4. 65. On the making of the lower Danube into a barrier in Augustus' time, see below, n.322.

**251**  Neustupny, *op. cit.* (n.240), 169. Later, in the second century A.D., trade within the frontier, between the Rhineland and the Danubian provinces, was much more important than trade between the Empire and Germany: cf. Petrikovits, *Das römische Rheinland*, 116–20.

**252**  Individual finds of Roman coins in and around Linz include six republican, six of Augustus, four of Tiberius and twelve of Claudius (Alföldy, *Noricum*, 179, from L. Eckhart, *Linzer Fundkatalog* II (1966)), but these probably reflect the posting of an auxiliary unit there under Claudius (Alföldy, 103–4).

**253**  Strabo 5. 1. 8, p. 214 (who strangely supposed that traffic could go by river all the way from Aquileia to Noreia; Noreia was probably the name of the town on the Magdalensberg); Hermann Vetters, *RE*, *s.v.* Virunum (1961); Rudolf Eggers, *Denkschriften der Akademie der Wissenschaften in Wien* 79 (1961). The reports of the excavation on the Magdalensberg since 1948 include detailed accounts of the coin finds: see *Carinthia* I, 142 (1952), 143 (1953), 146 (1956), 148 (1958, with an important article on the Celtic coins by Karl Pink), 149 (1959), 151 (1961), 153 (1963), 156 (1966), 159 (1969). (I have not seen the comprehensive publication, including also earlier finds, by H. Bannert and G. Piccottini, *Die Fundmünzen vom Magdalensberg* (1972).)

**254**  For the problem of dating see above, n.143.

**255**  Pliny, *NH* 37. 45 (our only literary evidence for a trade route reaching deep into Germany); M. P. Charlesworth, *Trade Routes and Commerce of the Roman Empire*[2] (1926), 176.

**256**  Rostovtzeff, *SEHRE*[2] 69, 567: cf. Pliny, *NH* 37. 44. When T. R. S. Broughton points out that the amber brought back by 'the anonymous Roman knight who travelled the amber route to the Baltic under Nero . . . was used for imperial display—hardly a commercial proposition' (*Deuxième Conférence Internationale d'Histoire Economique*, 1962, I (1965), 162), he evidently means to illustrate not the insignificance of the amber trade but the insignificance of the part played in it by *equites*.

**257**  Pliny, *NH* 37. 45. In Strabo's time no Roman had travelled beyond the Elbe (7. 2. 4, p. 294), and probably none had ventured even that far on any peaceful mission: cf. Eggers, *op. cit.* (n.209), 77.

**258**  Strabo (5. 1. 8, p. 214) speaks of the bartering of goods at Aquileia by natives from the hinterland, who brought slaves, cattle and hides, to exchange for wine, oil and products of the sea, which they carried inland on their wagons: largely, no doubt, by way of the road across the Julian Alps to Nauportus (Strabo 4. 6. 10, p. 207, 7. 5. 2, p. 314), which formed the first part of the easiest route to Carnuntum.

**259** *Corpus Inscriptionum Latinarum* III, 5143, 5227; G. Alföldy, *Noricum* (1974), 81–2.

**260** Two were found in 1895, one (*RRCH*, 462) at Celje (Celeia), comprising twenty-four *denarii* down to the legionary issue of M. Antony, the other (*RRCH*, 492) at Ptuj (Poetovio), comprising twenty-eight *denarii* down to *c*. 16 B.C.; a third was found in 1930 at Licka Ribnica, somewhat away from the route, comprising 209 republican *denarii*, one of Juba I and thirty-six of Augustus, down to the issue celebrating Gaius and Lucius (Josip Klemenc, *Numismatika* I (1933), 12–14; *RRCH*, 546). For the route from Nauportus down the Save, see below, p. 38.

**261** Tac., *Ann.* 2. 62.

**262** A map compiled by H. J. Eggers (*op. cit.* (n.209), No. 39) shows the distribution of finds within free Germany of 'Kasserollen mit Schwanenkopfbügeln', a type of bronze vessel attributable to the later part of Augustus' reign (*ibid.*, 47–8, 51). Twenty-three have been found; thirteen at different sites in Bohemia, one in Moravia, on the route to Bohemia, and the other nine at various points in central and northern Germany to which they could quite easily have travelled from Bohemia, as gifts, for instance, or as booty. This suggests, and other finds seem to confirm, that beyond the frontier zone, the zone inhabited by Tacitus' *proximi* (*Germ.* 5), the one German tribe with which the Romans had close friendly contacts, at least in the later years of Augustus and in the early years of Tiberius' reign, were the Marcomanni, contacts persisting until the fall of Maroboduus.

**263** Tac., *Germ.* 5.

**264** For Bohemia (which corresponds roughly with the area within which the Marcomanni were living during the reign of Tiberius), reasonably well-attested finds of single Roman coins that might have found their way there before the death of Tiberius comprise nineteen republican *denarii* and one *quinarius*, one *denarius* of Augustus and two of Tiberius; five republican *asses* (four from the Celtic site Stradonice), six Augustan *aes* coins (three Nemausus *asses*, one Lugdunum *as*, two unidentified) and five Tiberian (see Eugen Pochitonov, in *Nalezy Mincí v Cechách, na Moravě a ve Slezsku*, ed. Manuela Nohejlová-Prátová I (1955).

**265** T. Pekary, *Arch. Ertesíto* 80 (1953), 106–14. Zdenka Nemeskalová-Jiroudková pointed out the similarity, *Num.Sbornik* 7 (1962), 43–59.

**266** One contained over one hundred; the thirty-five (including thirty *serrati*) of which there is detailed knowledge extend down to *c*. 60 B.C. (*RRCH*, 328). The other consisted of about twenty, said to be of the second century B.C. (see n.264). The earliest two imperial hoards extend down to Hadrian and so do not concern us.

**267** Twenty-five republican and two Augustan *denarii*, one republican and one Nemausus *aes*, three other Augustan and three Tiberian *aes* coins: also three small hoards of republican silver, in one of which the latest coin specified is a *quinarius* of the eighties B.C., in the second a *denarius* of *c*. 80 B.C., in the third a *denarius* of Julius Caesar (Pochitonov, *op. cit.* (n.264)).

**268** Seventeen republican *denarii* and one *victoriatus*, two legionary *denarii*, two Augustan *denarii* and one *quinarius*, six Augustan *aes* coins from the Roman mint, nothing of Tiberius (see Vojtech Ondrouch, *Nalezy Keltskych, Antikych à Byz. Minci na Slovensku* (1964); also one hoard of one hundred coins, found near Trencin, not mentioned by Ondrouch, which is listed below, n.275).

**269** Comprising seventeen republican and three Augustan silver coins and three Augustan *aes* coins. The earliest hoards were Hadrianic.

**270** Andrzej Kunisz, *Rocznik Muzeum Swiętokrzyskiego* 6 (1970), 104–58, a report kindly lent me by Mr Michael Crawford.

**271** Kunisz, *op. cit.*, English summary, p. 158.

**272** Cf. the evidence from Romania, below, nn.297 ff.

**273** Pink, *Die Münzprägung der Ostkelten* I (1939), 129, 131 and find-map; cf. A. Kerenyi, *Num.Közl.* 58–59 (1959–60), 3–6 on a more recent large find at Intercisa.

**274**  Pink, *op. cit.* (n.273), 125; *Einführung in die keltische Münzkunde*, 31.

**275**  The hoards in question are as follows:

   (i)  Ö. Gohl, *NZ* 35 (1903), 146; *RRCH*, 330: hoard found near Trenčin in Slovakia, comprising about one hundred coins, including at least twenty-nine imitations; according to Crawford, the latest coins are imitations of *CRR* 915, giving a terminal date near 50 B.C., but according to Gohl there is one later *denarius*, *RIC* I Augustus, 27/28).

  (ii)  *Archiv für österreichische Geschichtsquellen* 24 (1860), 349; cf. Gohl, *NZ* 35 (1903), 147; *RRCH*, 370: hoard found at Bia near Pest of four *denarii*, to *c.* 47 B.C., and seven imitations.

 (iii)  A. Kerenyi, *Num.Közl.* 56–57 (1957–58), 63; cf. 62–63 (1963–64), 97: hoard of fifty-two *denarii* found at Erd, on the Danube, a little south of Pest, the latest being of 46 B.C. = *RRCH*, 373 (curiously, two varieties, *CRR*, 752 (eighteen, plus one incuse) and 785 (eight) make up more than half the hoard—are they copies? Cf. below, pp. 42 f.).

  (iv)  Gohl, *Num.Közl.* I (1902), 17; *NZ* 35 (1903), 146: hoard found at Lagymanyos near Pest, comprising 119 *denarii*, to 11 B.C., and 365 imitations = *RRCH*, 510).

   (v)  Gohl, *NZ* 35 (1903), 147 (citing earlier literature), *Budapest Regisegei* 8 (1904), 182: hoard found in 1796 at Bia, near Pest, containing eighty imitations together with 600 *denarii*, including some of Augustus and Tiberius and one of Gaius.

  (vi)  A. Mocsy, *Num.Közl.* 60–61 (1961–62), 15–18: hoard of fifteen coins found at Tokod, near the Danube, north of Pest: twelve *denarii*—nine republican, one legionary, one Augustan, one Tiberian—and three *asses* of Tiberius.

 (vii)  A. Alföldi, junior, *Magyar Muzeum* 1946, 52–7, 95–6: hoard of eleven *aes* coins found at Mucsi, Kurd: (*a*) one *uncia* of the third century B.C., one *as* of the first century B.C., one *aes* coin of Hieron II; (*b*) eight Augustan and Tiberian coins: Alföldi suggests that the coins in group (*a*) had reached the district about a century earlier.

According to Pârvan, coins of the Eravisci were found also in a Dacian fortress at Costeşti (*Dacia*, 137; *Getica*, 603, 778), but there is perhaps a confusion with Dacian imitations of *denarii*, two of which are reported from the excavation of Costeşti in Maria Chiţescu's list (see below, n.324).

**276**  Gohl, 'Die Münzen der Eravisker', *NZ* 35 (1903), 145–68; A. Alföldi senior, *Zur Kenntnis der Geschichte des Karpathenbeckens im I. Jh. v. Chr.* (1942), 26 ff., 44 f.; cf. J. Szilagyi, *Aquincum* (1956), 9; Mocsy, *Num.Közl.* 60–61 (1961–2), 15–18.

**277**  Mocsy, *Die Bevölkerung von Pannonien biz zu den Markomannenkriegen* (1959), 97; *Num.Közl.* 60–61 (1961–62), 15 ff.; *Acta Archaeologica Academiae Scientiarum Hungaricae* 23 (1971), 41 ff.

**278**  See Walter Schmitthenner, *Historia* 7 (1958), 189–236.

**279**  Bellinger, *Alexander*, 65–6.

**280**  See *GCH*, 1634–45; cf. Colin Kraay, *JHS* 84 (1964), 83, 87–8.

**281**  Szilagyi, *loc. cit.* (n.276); cf. P. Oliva, *Pannonia and the Onset of Crisis in the Roman Empire* (1962), 155–7; Ondrouch, *op. cit.* (n.268), 191. Gohl, *op. cit.* (n.276), 166–67, argued that their production must have begun around the middle of the century, but their presence in hoards containing early imperial *denarii* led him to suggest that it continued down into, and perhaps through, the reign of Augustus. However, he held also that type-links between the various coins of this character prove that all must have been produced 'innerhalb eines kurzen Zeitraumes'; and, even if their production did not extend beyond the fifties, there would be parallels from Gaul (Lumigny, *Revue belge de numismatique* 1959, 59–94); Sark (*NC*[7] 8 (1968), 40) and Germany (Haltern, Neuss: Chantraine, *Novaesium* III, 33–4) for the presence of coins struck in the fifties in a hoard closed as late as 11 B.C., and even beside coins of Gaius.

**282** Geza Szepressy has compiled a survey (*Num.Közl.* 64–65 (1965–66), 73–5) of isolated finds of Roman coins in the region south and west of the Danube and north of Pest: too much significance must not be attached to them, as many of the coins may have arrived long after they were minted, but it is worth mentioning that he lists only fifteen Julio-Claudian coins (including five of Augustus and two of Tiberius), as against twenty-seven Flavian and sixty-three from Nerva to Hadrian. Cf. the Slovakian evidence (n.268) and the evidence from Linz (n.252).

Several hoards containing *denarii* found in parts of Pannonia lying within present-day Hungary but on the route into Dacia are considered below, nn.298, 305. On finds of Roman *aes* coins in Pannonia, see also p. 56.

**283** Strabo 4. 6. 10, p. 207; 5. 1. 8, p. 214; 7. 5. 2, p. 314. It may well have been at some point or points along this route that Roman citizens and *negotiatores* were butchered at the outbreak of the Pannonian revolt (Velleius 2. 110. 6: *oppressi cives Romani, trucidati negotiatores*). If the *negotiatores* were *cives Romani* (which Velleius' words neither imply, although this is commonly assumed, nor exclude), they may well have been moneylenders, helping to finance the development of trade along this route (cf. the references in inscriptions from the Magdalensberg to loans in connection with the iron trade (Egger, *Denkschriften Akad. Wien* 79 (1961)) and the role of debt in the revolt of Sacrovir (Tac., *Ann.* 3. 40)). But *mercatores* themselves, like those at the court of Maroboduus (above, p. 36) could be so described, if one wished to make them sound respectable.

**284** Strabo 5. 1. 8, p. 214; Mocsy, *RE* Supplementband IX, *s.v.* Pannonia, 693. In *GCH* there are only two hoards from the interior of Croatia, both of *c.* 100 B.C. (569, 644).

**285** Pârvan, *Getica* (1926), 613 ff.; *Dacia* (1928), 154–5; Ceka, *Studia Albanica* 3. 1 (1966), 222. A list of some of the finds of coins of Dyrrhachion and Apollonia, down to 1938, has been compiled by Mitrea, *Ephemeris Dacoromana* 10 (1945), 83–7; for finds in Bosnia and Herzegovina, cf. Partsch, *Wissenschaftliche Mitteilungen aus Bosnien und der Herzegovina* 4 (1896), 113 ff.; 6 (1899), 100–2; and for hoards from this area that include them see now *GCH* (556–60, 578–9, 665–7). Abundant finds in north-western Bulgaria: Gerassimov, *Arheološki Vestnik* 23 (1972), 74 ff.

**286** Cf. John Wilkes, *Dalmatia* (1969), 7–8, 410.

**287** Ceka, *Studia Albanica* 3. 1 (1966), 213–23, argues that production continued until *c.* 27 B.C. but was declining during the first century in face of the competition of *denarii*; he refers to two mixed hoards from Albania (*GCH*, 665–6) in which the latest *denarii*, mint-fresh, are of 49 B.C. and in one of which one of the Dyrrhachion drachmas is mint-fresh. Of the only two hoards from the Sirmium region that are known to have contained republican, but not imperial, *denarii*, one, from Vukovar (Cornacum, near Mursa), included forty-eight drachmas of Dyrrhachion and eighty-eight of Apollonia with four *denarii* down to *c.* 80 B.C. (Brunsmid, *Vjesnik hrvatsk. arheol. društva* 12 (1912), 260–4; *RRCH*, 276; not in *GCH*) and the other, from Szeged (i.e. on the route from the Danube by the Tisza and the Mures into Dacia) contained a drachma of Dyrrhachion and an unspecified number of *denarii* (Mitrea, *op. cit.* (n.285), 86–7): cf. similar Dacian hoards (n.303). The persistence of the drachmas of Dyrrhachion and Apollonia, at least in people's savings (cf. Winkler, *JbNumG* 17 (1967), 140) is shown by the contents of a hoard found at Vacz-Hartya (Pest) containing a drachma of Apollonia and three of Dyrrhachion with ten imperial *denarii* (*Num.Közl.* 4 (1905), 98; Winkler, *op. cit.*, 157), and another, from Potoc in the Banat, with a drachma of Apollonia, 171 republican *denarii* and one of Vespasian (Winkler, *op. cit.*, No. 116). A hoard found at Tisa in Transylvania in 1872 combined thirty-two drachmas of Dyrrhachion and nineteen of Apollonia with fifty Thasos tetradrachms, two imitations, 833 republican and thirteen imperial *denarii*, to A.D. 229 (Winkler, *Sargetia* 7 (1970), 27–42).

**288** For some hoards from points along this route see Klemenc, *Numismatika* 2

(1934–36), 124. Unfortunately many coin finds in the regions now comprised in Yugoslavia remain unpublished. There are tantalising allusions in *Arch.-Epigr. Mitteilungen aus Österreich-Ungarn*, e.g. 4 (1880), 99, 103, 105, 122; 19 (1896), 169, 177–8.

**289**    That was the view of Karl Pink (*Die Münzprägung der Ostkelten* I (1939); *Einführung in die keltische Münzkunde* (1950)), followed by A. Alföldi senior (*Zu den Schicksalen Siebenbürgens im Altertum* (1944), 70) and Maria Alföldi (*JbNumG* 8 (1958), 203; 11 (1961), 189); cf. Vasile Pârvan, *Getica* (1926), 599–605.

**290**    See Bucur Mitrea, 'Penetrazione commerciale e circulazione monetaria nella Dacia prima della conquista', *Ephemeris Dacoromana* 10 (1945), 1–154. This view has been developed in numerous articles by Constantin Preda (e.g. 'Einige Fragen der geto-dakischen Numismatik', *JbNumG* 16 (1966), 63–82; 'Über die Anfänge der "barbarischen" Münzprägung vom Typ Philipps II', *JbNumG* 20 (1970), 63–77; his *magnum opus*, *Monedele Geto-Dacilor* (1973) appeared after my work was completed), and Judita Winkler (e.g. *Num.Sbornik* 5 (1958), 5–40; *JbNumG* 21 (1971), 109–13). It is held to be in general correct by Harald Küthmann, *Congresso internazionale di numismatica* (Rome, 1961), *Relazioni*, 23 (but he adds: 'Die handelspolitischen und kulturellen Gegebenheiten und die damit zusammenhängenden Fragen dürften allerdings noch nicht restlos erschöpfend bearbeitet sein'). It has been given further support recently at its upper end by Virginia Joyce Hunter (ANS *Museum Notes* 13 (1967), 17–40). Her reconsideration of a hoard of Greek and Celtic silver coins found at Zemun near Belgrade in 1924 (*GCH* 458) shows almost conclusively that 'at least three distinct types of East-Celtic coins' found in Serbia, derived from the silver tetradrachms of Philip II, which in Pink's view did not begin to be produced until after 107 B.C., 'can be dated before 220': she hold that at least one of them, dubbed by Pink the *Eselohrtyp*, probably began to be struck about 270.

**291**    See above, n.161.

**292**    Pârvan, however, believed that 'a large number of Dacian imitations . . . singularly poor in metallic content' were produced in Transylvania (*Dacia* (1928), 100), and it is said that many have been found in the region of the Dacian fortresses in south-western Transylvania (H. Daicovicu, quoted in *Acta Musei Napocensis* 8 (1971), 77 n.10). Many Dacian hoards of the first century B.C. including such imitations are listed in *GCH*: 622–41, 652, 656, 662, 683 (hoards containing imitations only are not listed); most of these can be located on a find map compiled by I. Glodariu, *Acta Musei Napocensis* 8 (1971), 79–80.

**293**    About 2,900, and about 450 of Macedonia Prima, have been found in Dacia, approximately 1,700 in Transylvania, approximately 1,200 in Muntenia: Glodariu, *op. cit.* (n.292), 72–6; he provides a map of find-spots (unfortunately too poorly printed to be wholly legible); he does not distinguish dates of hoards, but details of most that he lists can be found in *GCH*.

**294**    In fifteen Dacian hoards, according to Glodariu, *op. cit.*, 72.

**295**    See Katzarova, *op. cit.* (n.161).

**296**    Cf. Dunant and Pouilloux, *op. cit.* (n.161), 7, 9; Pârvan, *Getica*, 796.

**297**    Hoards containing no *denarii* that were struck (if they are genuine) after 70 B.C.: ten containing only *denarii* are listed by Crawford in *RRCH* (120, 177, 224, 254, 270, 274, 275, 280, 291, 318); another four, not included in his inventory, are in a list compiled by Winkler, *JbNumG* 17 (1967) (Nos. 4, 73, 91, 95). Five others contain also coins of Dyrrhachion: *GCH*, 652 (not in *RRCH*), 651 (*RRCH*, 285—different details), 650 (*RRCH*, 321), 655 (*RRCH*, 303), *RRCH* 296 (not in *GCH*); one also coins of Apollonia: *GCH* 657 (not in *RRCH*); three others contain also coins of Thasos: *RRCH*, 295 (not in *GCH*), 322 (ditto), 320 (*GCH*, 656). Correspondingly, the majority of Dacian imitations of *denarii* are derived from *denarii* struck before 70 B.C.: see below, p. 42.

**298** The only certain cases known to me are:
  (i) a hoard from the Banat, which included one pseudo-Philippic didrachm of Pink's *Ringellocken* class, along with three drachms of Apollonia, ten of Dyrrhachion and thirty-eight *denarii*, the latest being of the seventies B.C. (No. 83 in Winkler's list (see n.297), No. 21 in Mitrea's list (see n.285), *RRCH*, 293).
  (ii) a hoard from Bekes-Gyula, just across the Hungarian border, containing one pseudo-Philippic tetradrachm along with sixty-three *denarii* and many drachms of Apollonia and Dyrrhachion (Mitrea No. 91).
  (iii) a hoard from Muntenia including one 'Lysimachos' tetradrachm of Pink's *Sattelkopf-pferd* class along with seventy-seven *denarii*, the latest being of the fifties B.C. (Winkler No. 24, Mitrea No. 106, *RRCH*, 346).
  (iv) a hoard from Oltenia, *c.* 70 B.C. (*GCH*, 658) containing nine 'Geto-Dacian' coins along with one imitation *denarius*, thirty-nine Dyrrhachion drachmas and one imitation).
  (v) a hoard from Körösszakál, near Bekes-Gyula, comprising one tetradrachm of Pink's *Ringellocken* group, 269 *denarii*, one drachma of Dyrrhachion and one imitation (ANS *Numismatic Literature* 83 (1969), No. 164).
**299** See the analysis by Winkler (who was following Grueber's dating in the *British Museum Catalogue of Coins of the Roman Republic*), *JbNumG* 17 (1967), 137–9 and Beilage III.
**300** Pârvan, *Getica* (1926), 612. He, indeed, held that they 'made their appearance towards the end of the third century' (*Dacia* (1928), 136).
**301** Mitrea, *SCN* 2 (1958), 126 ff.; cf. Lupu, *JbNumG* 17 (1967), 118 ff.; Chiţescu, *Memoria Antiquitatis* 3 (1971), 219.
**302** See Winkler, *op. cit.* (n.297), 137.
**303** Nearly twelve thousand of the drachmas of Dyrrhachion and Apollonia, together with Illyrian imitations, have been found in Dacia (Glodariu, *op. cit.* (n.292), 77–80, with map of find-spots). There is a cluster of finds in the Banat, close to the Danube, but they occur chiefly (about 9,500 altogether) in Crişana and western Transylvania, indicating that it was chiefly by way of the Tisza valley that they reached Dacia. Another cluster of finds in south-eastern Transylvania and just beyond, in Moldavia, suggests that some of those who brought them to Dacia travelled on into that area. Fifteen Dacian hoards in which drachms from one or both of these mints, nearly one thousand in all (those of Dyrrhachion being far the more numerous), are combined with over 2,600 republican *denarii* have been listed by Mitrea (*op. cit.* (n.285), 102–13) and Winkler (*op. cit.* (n.297), 123–56), and at least five more have since been published, comprising altogether: three from the Banat, eight from Transylvania (the three recent examples: *SCN* 4 (1968), 355–62; *Sargetia* 6 (1969), 7–26; 7 (1970)), two from Crişana, two from Oltenia, three from Muntenia (the two recent examples: *SCN* 4 (1968), 452–5; 5 (1971), 377–9). Two hoards of similar composition have been reported from Hungary, just across the boarder from Crişana (see above, n.287) and a third from Szeged, on the route from Sirmium into Transylvania (*Num.Közl.* 11 (1912), 13). These mixed hoards illustrate the adoption of *denarii* by those who had previously carried the coins of Apollonia and Dyrrhachion beyond the Sirmium region along the routes indicated above. Another such hoard, including also Thasos tetradrachms, has been reported from subcarpathian Russia (Mitrea, *op. cit.* (n. 285), pp. 69, 87).
**304** Ceka, *op. cit.* (n.285), 221–2; cf. Gerassimov, *loc. cit.* (n.285). Pârvan believed that these were the routes by which most of the *denarii* that reached Dacia before the time of Augustus travelled: *Getica*, 610–13, 797–8; *Dacia*, 154–5.
**305** Glodariu (*op. cit.* (n.292), 85) estimates that about sixteen thousand pre-conquest *denarii* have been found in Transylvania, about nine thousand in other parts of Romania (excluding Dobrugia). Less comprehensive but more precise information

is provided by Crawford in *RRCH*: his survey omits a large number of the hoards listed by Glodariu, but gives some data for forty Dacian hoards which include republican *denarii* with closing dates down to 45 B.C., a total exceeded only by the combined total (forty-seven) from Spain and Portugal, where the circulation of *denarii* probably began much earlier. Known contents of these forty hoards amount to more than three thousand *denarii* (no other Roman coins being represented). Another eight hoards for which Winkler (see n.297) gives terminal dates down to 45 B.C. included another 375 *denarii* (Winkler Nos. 1, 4, 15, 29, 73, 91, 95, 149) and more have been reported since, e.g. *SCN* 4 (1968), 375–9, 450–2; 5 (1971), 372–6; *Historica* 1 (1970), 53–72. (Pârvan (*Dacia*, 138; cf. *Getica*, 612, 797) somewhat exaggerated the proportion of hoards ending with *denarii* of 45 or 44 B.C., when 'Caesar was preparing against Burebista', but one may agree that some were probably buried at that juncture.) For the period 44–27 B.C. Crawford has another twelve, with over 1,800 *denarii*, and one from just across the Hungarian border (*RRCH*, 411) with 169; Winkler a further eleven, with over one thousand; and here again additions can be made, e.g. *SCIV* 21 (1970), 429–50, *Pontica* 3 (1970), 31–7, making another 250. In Winkler's list there are also about fifty other hoards containing *denarii*, details of which are not available but which are said to be all republican.

**306** For this interpretation of the Dacian finds see e.g. Dunant and Pouilloux, *op. cit.* (n.161), 7 ff.; Winkler, *JbNumG* 17 (1967), 132, 136–7, 140; Lupu, *ibid.*, 103: 'das römische Geld ist in Dakien in weitaus stärkerem Masse vertreten als das griechische, sowie dessen einheimische Nachprägungen, woraus sich der Schluss ergibt, dass die Handelsbeziehungen mit Rom intensiver waren'; 119–20: cf. Pârvan, *Dacia*, 96–101, 135–9, 154–6.

**307** Pârvan, *Getica*, 794. Hoards of gold coins in particular may well have been acquired in such ways, e.g. *GCH*, 465–7, 853, 866, 876–7 (third century B.C. ?), 958 (early first century B.C. ?).

**308** Justin 24. 4. 7; Byzantion paid twenty-four thousand gold staters per annum for a time: Polybius 4. 46. An inscription from Histria attests similar payments by Greek states of the western Euxine to Thracian or Geto-Dacian potentates, *c.* 200 B.C.: Institut Fernand-Courby, *Nouveau choix d'inscriptions grecques* (1971), No. 6; Pippidi, *I Greci nel basso Danubio* (1971), 102 ff.; but such payments cannot be the source of most of the Greek currency found in Dacia, since the coins chiefly found there are not those that were in use in Histria, for instance (C. Preda, 'Monedele grecești', in *Histria* III: *Descoperirile monetare 1914–70* (1973)).

**309** Polyainos 4. 16.

**310** Thucydides 2. 98. In the following centuries Celts, Illyrians and Thracians served individually as mercenaries in large numbers (Launey, *Recherches sur les armées hellénistiques* (1950), 366–98, 410–18, 490–534), but we know of only one Getan (Launey, 1202), though Pârvan, *Getica*, 150, argued that there were more.

**311** Plutarch, *Antony* 64; cf. Dio 51. 22. It has been suggested that this might account for the large number of legionary *denarii* found in Dacia (Marie Chițescu, *SCN* 4 (1968), 655–65), but the fact that many of these were found in hoards of much later date and the ubiquity of this phenomenon in the Roman world show that it neither requires nor admits this explanation, as Judita Winkler has pointed out, *SCN* 5 (1971), 283 ff.

**312** See *GCH*, 670–2; Glodariu, *op. cit.* (n.292), 84–5 (about 1,200 in all).

**313** Ruzicka, *Buletinul societatii numismatice romane* 17 (1922), 10, pointed in particular to raids into Thrace by Burebista (Strabo 7. 3. 11, p. 304) as the likely source of large quantities of *denarii* and drachms of Apollonia and Dyrrhachion, and recently Winkler (*JbNumG* 17 (1967), 132) has again drawn attention to this possibility, but without attaching any great importance to it (cf. *ibid.*, 140). There were further Dacian raids across the Danube in the time of Augustus, but seemingly these did not go very deep or bring the Dacians to places where they would find much coined money: see Florus 2. 28. 18–19 (before Lentulus' campaign, *c.* A.D. 3); Dio 55. 30. 4 (A.D. 6); Orosius 6. 22. 2 (A.D. 10); Ovid, *epp. ex Ponto* 1. 18. 11–19 (A.D. 12); 4. 9. 75–86 (*c.* A.D. 14 ?).

**314** Objections to this explanation have been set forth at length by Mitrea (*Ephemeris dacoromana* 10 (1945), 12–22).

**315** E.g. *GCH*, 917, 924, 952, 963, 974, 975, 976, 977, 978. Maria Alföldi, in criticising the commercial explanation, has suggested briefly that coins may have reached Dacia from the Adriatic and the Aegean by being passed from tribe to tribe (*JbNumG* 11 (1961), 189). A similar explanation has been proposed for the movement of copper over long distances in Africa in the Early Iron Age, where the role of copper *vis-à-vis* iron was similar to the role of silver in the European Iron Age: 'While some sites containing copper are hundreds of kilometres from any ore deposits, there is no reason to postulate organised long-distance trading in this metal . . . Small numbers of ingots or finished ornaments could easily pass through local barter networks or be passed from village to village as a part of bridewealth' (Michael S. Birzan, *World Archaeology* 6 (1975), 281). However, this does not carry conviction as an explanation of the travel of coins from the Adriatic and the Aegean to Dacia in such large numbers.

**316** Crawford's view of the republican *denarii* found in Dacia is that 'in the absence of small denominations they can hardly have played a meaningful rôle in any kind of monetary economy' ('Roman republican numismatics', in *Survey* (see n.127), 299). This seems too categorical: Giard (*ibid.*, 320) is more cautious: 'Prenait-on plaisir à amasser de bons deniers d'argent ou voulait-on privilégier ici un moyen d'échange durable et sûr, destiné à servir une économie relativement évoluée dans laquelle la monnaie entrait en jeu ?'

**317** Cf. the remarks of M. I. Finley, *op. cit.* (n.124), 20. The belief that the coin finds prove that large numbers of Romans were trading in Dacia already in the second century is expressed strongly by Pârvan, *Dacia*, 138–9. Mitrea, *op. cit.* (n.314), 21, went so far as to say that it is only if very few coins of some state are found that 'possiamo ammettere che siano giunte per vie indiritte e non portate da commercianti dai paesi dalla loro emissione': and, taking this as axiomatic, he deduced, from the ascendancy attained in the first century, to judge from finds, by the *denarius*, the ascendancy of Roman traders.

**318** Mitrea, 'Monede antice şi feudale descoperite la Zimnicea (Dunarea de Jos)', *SCIV* 16 (1965), 240–56. The finds comprised nine *aes* coins of Philip II and Alexander the Great, three *aes* coins of Odessos, two Geto-Dacian billon coins and a couple of unidentifiable *aes* coins, as well as two drachmas of Alexander and three Thasian tetradrachms.

**319** Two finds, comprising twelve coins, of *aes* of Philip II in the Dolj region in Oltenia (E. Isăcescu, *SCN* 4 (1968), 319–25); a find of thirty-six *aes* coins of Cyzicus, of the late second or first century B.C., at Curcani, 50 km south-east of Bucharest (*GCH*, 618). (A fourth-century Dobrugian hoard: *Pontica* 7 (1974), 147–55.)

**320** Finds in the district to the east of Lake Potelu, where a natural route from Macedon by the Strymon valley northwards to Transylvania crossed the Danube, comprise one *aes* coin of Mesembria of the third or second century, two *asses* of Augustus, one of Tiberius, two of Claudius, two of Nero (and later *aes*), as well as one plated 'barbarous' copy of an Alexander drachma of Mesembria, two Thasos tetradrachms, one Apollonia and two Dyrrhachion drachmas, twenty-one republican *denarii* (two plated), one of Augustus, one of Nero (and later silver) (J. Winkler and C. Baloi, *Acta Musei Napocensis* 10 (1973), 181 ff.). Finds at Sucidava, a settlement a little further downstream, are said to include, in addition to a hoard of four *aes* coins of Maroneia of the fourth century (*GCH*, 422), *aes* of 'Augustus, Tiberius,

Claudius etc' (D. Tudor, *Sucidava* (1965), 123–4, referring to his reports, which I have not seen, in *Arhivele Olteniei* 20 (1941) and 21 (1942)). Tudor considers the finds of early imperial *aes* 'not surprising in view of the close economic relations linking the two banks of the Danube', but, although both these sites lie at the intersection of long-distance trade routes, up the Danube valley and from the Aegean to Transylvania, along which there was probably already some use of silver currency, the rarity of *aes* finds even along these routes suggests that the trade did not involve the use of money in small denominations (cf. p. 134 on Moesia). A map of finds of coins of Histria records no finds of *aes* in Dacia beyond the Dobrugia (Pippidi, *op. cit.* (n.308), 112–13).

**321**  Geto-Dacian silver coins which, though similar in character to the tetradrachms, might appear to be of smaller denominations should, in the view of those who know the find-evidence best, be regarded, generally speaking, as late, light-weight tetradrachms (Castelin, *JbNumG* 13 (1973), 174, quoting the opinion of Winkler).

**322**  Stančuta hoard: C. Preda, *SCIV* 8 (1957), 113–22 = *RRCH*, 331 = *GCH*, 662. Transylvanian hoard: No. 36 in Winkler's list (see n.297). There are also some Dacian hoards in which Greek and/or Roman coins are associated with silver jewellery (*GCH*, 586, 600, 625, 641, 648, 650, 674, 685), but it does not follow that the coins were to be melted down: the hoard could represent a store of wealth. Thus for instance in Britain, later, 'with their coins Romano-Britons often kept and concealed other valuables' (Robertson, *Mattingly Essays* (see n.54), 265).

**323**  Cf. Pârvan, *Dacia*, 174.

**324**  Marie Chiţescu has published a catalogue of all the indubitable imitations found in Romania or included in Romanian collections which she could trace, 181 in number: 150 from thirty-five hoards and other accurately recorded finds, thirty-one of unknown provenance (*Memoria Antiquitatis* 3 (1971), 209–58). The hoards in question appear to include *RRCH* 120, 285, 320, 323 (one imitation), 329, 335, 338, 347, 348, 367, 368, 378—none of these extending below 45 B.C.—412, 420, 426, 428 (one imitation), 436, 439, 472; several other republican hoards included in Winkler's list (see n.297): 15, 32, 72, 91; and several that are in neither list. She also mentions (but does not include in her list) twenty-two imitations found with 169 republican *denarii* in a hoard from Nagykagy, just across the Hungarian frontier (*RRCH* 411). Relatively few of the imitations in her list are from hoards of imperial date: a hoard from Transylvania (No. 7 in Winkler's list) contained 293 *denarii* and one imitation; a hoard from Muntenia (*RRCH*, 512) contained 213 *denarii* to 11/9 B.C. and three imitations); and of two from Moldavia, which contained the only imitations of Augustan *denarii* listed, one (*RRCH*, 531) had two (or, according to *RRCH*, four) imitations of Augustan and ten (or, according to *RRCH*, eight) of republican *denarii* with twelve Augustan and 492 republican originals, while the other (Winkler 112) had one imitation of an Augustan and three of republican *denarii* with sixty-two originals to Vespasian. A hoard found at Russe, just south of the Danube and thus outside Dacia, also included imitations among about one hundred republican and early imperial *denarii* (*Bull. de l'inst. arch. bulg.* 1913, 336; Seure, *Rev.num.*[4] 26 (1923), 17). What emerges clearly, despite some divergences between lists, is that the great majority of imitations, especially those found in Oltenia and Muntenia, are derived from *denarii* struck before 70 B.C.

**325**  Chiţescu's list (see n.324) mentions only two that are not: No. 19, of unknown provenance, in Bucharest, plated; No. 147, from a recently found Moldavian hoard, with only 75 per cent silver content. Elsewhere (*SCN* 4 (1968), 127–35) she alludes to the finding of plated coins in Romania, but the only plated *denarii* which she mentions are from a Flavian hoard (see below, n.335) and from a post-conquest hoard.

**326**  Included in Mitrea's inventory of finds (see above, n.285) as No. 35; described and discussed, with references to earlier discussions, by E. Stoicovici and J. Winkler, *Acta Musei Napocensis* 8 (1971), 477–9.

**327**  N. Lupu, *Forschungen zur Volks- und Landeskunde* 7 (1964), 5–31 (*non vidi*), *JbNumG* 17 (1967), 103–21; cf. Winkler, *ibid.*, 129–31.

**328**  It was voiced by Dr Winkler (*loc. cit.*, n.327) before the discovery of the Breaza hoard mentioned below.

**329**  G. Poenaru Bordea and C. Stirbu, *SCN* 5 (1971), 265–82.

**330**  This hypothesis has been persuasively expounded by Preda, *Monedele Geto-Dacilor* (1973), 448; cf. 451; see also Chiţescu, *op. cit.* (n.324), 219.

**331**  Compare, for example, the coins of the Eravisci (p. 37) and the Boii (n.24) and various Gallic tribes (above, p. 21).

**332**  Wine: Strabo 7. 3. 11, pp. 303–4. Cf. Pippidi, *op. cit.* (n.308), 149–50.

**333**  But I do not understand the reasoning of Stoicovici and Winkler (see n.326) in their comment on the die derived from a die of C. Marius Capito: 'Der Umstand, dass die Stanze von Ludeşti sich von ihrem Vorbild unterscheidet, bestätigt die These, dass die Nachahmungen römischer Denare von Falschmünzern geprägt wurden und widerlegt demnach die Meinung, der zufolge die Nachahmung des Denars im 1. Jh. v.u.Z. auf gesetzlichem Wege erfolgt wäre, um das nötige Bargeld in Umlauf zu bringen', especially as this seems to carry the implication that coins struck, for instance, from the Tilişca dies, which they refer to as 'einfach genau nachgeahmt', must have been produced officially.

**334**  Cf. the comment of Giard (*op. cit.* (n.321), 307): 'Les coins monétaires mis au jour à Tilişca sont un indice de la faveur croissante rencontrée par le denier romain dans les pays que Rome n'avait pas encore soumis . . . [Ils ont] contribué à répandre en Dacie des monnaies que Rome était sans doute incapable de produire en quantités suffisantes.'

**335**  No. 18 in Winkler's list (see n.297): Maria Chiţescu and Vasile Ursache, *SCIV* 17 (1966), 703–7; Chiţescu, *SCN* 4 (1968), 127–35. For careful copying of Roman dies elsewhere at an earlier date, for the making of plated coins, see Crawford, *NC*⁷ 8 (1968), 56–7.

**336**  So Constantin Deculescu, *SCIV* 17 (1966), 577–92. His find statistics are vulnerable in detail, but there can be no doubt about the validity of his main contention concerning the composition of hoards. However, if tension between Romans and Dacians led to an interruption of commercial contacts, one would expect the interruption to date from Augustus' reign, when from *c.* 4 B.C. Roman policy on the lower Danube was at its most forceful (Strabo 7. 3. 10–13, pp. 303–5; Florus 2. 28–29. 18–20; Augustus, *Res Gestae* 30–1: see Syme, *JRS* 14 (1934), 113–37), if not from Burebista's time (cf. n.313).

**337**  Compare the evidence from Bulgaria: between 1891 and 1916 five hoards were found with a closing date before Actium, one with a closing date under Vespasian, and one with an unspecified closing date in the first century A.D.: Seure, *Rev. num.*⁴ 26 (1923).

**338**  See n.305.

**339**  To hoards listed by Winkler (see n.297) I have added five Augustan hoards (*SCN* 4 (1968), 363–72; 5 (1971), 380–4, 265–82; *Carpica* 2 (1969), 131–44; *Sargetia* 8 (1971), 61–6) and also one with a coin of Gaius as its latest (known to me from ANS *Numismatic Literature*, 85 No. 207) and one with a coin of Nerva (*Acta Musei Napocensis* 5 (1968), 429–32). The imperial hoard consisting wholly of imitations (above, n. 324) has been left out of the reckoning. For the sake of completeness it may be added that there are nine hoards (Winkler, Nos. 10, 21, 26, 39, 104, 107–9, 120) of which it is known only that they contained imperial as well as republican *denarii*, so that it is uncertain whether they were deposited before the conquest.

**340**  E.g. from Pompeii (Enrica Pozzi, *AIIN* 5–6 (1958–59), 211–29 (one of Nero);

*FMRD* I, 1082 (one of Nero), 1267 (one of Galba), IV, 1151 (two of Augustus; *aurei* of Nero).

**341** Rostovtzeff, *SEHRE*², 95. The finds of *aes* coins in excavations at Susa indicate, in the view of Le Rider, that trade between Susa and Seleuceia, in goods brought to Susa from the Persian Gulf, was at a low ebb in the time of the later Seleucids and the Roman Republic, but that there was a temporary slight revival in the early first century A.D. (*Suse sous les Séleucides et les Parthes* (1965), 446 ff.).

**342** Strabo 16. 1. 28, p. 748.

**343** Rostovtzeff evidently believed that the route from Palmyra to the Persian Gulf passed through Parthian territory, for he says (*SEHRE*², 95) that 'in the first century A.D. . . . the Romans had found a *modus vivendi* with the Parthians', and the same view is reflected in the marking of trade-routes in the *Grosser historischer Weltatlas* edited by H. Bengtson and V. Milojčič (I⁵ (1972), 47), but others hold that until the Sassanid seizure of Mesene, the region lying south of the Tigris delta, there was a route that wholly avoided Parthian territory: see e.g. E. W. Gray, *JRS* 60 (1970), 223; Sir Mortimer Wheeler, in *Aspects of Archaeology in Europe and Beyond, Essays in Honor of O. G. S. Crawford*, ed. W. F. Grimes (1961).

**344** Rostovtzeff, *loc. cit.* (n.343).

**345** Peter A. Clayton, *Iraq* 29 (1967), 143–54.

**346** See *Dura* VI.

**347** E. T. Newell, *The Seleucid Mint of Antioch* (1918), 123–4, 126; Bellinger, *Dura* VI, 200–2. Cf. above, n.183.

**348** See above, n.166.

**349** *Dura* VI; Le Rider, *op. cit.* (n.341), 443 ff.: cf. *GCH*, 1744, 1784, 1786, 1813–14, mixed hoards of the first century B.C., in which Seleucid and Arsacid coins predominate; and above, n.165; and below, n.352, hoard from Nineveh.

**350** Bellinger, *Dura* VI, 203.

**351** See above, p. 25.

**352** See above, n.166. It is interesting to compare the contents of a hoard from Nineveh, in which the latest coin is a *denarius* of A.D. 205: the earliest of 142 *denarii* is of Galba and the earliest of twenty-nine imperial tetradrachms is of Nero, but there are 121 pseudo-Seleucid tetradrachms, struck between 31 and 18 B.C. and ninety-two Arsacid drachmas, the earliest being of Gotarzes: *NC*⁵ 11 (1931), 160–70.

**353** *Dura* VI.

**354** Henri Seyrig, *Rev.num.* 1955, 85–128; cf. Georges le Rider, *op. cit.* (n.341), 29, 446 ff. The Nisibis *aes* hoard, deposited after 31 B.C., published by Seyrig comprised 172 Seleucid pieces, mostly struck at Antioch, one Arsacid, eleven of Tigranes I of Armenia, 214 of Antioch, seventy-two of Seleuceia, eighteen of Aradus, twenty-four miscellaneous, 111 unclassified, and one plated *denarius*.

**355** Dorothy B. Waage, *Antioch* IV. 2, *The Greek . . . Coins* (1952).

**356** Strabo 2. 1. 15, p. 73; 11. 2. 17, p. 498; 11. 3. 4, p. 500; Pliny, *NH* 6. 52; M. P. Charlesworth, *Trade Routes and Commerce of the Roman Empire*² (1926), 104–7; E. H. Warmington, *The Commerce between the Roman Empire and India* (1928), 26–30, 42–3.

**357** There is a useful short account of coins struck in Colchis by David M. Lang ('Studies in the numismatic history of Georgia in Transcaucasia', ANS *Numismatic Notes and Monographs* 130 (1955), 9–11). Konstantin Golenko has composed a brief survey, with full bibliography, of finds in Colchis of coins of Greek character (*Chiron* 2 (1972), 565–610; cf. *Chiron* 3 (1973), 467–99 for finds, mostly on the coast, of silver and *aes* coins struck for Mithridates VI, brought in mainly, Golenko suggests, to pay his garrisons).

**358** Golenko, *Chiron* 2 (1972), 572.

**359** Golenko, *VDI* 1971. 4, 73, ascribes the imitations to the third century A.D., since many have been found in graves in association with third century *aurei* (cf. Kapanadze, *VDI* 1955.1. 160–73; *Sovietskaja Arkheologija* 1957.3. 159–75).

**360** Several hoards from points on or near to the route from the Black Sea to the Caspian illustrate the coming of *denarii*; I list them in order of closing date:

(i) From Khinisli in Azerbaijan (closing date *c.* 50–25 B.C.?): one *denarius* (*CRR*, 732), one tetradrachm of Mithridates VI, three tetradrachms of Bithynian kings, five or six Athenian tetradrachms, seventy-two posthumous drachmas of Alexander the Great, three posthumous tetradrachms of Lysimachos, eighty-four Seleucid tetradrachms to Philip I, 162 Arsacid drachmas to Phraates III (E. A. Pakhomov, *Monetniie Kladii Azerbajdzhana i drugikh respublikh i oblastei Kavkaza* IX (Akad. Nauk. Azerb. SSR, 1966), No. 2080; *GCH*, 1745; *RRCH*, 246).

(ii) From a tomb at Mingechaur on the river Cyros in Azerbaijan: two drachmas of Tigranes I, four republican *denarii* to *CRR* 959b (Pakhomov VI (1954), No. 1548; *GCH*, 1743; *RRCH*, 387).

(iii) From Sarnakunk on the Araxes, 120 km from Artaxata, in Armenia (i.e. on a more southerly route) (closing date 30–25 B.C.): one tetradrachm and one drachm of Alexander the Great, fifty-eight Seleucid tetradrachms to Philip I (including at least one pseudo-Philip), one tetradrachm of Mithridates VI, twenty-two Arsacid drachmas to Orodes II, one tetradrachm and one drachma of Tigranes I and two drachmas of Artavasdes (ten Armenian in all), thirty-seven tetradrachms of Tyre to 37 B.C., one of Sidon, one of Aradus, one drachma of Ariarathes IX and two of Ariobarzanes I of Cappadocia (eight Cappadocian in all), fifteen *cistophori* (five of Pergamon with monogram *ΠPYT*, one of Claudius Pulcher, two of Ephesos, seven of Antony), eight tetradrachms of Antony and Cleopatra struck at Antioch, and 210 republican denarii to 34 B.C. (Pakhomov VI No. 1536; *GCH*, 1746; *RRCH*, 455; the figures are from a republication, incorporating further coins: ANS *Numismatic Literature* 92 (1974), No. 295, citing X. A. Mushegyan, *Hayastani dramakan ganjer* I (Erevan, 1973). (Cf. *Coin Hoards*, I (London, Royal Numismatic Society, 1975).)

(iv) From Nazodelavo in the Kutais district of Georgia: one drachma of Archelaos of Cappadocia, twenty-four republican *denarii*, one of Augustus (Noe, *Bibliography of Greek Coin Hoards*[2] (1937), No. 734; Pakhamov VIII, k29; *RRCH*, 541).

(v) From near Artaxata in Armenia: one drachma of Artavasdes II, three of Tigranes II, one Parthian coin, three republican *denarii* (P. Naster, *Survey* . . . (n.127), 155, quoting an Armenian publication).

(vi) From Gori: a *cistophorus* of Antony and a number of *denarii* of Augustus, *RIC* I Augustus, 350 (Pakhomov I, 28; 37; *RRCH*, 532).

With these one may compare the excavation finds from Vari, a fortress on the Black Sea coast garrisoned by Mithridates, captured by Pompey and destroyed by Pharnaces: two republican *denarii*, one proconsular *cistophorus*, one drachma of Sinatruces of Parthia, several drachmas of Ariarathes VI and IX and Ariobarzanes I of Cappadocia, one Athenian tetradrachm, one tetradrachm of Mithridates VI, twenty-six Mithridatic *aes* of Pontic towns (résumé by Golenko, *Chiron* 1972, 583).

One of the most striking features of coin finds in Transcaucasia is the predominance among Roman coins of *denarii* of Augustus, nearly all, it seems, belonging to the issue in honour of Gaius and Lucius Caesar. Published finds of Roman coins, of which the fullest list is that given by Golenko, *VDI* 1971.4. 47–73, comprise (hoards excluded) well over two hundred Augustan *denarii* (but only about seven 'barbarous' imitations), against twelve republican *denarii* (all different), three *denarii* and one *aureus* of Tiberius, and only thirty-five other *denarii*, spread fairly evenly over the reigns from Domitian to Caracalla, and thirty-nine other *aurei*, from Nero to Caracalla. The coins most commonly found in association with Augustan *denarii* are imitations of Alexander staters (cf. above, n.358) and Parthian drachmas, among which those of Artabanos II predominate. Many coins of these three classes have been found in native tombs in Georgia. In some tombs they have been found in association with *aurei* of the third century A.D. (cf. above, n.359): one possible explanation of this is that those who traded into this area were continuing to put coins of Augustus and of Artabanos II into circulation long after their reigns, selecting them from the circulating medium (if not arranging for their continued production, as in the case of Maria Theresa dollars) because they were popular (unless one supposes that they had been imported into Georgia solely for use as grave-goods). It would follow that there was probably not as great a rise in demand for *denarii* for trade along these routes in the latter part of Augustus' reign or under Tiberius as the finds would *prima facie* suggest; but there would still be reason to believe in a considerable increase in the use of Roman currency at that time, since it would otherwise be hard to explain why an Augustan coin became so popular in the first place.

**361**   As Regling asserts, *RE*, *s.v.* Münzwesen, referring to the imperial epoch as a whole. One can not, of course, exclude the possibility that, in addition to the use of a few Augustan coins as tomb offerings in Georgia (but mainly long afterwards?), some coins that went eastwards along this route were melted down.

**362**   Strabo 2. 5. 12, p. 118; 17. 1. 13, p. 798.

**363**   Rostovtzeff, *SEHRE²*, 94–7; Warmington, *op. cit.* (n.356), 10–18.

**364**   On the commerce of Petra see Strabo 16. 4. 18, p. 776; 21, p. 779; 23–4, p. 781; cf. *Periplus Maris Erythraei* 19 (for the date see n.405). Still richly stocked in A.D. 107: *Michigan Papyrus* 465. 1–17: but J. Schwartz (*Annales* 15.1 (1960), 2–21) doubts whether this passage really proves that Petra then still lay on a main route; similarly Bowersock (*JRS* 61 (1971), 228). 'It is becoming clear', he says (*ibid.*, 223), 'that the reign of Aretas IV, 8 B.C.–A.D. 40, was the period of greatest prosperity for the Nabataeans.'

**365**   For the coinage of the Nabataean kings, in whose territory Petra lay, who began to strike silver early in the first century B.C., see Head, *Historia Numorum²*, 810–11; Robinson, *NC⁵* 16 (1936), 209 f; Parr, *VIIIᵉ Congrès International d'Archéologie Classique*, Paris 1963 (1965), 530. For that of the Himyarite kings, who dominated southern Arabia at this time, see above, n.200.

**366**   As the placing of a portrait of Augustus, derived from *denarii*, on Himyarite coinage implies: cf. n.200. The author of the *Periplus Maris Erythraei* speaks of the use of δηνάριον οὐ πολὺ χρυσοῦν τε καὶ ἀργυροῦν (8; cf. 6), 'a small quantity of *denarius*, both gold and silver' in trade with east Africa in his time (cf. below, n.405).

**367**   Strabo (16.4.26, p. 784) lists some of the things for which the Nabataeans were, according to him, wholly dependent on imports, including bronze and iron (but see Rostovtzeff, *Social and Economic History of the Hellenistic World*, 1173–74, 1614–22), purple garments, and works of painting and sculpture. They are likely to have imported these from the Mediterranean world rather than from anywhere else: likewise some of the textile products which are listed by the anonymous author of the *Periplus Maris Erythraei* (24, 28, 32) among goods imported into southern Arabia in his time (cf. below, n.405); he mentions also gold and silver plate, but only among gifts made to the kings and their chief vassals. Ostraca of the first century A.D. (the so-called Archives of Nicanor: J. G. Tait, *Greek Ostraca in the Bodleian Library* I (1930)) relating to the transit trade from the Nile to the Red Sea coast mention various other goods, some of which were probably on their way to Arabia: some of them are among the goods for which, according to the author of the *Periplus Maris Erythraei*, there was a market in India or east Africa, and such goods would be wanted by the Arabians for use in that trade.

**368**  Cf. Pliny, *NH* 6. 162.
**369**  Strabo 16. 4. 26, p. 784.
**370**  Strabo 16. 4. 22, p. 780.
**371**  Strabo 16. 4. 19, p. 778: ἐκ τῆς ἐμπορίας.
**372**  Tac., *Ann.* 3. 53: *ad externas aut hostiles gentes.*
**373**  *Mineral Resources of Saudi Arabia* (Kingdom of Saudi Arabia, Ministry of Petroleum and Natural Resources, *Bulletin* I, n.d. (1965)), 20, 25 (my colleague Professor Barri Jones kindly drew my attention to this report).
**374**  Strabo 2. 5. 12, p. 118; cf. 17. 1. 13, p. 798. The sea route to northern India probably became known *c.* 120–90 B.C., but before Augustus' time, as Strabo indicates, it was not of much importance. 'Lack of public resources and energy in the troubled century which succeeded the discovery, and the effect of that lack on private enterprise' inhibited its exploitation (P. M. Fraser, *Ptolemaic Alexandria* (1972), 184).
**375**  Pliny, *NH* 6. 101.
**376**  Pliny, *NH* 12. 84.
**377**  Most recently, M. P. Charlesworth, in *Studies in Roman Economic and Social History in Honour of Allan Chester Johnson*, ed. P. R. Coleman-Norton (1951), 138–42; Sir Mortimer Wheeler, in *Aspects of Archaeology* (see n.343), 345–81; J. Schwartz, 'L'Empire romain, l'Egypte et le commerce oriental', *Annales* 15.1 (1960), 18–45. Fullest treatment, with references to earlier literature, by E. H. Warmington, *op. cit.* (n.356), 35–83.
**378**  Sir Mortimer Wheeler has included a list of fifty-eight finds (and of twenty-two in Ceylon) in his report in *Ancient India* 2 (July 1946), 116–21), and an amplified list of sixty-nine finds in *Aspects of Archaeology* . . . (see n.343). Most of these were described by Thurston in the *Catalogue of the Madras Museum* No. 2, *Roman* . . . *Coins*[2] (1894), or in reports of subsequent accessions to the museum; Wheeler has checked and improved these descriptions by autopsy, so far as possible, but he has omitted some valuable details given by Thurston and by Sewell (*Journal of the Royal Asiatic Society, Bombay Branch*, 1904, 623–31). He has also for some reason omitted from his later list one of the finds (No. 56) included in his earlier list: a pot hoard, found near Bangalore, of 163 *denarii*, described by Thurston (*op. cit.*, 26–8) merely as running from Augustus (IMP X) to Claudius (this hoard has been noted also by Warmington, *op. cit.* (n.356), 284 and by M. Seshadri, 'Roman contacts with south India', *Archaeology* 19 (1966), 244–7). Seshadri (*loc. cit.*) also reports a new find, a pot hoard of 256 *denarii* of Augustus and Tiberius unearthed in 1965 by labourers laying the runway of the airport at Bangalore. A hoard of thirty-nine *denarii* found at Nasthullapur in 1952 has been published by Parmeswari Lal Gupta in the *Journal of the Numismatic Society of India* 19 (1957), 1–8, and he has further discussed it in publishing a hoard of 1,531 *denarii* found at Akkanpalle in 1959 (*Roman Coins from Andhra Pradesh*, Andhra Pradesh Government Museum Series No. 10, known to me only from D. M. MacDowall's review, *NC*[7] 10 (1970), 340–1). See Table V.
**379**  Respectively Nos. 51, 49–50, 47–8 in Wheeler's later list (see n.378).
**380**  Wheeler (*op. cit.*, n.343). Schwartz (*loc. cit.* (n.377), 37) agrees; he also points out that finds at Begram in Afghanistan, near the sources of the Indus, not only show in their character notable similarity with finds at Pompeii, but that one of them, a glass model of the Pharos at Alexandria, had surely been brought back as a souvenir: one of several indications which he notes that these goods had arrived by the sea route and the Indus valley.
**381**  Strabo 15. 1. 30, p. 700. However, according to the author of the *Periplus Maris Erythraei*, 49, Barygaza, one of the chief trading posts in northern India (Broach, near Baroda) was the one place in India at which there was a demand for gold and silver coins as an import, and Schwartz (*loc. cit.*, n.377), noting that some

of the Roman coins found near the north-west frontier were found along with coins of the Kushana kingdom, accepts Wheeler's view that they will have been serving as currency, not as bullion, while D. M. MacDowall and N. G. Wilson (*NC*⁷ 10 (1970), 221 ff.) have suggested that gold and silver coins were wanted at Barygaza for melting down to create 'a precious-metal coinage that was minted with a mint surcharge': cf. R. S. Sharma, *Journal of the Numismatic Society of India* 31 (1969), 3, who suggests that only *aurei* were melted down, the Kushana coinage being of gold, and that this would explain why no *aurei* have been found in northern India. Sharma suggests that the mines mentioned by Strabo may have lain outside Kushana control. But none of these phenomena seem to fall within the period with which we are chiefly concerned: the hoards are of the second century A.D.; the *Periplus Maris Erythraei* has been variously dated between A.D. 50 and 130 (see below, n.405) and the king who in the view of MacDowall and Wilson instituted the coinage which they have in mind did not come to the throne until *c.* A.D. 95.

**382**   Five of Augustus and Tiberius, one unidentified. Having been found on different parts of the site, they figure as six separate items (Nos. 60–5) in Wheeler's later list (n.378).

**383**   See Table V. Since no hoard has an Augustan closing date, there is no apparent ground for Warmington's assertions (*op. cit.* (n.356), 38–9) that of Augustus' coins 'at least some came in his reign' and that 'even . . . under Augustus . . . the Roman Empire was unable to counterbalance the inflow of Indian products by a return of imperial products, with the result that the Romans sent out coined money which never returned to them'.

**384**   Of the 371 identified *denarii* of Augustus in the finds published by Wheeler and Seshadri, 368 are of this issue (*RIC* I Augustus, 350), of the 1,033 of Tiberius 1,029 (*RIC* I Tiberius, 3). They predominate also in the Akkanpalle hoard published by Lal Gupta. Seshadri (*op. cit.* (n.378), 245) revives the old suggestion that the former 'may have been struck by Augustus especially for trade with south India': he was presumably unaware of its widespread abundance. However, in the Akkanpalle hoard there are '55 imitations which have badly blundered legends . . . Lal Gupta argues convincingly that they were produced by Roman traders.' (MacDowall, *loc. cit.* (n.378)).

**385**   See Table V.

**386**   Of the forty-two identified *aurei* of Augustus, twenty-two are of this issue; of the 171 of Tiberius, 165. But, considering that each *aureus* is worth twenty-five *denarii*, it is somewhat misleading to say (Warmington, *op. cit.* (n.356), 292–3) that coins of Claudius 'are not numerous' and that of Nero 'not very many' have been found: see Table V.

**387**   The *aurei* which are known to have been defaced are indicated on Table V.

**388**   Prior to Lal Gupta's publication (n.378), only one *denarius* was known to have been thus defaced, but in the Akkanpalle hoard all but twenty-six of them were defaced.

**389**   Only two republican *denarii* are known to have been found in southern India; these were in a hoard (Wheeler (n.378), No. 13) found in the Coimbatore district, comprising these two 'worn' coins, of *c.* 50 B.C. and 39 B.C., 'other coins', presumably not Roman, and gold and silver jewellery. These two may have made the journey in one way or another before the direct sea route from Egypt to India was in regular use (Seshadri, *op. cit.* (n.378), 247) (Seshadri refers also (*ibid.*) to a pot hoard (Wheeler No. 57) found in Cochin in 1945, which according to Wheeler comprised twelve fresh *aurei*, the latest of A.D. 99, twenty-five-plus worn *denarii*, Augustus to Nero, and thirty-plus punch-marked indigenous silver coins, but gives quite different data: no *aurei*, twelve indigenous coins, 'and 50 silver coins, late Republican to Augustus'. There is yet another account in *Journal of the Numismatic Society of India* 23 (1961): twelve *aurei*, thirty-three indigenous punch-marked silver coins, seventy-one Roman silver coins, 'Antony to Nero'. Clearly nothing can be built on reports of this hoard unless a detailed inventory becomes available.)

**390**   Bruck, *Carinthia* 1. 151 (1961), 168–70. For hoards from Pompeii see Table I. Finds in Transcaucasia have some similarity with the Indian finds, but there some republican *denarii* occur (see above, n.360).

**391**   As A. C. Johnson pointed out (*ESAR* 11, 427), 'Roman *denarii* are extremely rare in hoards of coins found in Egypt (Weber, ANS *Numismatic Notes and Monographs* 54.4) and the theory [propounded by Mommsen] that they circulated freely [but at a premium] must be regarded with considerable reserve.' (Cf. Louis C. West and Allan Chester Johnson, *Currency in Roman and Byzantine Egypt*, 1–2.)

**392**   *Gnomon of the Idios Logos*, 106. Cf. Rostovtzeff, *op. cit.* (n.367), 402.

**393**   West and Johnson (*op. cit.* (n.391), 78) propound an alternative possibility, that gold and silver currency 'passed through in bond'. Schwartz (*op. cit.* (n.377), 39–40) takes a similar view: 'il est certain que les Romains laissent passer par Alexandrie la monnaie d'or et d'argent à destination de l'Inde.' This is possible, but it seems unlikely that all or even most movements of money from the Mediterranean to regions beyond Egypt would have arisen from direct transactions between Mediterranean merchants and merchants trading southwards from Egypt, which is what this view would seem to presuppose.

**394**   Tests in the Madras Museum revealed no plated coins (Wheeler, *op. cit.* (n.343)). Similarly in the Akkanpalle hoard all the coins, even the imitations, are of good silver.

**395**   Warmington, *op. cit.* (n.356), 39; cf. 284, 292, 341 n.15, 388 n.49. Hill and Willers (*NZ* 31 (1899), 363–6) had accepted it on the authority of Mommsen (*Geschichte des römischen Münzwesens* (1860), 726, 760), who suggested that they were specially produced for trade with India. Mommsen must have derived the story that most of the *denarii* of this variety were plated either from Akerman (*NC* 6 (1843–4), 70, who said 'all') or from Eckhel (*Doctrina Numorum Veterum* (1796) VI, 171): an admirable illustration of the dangers of received opinions; but Warmington made matters worse by implying (*op. cit.* (n.356), 39, 284) that the same was true of *aurei* bearing this type and by stating (388 n.49) that 'in the Coimbatore district 131 of them [i.e. the plated coins] have been noticed', a statement for which there appears to be no foundation. The only example of a plated coin which Wheeler mentions is a Livia-Pax *aureus* of Tiberius with a base-metal core, found in isolation, and now in the Hyderabad Museum; but even this may represent not Roman deception but local imitation, for this 'coin' may be akin to the numerous clay pendants, originally no doubt gilded, bearing these types which have been found in southern India, showing that the image of Tiberius must have been much more popular among Indians than the reality was among his fellow senators.

**396**   The parallel was pointed out by Rostovtzeff (*SEHRE*[2], 576 n.17), who suggested that 'it is possible that the coins of Tiberius, because of their popularity with the Indians, were struck as a real "commercial money" (*Handelsmünze*) by his successors'. If so, the nearest ancient analogy would be with the pseudo-Philippic tetradrachms of Antioch. But Rostovtzeff himself remarked on the very next page (577 n.18) that 'we have not the slightest ground for supposing the existence of any economic policy on the part of the emperors of the first century' (see *ibid.*, 74 for a fuller expression of this view, with reference to Augustus). A similar possibility is suggested by Warmington (*op. cit.* (n.356), 285)—that in Nero's time the traders themselves, at his instigation, carefully collected 'good coins belonging to previous emperors' to take to India: this rests on the belief that Nero 'debased the silver currency', on which see above, n.25. However, the presence in the Akkanpalle hoard of imitations, in good silver, of the most popular *denarii* (see nn.384, 394) seems to show how the traders did help themselves if for some reason they could not get enough of these.

**397**  Mr Michael Crawford has suggested to me an attractive explanation: 'Augustan and Tiberian coins perhaps go to India because they were picked out of the circulating medium by merchants as being fresh and therefore suitable to an area interested in coins as bullion.'

**398**  'With Nero a change takes place': Warmington, *op. cit.* (n.356), 278. There is an obvious (but common) fallacy in Seshadri's assertion, *op. cit.* (n.378), 246, that, 'since the various South Indian hoards contain a large majority of coins of Augustus and Tiberius, we must presume that the peak period of this trade was during the reigns of these two emperors': cf. the assertion of Mazzarino (*Trattato di storia romana*[2], 96) that under Tiberius trade with India was particularly encouraged 'come chiaramente attestano i reperti numismatici in quella regione'.

**399**  After listing a number of the hoards, Warmington said: 'From the lists given above we may conclude with safety that down to the time of Nero deliberate exportation of both metals took place not only for wholesale purchases but in order to create in India a gold and silver currency of a Roman type among the Tamils in general' (*op. cit.* (n.356), 284; cf. 292). It is not clear why he drew this conclusion, since he produced no evidence to prove that they were not regarded simply as bullion. There is in fact one piece of evidence which suggests, as Wheeler pointed out (*Aspects of Archaeology* (see n.343), 367), that *denarii* may have been used as currency to some extent: the discovery of five isolated examples at various points in the excavation of an ancient town at Chandravalli, within the Andhra zone, 'which had an extensive local potin currency' (cf. Parmeswari Lal Gupta, *Journal of the Numismatic Society of India* 19 (1957), 1–8). But the total absence of coins from the finds at Arikamedu, which include considerable quantities of pottery fragments, led Wheeler to conclude 'that the imported currency did not normally circulate at all, save in bulk' (*op. cit.*, 365; cf. Schwartz, *op. cit.* (n.377), 39).

**400**  Warmington, *op. cit.* (n.356), 9, 43–51. Rostovtzeff's view seems to have been similar: *SEHRE*[2], 97.

**401**  Wheeler, *Aspects of Archaeology* (see n.343), 358; *Ancient India* 2 (1946); *Rome beyond the Imperial Frontiers*, 146; cf. Schwartz, *op. cit.* (n.377), 24. Wheeler's dating was based partly on an assessment of the fragments of Arretine ware that the excavation yielded; he attributed them to the last period of production, between A.D. 20 and 50. However, Ludwig Ohlenroth (*Germania* 30 (1952), 309–92) has pointed to the absence from the Arikamedu sherds of the decoration characteristic of that period, and from a comparison of them with the Arretine ware found in datable contexts, in Roman camps in Germany, Oberaden, Oberhausen and Haltern, he concludes that they should rather be attributed to the later years of Augustus; for the kind found is that which predominates among the later finds at Haltern, a camp destroyed in A.D. 16.

**402**  As Rostovtzeff believed, *SEHRE*[2], 67.

**403**  As Charlesworth points out, *op. cit.* (n.356), 137.

**404**  Writing before these finds at Arikamedu had been made, Warmington emphasised (*op. cit.*, 272) the shortness of the list of known exports: but in reviewing Warmington's book Ensslin commented that we must allow more for 'Zufall der Überlieferung' than he did, and that we also do not know in what quantity the goods mentioned were exported, or what prices they fetched (*Philologische Wochenschrift* 50 (1930), 13–14: note his comment (*ibid.*, 11) on Warmington's use of literary evidence in general: 'die Auswertung gelegentlicher Hinweise bei Dichtern und Moralisten für eine Handelsgeschichte wird immer eine umstrittene Sache sein'). Petit (*La Paix romaine*, 326) adds 'des objets de métal, des toiles, et même du blé'. The fact 'that ships plying between Puteoli and Alexandria . . . always returned to the Egyptian capital less heavily laden than when they left for Italy' (Warmington, *op. cit.*, 272, referring to Strabo, 17. 1. 7, p. 793) proves nothing about the trade between Italy and India, since, for one thing, grain was, in terms of bulk and weight, the chief cargo carried from Egypt to Italy.

**405** For the date see D. W. MacDowall, *NC*[7] 4 (1964), 271 ff. (A.D. 120–30); D. C. Sircar, *NC*[7] 6 (1956), 241 ff. (*c.* A.D. 80); A. Dihle, *Umstrittene Daten: Untersuchungen zum Auftreten der Griechen im Roten Meer* (1965), 9–35 (middle or second half of first century A.D.); J. L. Miller, *The Spice Trade of the Roman Empire* (1969) (*c.* A.D. 79–85); D. W. MacDowall and N. G. Wilson, *NC*[7] 10 (1970), 221 ff. (*c.* A.D. 100); G. W. Bowersock, *JRS* 61 (1971), 223–5 (probably in the time of the Nabataean king Malichus II, who ruled A.D. 40–70). Cf. n.407.

**406** *Periplus*, 39 (Punjab; gold and silver plate), 49 (Barygaza, gold and silver δηνάριον (cf. n.366), also silver plate among gifts for the king).

**407** *Ibid.*, 56 (χρυσώματα πλεῖστα). The fact that he does not mention coins at all among exports to southern India (*pace* Wheeler, *Rome Beyond the Imperial Frontiers,* 139), may mean that he was writing at a time at which the use of *aurei* for exports had declined, i.e. after Vespasian's reign.

**408** Pliny *NH*, 6. 101: *nullo anno minus HS* $\boxed{D}$ *imperio nostro exhauriente India et merces remittente.*

**409** Charlesworth, *op. cit.* (n.356), 137. Speaking generally of routes beyond Rome's eastern frontiers, Petit remarks: 'On discute de l'importance relative de ces cheminements et de la chronologie de leur utilisation sans pouvoir en aucun cas évaluer quantitativement la valeur des échanges' (*La Paix romaine*, 324).

**410** As Schwartz has said (*op. cit.* (n.377), 42)—though he dates the change too early—'on peut se demander si, dès le milieu du 1er siècle après J.C. . . ., l'administration romaine, plotôt que de fournir de l'argent et de l'or monnayé . . . n'a pas préféré livrer à ceux qui trafiquaient avec l'Inde des lingots . . . Dans ce cas d'ailleurs la densité des trouvailles de monnaies romaines aux Indes serait moins révélatrice d'époques et de courants de trafic.' Wheeler states that by the time of Vespasian 'the export of bullion from the Roman Empire was restricted' (*op. cit.* (n.343), 363) but he cites no evidence for such a restriction.

## Chapter IV: notes 411–573

**411** Frank's only reference to *aes* is his remark that Gaius 'began his reign with a large emission of coins in all metals'. 'Official' is the term used by many numismatists to denote mints, and issues, under the direct control of someone vested with *imperium*, or of the Senate, as distinct from mints run by *coloniae, municipia,* non-Roman city states, or other authorities operating within the ambit of Roman power: not a very satisfactory term, but it is difficult to think of a better one.

**412** Note Kraay's comment on certain early imperial *aes* coins that have been countermarked with the letters NCAPR: 'the large number of surviving examples . . . can be explained by the interest which the countermark has aroused and the keenness with which specimens have been sought out, so that many coins, the condition of which would never have won them a place in any collection, have been included because of their countermark' (*Mattingly Essays* (see n.54), 133).

**413** Thus, for instance, of the sixty-seven hoards with terminal dates between 27 B.C. and 2 B.C. of which Crawford was able to obtain adequate particulars, only three (*RRCH*, 494, 515, 518) are solely of *aes*; they contain altogether the equivalent of about 4½ *denarii*; eight other mixed hoards contain in *aes* the equivalent of about thirty *denarii* and in silver the equivalent of about 720 *denarii* (disregarding non-Roman coins), while the fifty-six hoards with no *aes* contained the equivalent of well over eighteen thousand *denarii*.

**414** By examining collections that seem to be of this character in the museums of France and Italy (*NC*[7] 7, 11, 12 (1967, 1971, 1972) Richard Reece is laying the foundations for a more thorough study than mine; he believes that 'the obvious collector's pieces can usually be spotted'. Cf. G. K. Jenkins' comment, *NC*[7] 10 (1970), 329, on the catalogue of the collection of the Museo Arqueologico Nacional in Madrid, which 'gives for the first time, a really close view of the quantitative aspects of the Iberian coinage in the light of the relative frequency of the various coins which can be expected to occur in a comprehensive collection'. But even here *aes* coinage, one suspects, will be less accurately reflected than silver coinage.

**415**  D. M. Metcalf, *JbNumG* 9 (1958), 187 ff.

**416**  Mayenne: *Bulletin de la Soc. d'Archéologie de la Mayenne* 1865. Cesano: *Rassegna numismatica* 1930, 363. Liri: *NC*[7] 10 (1970), 89–109, 14 (1974), 42–52.

**417**  Bruce W. Frier and Anthony Parker, *NC*[7] 10 (1970), 91.

**418**  Cf. nn.172–183; add *Dura* VI; Kapenadze, *VDI* 1966.4 (Pityus in Kolchis: 234 *aes*, fourteen silver coins, excluding hoards); T. Hackens, *BCH* 92 (1968) (Delos, Rheneia: no silver); *Delos* XXVII (1970), 387 ff., with discussion on pp. 406–7. An admirable report by M. J. Price, *Hesperia* 36 (1967), 248 ff., on some Corinth finds relates only to the period before 146 B.C., but is of analogical value for our purpose.

**419**  The most valuable for our purpose are *FMRD, FMRL, Novaesium* III and *Vindonissa*.

**420**  Hans Gebhart and Konrad Kraft, *JbNumG* 7 (1956), 39; cf. Anne Robertson, *NC* 13 (1973), 230: 'In the first century A.D. the Roman army seems to have been using a currency made up almost entirely of *aes* coinage, usually Asses'.

**421**  *JbNumG* 10 (1959), 241: cf. Reece, *Britannia* 4 (1973), 227 ff. on the influence of the army's habits on coin finds in Britain.

**422**  It has, for instance, been pointed out that the published record of coins found in the excavation of the Koenen-Lager at Neuss seventy years ago must cover only a small proportion of the *aes* yielded by that site (*Novaesium* III, 9 n.4).

**423**  Confusion and losses: see Laura Breglia, *AIIN* 2 (1955), 155–8. One awaits anxiously the results of 'un'indagine approfondita sulla circolazione monetale pompeiana' which, according to Enrica Pozzi, *AIIN* 5–6 (1958–59), 275 n.3, is in progress.

**424**  See Laura Breglia, 'Circolazione monetale ed aspetti di vita economica in Pompeii', in *Raccolta di studi per il secondo centenario degli scavi di Pompeii* (1950), 1–6; cf. Robert Etienne, *La Vie quotidienne à Pompéi* (1966), 227, 229.

**425**  At Minturnae only one Augustan *denarius* turned up, and none of Tiberius, against *aes* coins of their time to the value of forty-seven *asses*, nearly three *denarii*. (*Excavations at Minturnae* I (1935), edited by Jotham Johnson). Finds of Augustan and Tiberian silver coins on the Magdalensberg (excluding hoards) amounted to 7½ *denarii*; finds of *aes* of their time were equivalent to more than 191 *asses*, i.e. nearly twelve *denarii*. (*Carinthia* I 142 (1952)–144 (1954), 145–146 (1955–6), 148 (1958), 149 (1959), 151 (1961), 153 (1963), 156 (1966), 159 (1969); *Die Ausgrabungen auf dem Magdalensberg 1969–72*, edited by Hermann Vetters and Gernot Piccottini (1973).) For comparison: at Vindonissa, a military site, occupied from *c.* A.D. 17, the Augustan and Tiberian silver found amounted to fifty-five *denarii* (nineteen of the *denarii* being plated), while finds of their *aes* amounted to 3,530 *asses*, equivalent to over 220 *denarii*; and in the temple area at Augusta Treverorum (Trier: *FMRD* IV, 3.1) three Augustan and Tiberian *denarii* (two plated) were found, while finds of their *aes* amount to about 210 *asses*, equivalent to over thirteen *denarii*.

**426**  E.g. at Alba Fucens (*L'Antiquité classique* (1955)), Ordona (De Boe, in Mertens, *Ordona* (1965), 67–87), Luni (*AIIN* 12–14 (1965–67)), Aquileia (Brusin, *Gli scavi di Aquileia* (1934)), Nemi (Cesano, *Scavi di Nemi: Le Monete*, 307 ff.), Vetulonia (*Studi Etruschi* 5 (1931)), Vulci (Hus, *Vulci étrusque et étrusco-romaine* (1971), 156); cf. also finds in excavations in and around the Forum at Rome (knowledge of which

I owe to Mr Michael Crawford): and Professor T. V. Buttrey tells me that excavation finds at Cosa (and Morgantina) show that '*aes* was abundant in circulation'.

**427**  Cf. Kraay, *Vindonissa* 6; Hackens, *Délos* XXVII (1970), 406. On the other hand, these are likelier to elude excavators: *ibid.*, 419.

**428**  Chantraine, *Novaesium* III, 35 n.213.

**429**  Geoffrey Crowther, *An Outline of Money* (1940), 118 f.

**430**  Cf. Kraay, *Vindonissa*, 9. Some *aes*, however, was probably sent by the government to frontier areas: see below, n.556: cf. the suggestion of M. J. Price, *Hesperia* 36 (1967), 362–3, 368 that large Ptolemaic *aes* may have been deliberately transported to the Peloponnese in the second century B.C.

**431**  Crowther, *loc. cit.* (n.429).

**432**  For a full analysis of the material from two of these sites, in all its aspects, see Kraay, *Vindonissa*, and Chantraine, *Novaesium* III.

**433**  *BMCRE*, p. xlviii. Elsewhere Mattingly unfortunately gave quite a misleading impression when he remarked, seemingly with reference to imperial, or at least Augustan, *aes* coinage in general, that 'the bronze coinage seems to have been . . . designed mainly for circulation in Rome and Italy' (*Roman Coinage*², 102; cf. 177: 'Roman "aes" was at first issued for Rome and Italy'), that is to say, for circulation among civilians. Presumably he must have intended this comment to apply only to the *aes* struck in Rome, for he went on to say that 'Augustus placed it'—the bronze coinage—'under the control of the Senate', whereas 'as paymaster of the armies, he must keep in his own hands the issue of the precious metals.'

**434**  Cf. Crawford, *JRS* 60 (1970), 47–8.

**435**  Sutherland, *CRIP*, 42.

**436**  Cf. Anne Robertson, *NC*⁷ 8 (1968), 66. The part played by the Augustan *aes* mint at Rome in satisfying these needs is discussed below, pp. 66 ff.

**437**  On the slow growth of a demand for coined money in country districts, see Crawford, *JRS* 60 (1970), 43 ff.

**438**  Pannonia: Pink, *Die Münzprägung der Ostkelten*, 109–10; Castelin, *Num.Közl.* 68–69 (1969–70), 3–12. Rhaetia: Castelin, *Schweizer Numismatischer Rundschau* 50 (1971), 92–124.

**439**  See n.275, hoards (vi) and (vii). These are the only finds known to me of pre-Flavian *aes* in a context not obviously military. According to Maria R. Alföldi (*Archaeologia Hungarica* 33 (1954), 143) *asses* of Claudius (but not of subsequent emperors before Domitian) have been found in considerable numbers along the north–south line of the *limes* in Pannonia, but she remarks that all of these Claudian *asses* are very worn, and concludes that 'der normale Geldverkehr setzt in diesem Gebiet unter Domitianus bzw. Traianus ein'. A mapping of stray coin finds in Rhaetia and Noricum does, however, suggest that already in the Julio-Claudian period there was a tongue of Roman influence and trading activity, reaching out from Vindonissa across Rhaetia to Augusta Vindelicum (Augsburg) and on to Iuvavum (Salzburg): see Gebhart and Kraft, *JbNumG* 6 (1956), 67.

On finds of pre-Flavian Roman coins in military stations in Noricum and Pannonia, see G. Elmer, *NZ* NF 26 (1933), 55–67 (Carnuntum); 27 (1934), 31–2 (Lauriacum and Ovilava); T. Pekary, *Arch. Értesítő* 80 (1953), 106–13 (English summary, 113–14) (Aquincum); Maria R. Alföldi, *Archaeologia Hungarica* 33 (1954) (Intercisa). The finds at Carnuntum, as reported by Elmer, provide a good illustration of the monetary effects of the presence of a legion from A.D. 6 onwards at a key point on a trade route, while the chance finds at Aquincum that have reached the museum, on which Pekary reports, show the effect of the presence of *auxilia* from the time of Tiberius at a place less favourably situated for the development of purely civilian trade. (Cf. T. Nagy, 'Der Vicus von Aquincum', *Acta Archaeologica Academiae Scientiarum Hungaricae* 23 (1971), 59–81.) The finds comprise fifty-three pre-Flavian against sixty-one Flavian coins: but the pre-

Flavian coins include thirty-three republican *denarii*, many of which will have remained in circulation down into and in some cases beyond the Flavian period, so a more meaningful comparison would be between the fourteen *aes* coins of Augustus, Tiberius and Gaius, the four of Claudius and Nero, and the fifty-one Flavian *aes* coins. Not surprisingly, the extensive excavations at Intercisa yielded only two pre-Flavian coins; one *aes* of Claudius, one of Nero. That there was scarcely even any Roman military presence in Pannonia north of the Drave in the time of Augustus and Tiberius is argued by A. Mocsy, *Acta Archaeologica Academiae Scientiarum Hungaricae* 23 (1971), 41 ff.: for the absence of finds of *terra sigillata* see D. Gabler, *ibid.*, 83 ff.

**440**    Tac., *Ann.* 4. 5; at least one of them was on the Danube, at Oescus, the other perhaps at Naissus (A. Mocsy, *Gesellschaft und Romanisation in der römischen Provinz Moesia Superior* (1970), 47–50: on currency circulation, 257–8).

**441**    This statement rests largely on the regular reports by T. Gerassimov in *Izv.BAI.* Two hoards from south Bulgaria of *aes* of Rhoemetalces I, one of eighty-four coins, the other of two to three kilograms, have been published by D. Tsontchev, *Godishnik na narodnija arkheologicheski muzei Plovdiv* 4 (1960). Hoards of silver coins are not rare, but one, of *c.* 125 B.C., found some 300 kilometres inland, at the nearest point to Odessos on the route from the Hebros to the Danube, was exceptional in including fifty *aes* of Odessos, with twenty-five tetradrachms—fifteen of Thasos, one of the First Region of Macedonia, four posthumous Alexanders of Mesembria and four native imitations of coins of Philip II (*GCH*, 522).

**442**    Cf. G. Mihailov, *Athenaeum* 39 (1961), 33–44.

**443**    Aquae Calidae: Iordanes, *Getica*, 109.

**444**    Summary publication by B. Filov, *Archäologischer Anzeiger* 1911, 349–56. T. Gerassimov has published some individual coins from this find, now in Sofia, in his discussion of countermarking by Greek city states from Thasos to Histria (*Izv.BAI* 15 (1946), 51–81), also eleven halves from the find (*ibid.*, 20 (1955), 579–81: see below, n.466). Among the Roman coins that could be more or less closely identified, there is such a marked disparity in number between those earlier than Claudius' reign (370, and five Greek imperials) and those of Claudius (231, and three of Perinthos), on the one hand, and on the other hand those of Nero (seven, and six of Perinthos), of Vespasian (seven), and of all later emperors combined (164, and thirty-seven Greek imperials) that it seems safe to conclude that the perforated stone floor over the spring, beneath which most of the coins are said to have been found, was laid during the reign of Nero: the more elaborate fitting up of the spa may even have been connected in some way with his philhellenic policies. It seems likely that many, if not most, of the coins that are simply said to be of Augustus were, like the fifty-three of 'Agrippa', struck under Tiberius (or later), in view of the fact that only two are said to be of Tiberius and only seventeen are clearly of the reign of Gaius.

There are no less than 181 Thracian coins said to be of Rhoemetalces I, portraying Augustus on the reverse (some of which could perhaps be really of Rhoemetalces II, with Tiberius), which suggests that these were the *aes* coins that circulated most abundantly in this area under Augustus; perhaps even until the reign of Claudius, though the fact that there are only one of Cotys IV and Rhescuporis and two of Rhoemetalces III and Caligula might indicate that, during a period marked by dynastic strife and popular risings, there was a gradual fading away of these issues, which, following the cessation of the issues of Apollonia and Mesembria, led to an increasing demand for Roman *aes*, a demand for the satisfaction of which the presence of Roman troops in Moesia accidentally created a gradually increasing supply. (In the Thasos finds, among thirty-six coins of the Augustan–Claudian period, there were eight of these Thracian royal coins alongside fourteen of Philippi and ten of Amphipolis; Dunant and Pouilloux, *op. cit.* (n.161), 214–15.)

**445**  Histria: two *asses* and one *sestertius* ( ?) of Tiberius, one *sestertius* of Claudius, one small *aes* of Titus ( ?), one *sestertius* ( ?) of Nerva, six other *aes* coins assigned to the first century A.D., one *sestertius*, one *dupondius*, two *asses* and four fragments assigned to the first or second century A.D. (also Trajanic and later coins): H. Nubar, 'Monedele romane', in *Histria III: Descoperirile monetare 1914–70* (1973). Thasos: *BCH* 75 (1951); 79 (1954: three coins); 79 (1955), 80 (1956: no mention of coins in later reports); the coins in question, being not further specified, may well all be representative of the same eastern official and Macedonian colonial series as the halves published by Gerassimov (see below, n.466).

**446**  Except in southern Noricum: see below, p. 60.

**447**  See above, p. 37. On *aes* in Dacia see pp. 41 f.

**448**  Jannoray, *op. cit.* (n.131), 341 ff.; J.-C. Richard, *Survey* (see n.127), 254–6, 260, who gives a full bibliography. They travelled beyond Gaul also, into the Po Valley, Switzerland and Spain: Richard, *Mélanges de la Casa de Velazquez* 8 (1972), 51 ff. 'Le monnayage de bronze a certainement continué après la guerre des Gaules pour satisfaire un commerce local' (Richard, *Survey*, 254).

**449**  Richard, *Survey*, 259; Colbert de Beaulieu, *ibid.*, 269–70. Pink, *Einführung in die keltische Münzkunde*, 9.

**450**  Harald Küthmann, *Jahrbuch des römisch-germanischen Zentralmuseums* 4 (1957), 73–80.

**451**  C. M. Kraay, *NC*[6] 15 (1955), 75–89.

**452**  A sample of the small change on which Roman soldiers on the Rhine had to rely during this period is provided by the *aes* coins found on the site of the camp at Oberaden, probably abandoned *c.* 12–8 B.C. Excluding a small hoard, the identified coins are as follows: Rome (Augustus) two; Spain (Sextus Pompeius) one half; Nemausus (main series) 118 and forty-four halves; Copia one half; Vienna one half; Spanish towns 2 and two halves; Leuci ( ?) one; other Celtic two (Bernard Korzus, *FMRD* VI.5 (1972), 5081). Chantraine (*Novaesium* III, 34) suggests that the scarcity of coins of Gallic *coloniae* and tribes is due to the camp's isolated forward position, for there is still a considerable proportion of Celtic coins even in the finds on the site of the Roman camp at Haltern, established in 11 B.C. and abandoned either in A.D. 16 or in A.D. 9 (788 of 2,685 non-hoard coins: Bernard Korzus, *FMRD* VI.4, 4057), and at Neuss, probably occupied from *c.* 15 B.C. to *c.* 104–10 A.D. (418 of 2,456 coins from the 1955–62 excavations: Chantraine, *Novaesium* III).

**453**  A subsidiary mint or mints: Grant, *SMACA*, 154; Kraay, *Vindonissa*, 26; Chantraine, *Novaesium* III, 14 n.45; Giard, *Rev.num.*[6] 9 (1967), 126–30.

**454**  Chantraine, *ibid.*, 14.

**455**  Chantraine, *ibid.*

**456**  *JbNumG* 16 (1966), 62.

**457**  See above, n.452, for finds of Gallic coins at Neuss and Haltern. Regling, in *Das Römerlager von Oberaden* I (1938), held that their circulation in these camps was 'illegal und nur stillschweigend geduldet', for in his view it was Augustus' policy, at least from 27 B.C., to give 'den kleinen Gewalten Kupferprägerecht nur unter seinem Namen oder Bilde'. But as with most theories about *Prägerecht*, there is no direct evidence; it is merely an inference from numismatic phenomena. A Gallic potin coin has been found in the Augustan or Tiberian *vicus* at Karlstein in Rhaetia, and others at the Tiberian settlement, Aquae Helveticae (Manfred Menke, *JbNumG* 13 (1973), 89–91). A hoard from Amiens comprised fifty-eight Gallic *aes* coins, mostly of Germanus Indutilli L(ibertus), along with a plated republican *denarius*, an *as* of Tiberius and an *as* of Nero (Hélène Huvelin, *Bulletin de la société française de numismatique* 28.10 (1973), 486–8).

**458**  A sample of the small change used by the Gauls is provided by finds at Bibracte, abandoned towards the end of the century (Gallic potin 707, Gallic *aes* 113, Tarraco one, Massalia five, Nemausus thirty-three, Cabellio one, Vienna three, Roman moneyers seven, Lugdunum altar four (*RRCH*, 567)), and Font-Garnier (see n.129); and for the last years of the first century B.C. by two predominantly base-metal hoards, one from Hussigny-Godbrange (Meurthe-et-Moselle) (*RRCH*, 516), in which 143 of the 151 base-metal coins are Gallic, while one is republican, five and a half are of Nemausus, and only one half is of Lugdunum; and from Port-Haliguen, near Quiberon (*RRCH*, 517, corrected by Giard, *Rev.num.*[6] 9 (1967), 119–39), in which, in contrast, only one of the 433 base-metal coins is Gallic, whereas eight and thirteen halves are republican, thirty-eight and twelve halves are of Nemausus (including two imitations), one half is of Vienna, 358½ are of Lugdunum (including four imitations), and one is a Roman *as* of c. 20 B.C.

**459**  *Annalen des Vereins für nassauische Altertumskunde* 40 (1912), 38. Chantraine, *Novaesium* III, 34 (cf. 11) supports Ritterling's view.

**460**  *FMRD* IV, 3.1. Only two Gallic *aes* coins have been recorded, against well over three hundred of Augustus and Tiberius.

**461**  See Ritterling, *op. cit.* (n.459).

**462**  Finds in the temple area at Trier (*FMRD* IV, 3.1) include a much higher proportion of *quadrantes* than the finds from any military site, which suggests that the chief demand for these smallest coins was from civilians, but even here the proportion that these coins represent of the total value of Augustan *aes* found is only about 3½ per cent: and it is significant that along with the twenty-five *quadrantes* there were twenty-four quarters of coins, evidently the result of cutting *asses* to create *quadrantes*. Cf. nn.475, 542.

**463**  Cf. Crawford, *JRS* 60 (1970), 48.

**464**  Kraay, *Vindonissa*, 21; Chantraine, *Novaesium* III, 11, cf. *ibid.*, 21 n.107; Doppler, *Schweizer Münzblätter* 17 (1967), 90 ff.: cf. Bellinger, *Dura* VI, 189–90.

**465**  This has long been the *communis opinio*: see H. Mattingly, *BMCRE* I pp. xxiv, lxxxv, and T. V. Buttrey, *AJA* 76 (1972), 31–48, who give references to the principal earlier discussions, by Blanchet, Strack and Cesano; and H. Chantraine, *Novaesium* III, 11, 17–22, the best discussion of the material from military sites, with clear tabulation (p. 19).

**466**  Italy and Sicily: see below, n.541. The Magdalensberg (see n.425): the excavations yielded in 1950–72 the following pre-Claudian *asses*: republican eight and four halves, Octavian one and a half, Nemausus four, Augustan moneyers' fifty-nine and fourteen halves, Lugdunum altar six and a half, eastern of Augustus (*SMACA*, 9–10, series 4) one half, Philippi under Augustus one, Tiberius forty-six, Augustus or Tiberius (unidentifiable) two and seven halves. Few halved coins have been found in Rhaetia, except on the Roman camp site at Oberhausen bei Augsburg, abandoned in A.D. 15/17, where the proportion of *asses* halved, and in particular the proportion of Augustan moneyers' *asses* halved, is larger than on any other site (*FMRD* I, 7011; *Novaesium* III, 20 n.94 and table on p. 19). Still fewer, if any, have been found further down the Danube frontier, because, as we have seen, *aes* hardly began to circulate in these regions before the practice of halving had virtually died out. There were, of course, Roman soldiers stationed in the Danubian provinces in the time of Tiberius, but in the north of these provinces they must have led very restricted, simple lives. Evidently there were still scarcely any goods or services to be bought with *aes* coins. (Cf. Chantraine's suggestion, *Novaesium* III, 21 n.107, that halves were for this reason less abundant at Oberaden and Haltern.) Perhaps halved *aes* coins would have been viewed with distrust by civilians who had scarcely seen Roman coins previously. There were, however, twenty-two halves in the Ajtoska Banja find along with the three to four hundred whole Roman coins that are or may be of the same period (see n.444). Of those which Gerassimov identified and published, two are of the same eastern official series as the Magdalensberg half (as are nineteen halves recently discovered at Sardes: Buttrey, *AJA* 76 (1972), 32 n.10); the others all appear to be of Macedonian mints, including one example (No. 4) of what Grant has called 'Julius Caesar's most important coinage' (*FITA*, 13).

**467** Oberaden: see above, n.452.

**468** I leave out of account quite separate earlier instances, which do not concern us. A hoard found at Terni in central Italy (*RRCH*, 415), which closed with *denarii* of 42 B.C., is said to have included three *asses* and a half, but Buttrey (*AJA* 76 (1972), 43 n.64) argues that they may be intrusive; he is also reluctant to accept a stratigraphic dating in the seventies B.C. for one of the halves found at Cosa.

**469** See Appendix A.

**470** At the camp sites for which figures are given by Chantraine, *Novaesium* III, 1,136 whole Tiberian *asses* have been found but only twenty-six halves. Halves of post-Tiberian coins are relatively far rarer: *ibid.*, 18 (one-third of the coins of Gaius found in the temple area at Trier were halves or quarters, but there may be special reasons for this unusual phenomenon—silver threepenny pieces used to figure more prominently in 'silver collections' than in general circulation). Kraft, *Bonner Jahrbücher* 155–156 (1955–56), 104 ff., has argued against the view of Strack, *ibid.*, 108–109 (1902), 1–25, and Regling, *Oberaden* (see n.457) that the practice was probably stopped by Tiberius, but Chantraine, *Novaesium* III, 17–21, after tabulating and analysing the German evidence very fully, argues that there is no reason to suppose that it continued under Tiberius to more than a very small extent. Examples of prices quoted by Crawford, *JRS* 60 (1970), 41, suggest that by the time of Pliny the Elder there was little need for coins of lower value than the *as*.

**471** Crawford, taking the view that a halved *as* was generally intended to count as an *as*, goes on to argue that the scarcity of coins of smaller denominations in finds from the northern provinces indicates that 'coinage was little used there as a means of exchange . . . mainly as a store of wealth and as a (compulsory) method of paying taxes'. It is no doubt true that there had been much less progress towards a monetary economy even in Gaul than in more urbanised regions, but what of the Gallic base-metal coinages ?

**472** *Rev.num.*⁶ 6 (1964), 151–7.

**473** For example, in two groups of coins that have been very carefully examined from this point of view, the Port-Haliguen hoard (see above, n.458) and a quantity of votive coins recovered from the river Aisne (J.-B. Giard, *Rev.num.*⁶ 10 (1968), 76–130), there were, respectively, six imitations among 409 Augustan *aes* coins of Lugdunum and Nemausus, and ninety-one imitations, mostly of Tiberian issues, among 844 Augustan and Tiberian *aes* coins of Lugdunum and Rome.

**474** A shortage would have been particularly likely in the early years of Nero's reign as a result of the suspension of official minting of *aes* during Claudius' last years, coming on top of the final cessation of local issues in Spain and North Africa.

**475** See below, p. 68 and n.561: M. Crawford, however, holds that they were not fiduciary; but he points out that many of the unofficial imitations of *asses* are underweight, and he believes that the fact that 'the circulating medium of the North and West was diluted with light-weight or poor quality forgeries' helps 'to explain the tendency . . . for the *denarius* to be worth more than the official sixteen asses' in outlying areas (*JRS* 59 (1969), 292, cf. 318; *ibid.* 60 (1970), 44–5). Heinrich Chantraine, noting the same phenomenon, suggests that these underweight coins were intended not to pass for *asses*, but to serve as *semisses* or even *quadrantes*, and were produced, unofficially, as a substitute for Gallic *aes* as it passed out of circulation (*Novaesium* III, 31–2).

**476** Even Blanchet's catalogue of hoards (see n.107) is not nearly informative enough. (The data published by Richard Reece (*NC*⁷ 7 (1967), 91–105; 12 (1972), 159–65) on the contents of some museums in France, though valuable as a basis for future research, are too general to help our purpose.)

**477** R. Egger, *Die Stadt auf dem Magdalensberg* (1961).

**478** Karl Pink, *Carinthia* I, 148 (1958), suggested *c.* 90 B.C., but Karel Castelin (*Mitteilungen der österreichischen numismatischen Gesellschaft* 17 (1971), 10–13) and Günther Dembski (*NZ* 86 (1971), 43–50) have argued for a later date.

**479** See the reports in *Carinthia*, cited above, nn.253, 425, on finds of Celtic and Roman coins on the Magdalensberg. Circulation of the Celtic coins into the reign of Tiberius: Castelin, *loc. cit.* (n.478); *Schweizer Münzblätter* 21.82 (1971), 33–7.

**480** Except in a sense and in a direction that do not here concern us—to throw light on 'les rélations permanentes imposées ou permises par la géographie' by tracing 'la circulation des hommes' which such finds attest: Robert, *Monnaies antiques en Troade* (1966), 113–14.

**481** Robert, *ibid.* There is the further difficulty that the value relationship of local, especially eastern, *aes* coins to official *aes* is extremely uncertain (see e.g. E. W. Klimowsky, *Proceedings* . . . (see n.122), 133 ff.), though there must have been recognised rates, since at Palmyra, for instance, from Tiberius' time customs dues were expressed in *asses*, but amounts of less than a *denarius* were customarily collected πρὸς κέρμα, which must mean in local *aes* (Dittenberger, *Orientis Graecae Inscriptiones Selectae*, 629, 154–7).

**482** 'Of course the coins so minted are true money . . . but they are too few to play an important part in the currency': Bellinger, *Troy: The Coins*, 194.

**483** 'Elles sont destinées avant tout à permettre les menus échanges dans une aire déterminée': G. le Rider, *Suse sous les Séleucides et les Parthes* (1965), 435; cf. T. Hackens, *Délos* XXVII (1970), 407; L. Kadman, *Proceedings* . . . (see n.122), 316 on Palestinian *aes* hoards. 'The purchasing power of coins in this period was still relatively great, and even when the *prutot* represent a very small denomination, they played a considerable rôle as "common coin" in the daily life, especially of the poorer classes' (B. Oestreicher, *ibid.*, 213). For retail transactions bronze coins had been gradually taking the place of silver throughout the Greek world since their first appearance in Sicily in the fifth century; gradually, because prejudice and mistrust had to be overcome: see M. Jessop Price, 'Early Greek bronze coinage', in *Essays in Greek Coinage presented to Stanley Robinson* (1968), 90 ff.; Anne E. Jackson, *NC*⁷ II (1971), 37 ff., discussing a decree issued at Gortyn in the second half of the third century (*Inscriptiones Creticae* IV, 162) enjoining the use of that state's new bronze coinage.

**484** Tom B. Jones, *Proceedings of the American Philosophical Society* 107.4 (1963), 308, 331; cf. Bellinger, *Dura* VI, 195 f; Franke, *op. cit.* (n.118), 220; Kadman, *op. cit.* (n.483), 314: 'The Talmud even describes the poor man who digs a hole in which to hide his few *prutot.*'

**485** In the case of Anatolian issues this has been shown by the careful researches of Louis and Jeanne Robert (e.g. L. and J. Robert, *La Carie* II (1954) on the Tabai plateau and its environs; L. Robert, *Études de numismatique grecque* (1951), *Monnaies antiques en Troade* (1966) on the Troad).

**486** Bellinger, *Troy: The Coins*, 188. The limited range of travel of most issues of *aes* is illustrated by a hoard of the first century B.C. from southern Asia Minor, containing 198 *aes* coins: of the fifteen mints represented (Perge with twenty-three, Termessus Maior with twenty-one, insignificant Ariassus (the find-spot?) with 131), fourteen are within about one hundred kilometres of Attaleia (Antalya): N. Olçay, *Istanbul Arkeologi Müzerleri Yilliği* 15–16 (1969), 289 ff.; cf. *GCH*, 1420, where coins from farther away—Apamea, Galatia, Pergamum—and extending into the first century A.D. are excluded as 'undoubtedly intrusive'.

**487** The limited range of travel of many issues of silver in the archaic and classical periods is emphasised by C. M. Kraay, *JHS* 84 (1964), 84–5. The silver coinages of the north Euxine states throughout antiquity provide an extreme example: though of perfectly good quality, they hardly circulated outside their own areas (Edith Schönert-Geiss, *VDI* 1971.2, 24–35; *GCH*, pp. 127–9). As to long-distance travel of *aes*, two instances may be cited from a slightly earlier period. On Crete, where Athenian silver 'a constitué le numéraire étranger le plus répandu' in the second century B.C. and in the early years of the first, Le Rider noted also 'la présence d'un grand nombre de bronzes d'Athènes' (*Monnaies Crétoises du Ve au Ier siècle av. J.-C., Études Crétoises XV* (1966), 295 n.5); while M. J. Price has shown that in the second century Corinth relied mainly on Ptolemaic and Macedonian coins to satisfy the need for large *aes*, thus refuting the suggestion of Le Rider (*op. cit.* (n.15), 187 n.3) that a previously published Corinthian hoard of Ptolemaic *aes* had been thrown away 'parce qu'il ne pouvait servir à rien'. No doubt, however, this was the fate of a small proportion of little-known civic *aes* that wandered too far in travellers' purses; hence some modern finds.

**488** For our period, Grant has singled out a number of cities—in his view, 'the chosen cities'—'whose mintages were extensive and regular', and has given examples of the travel of coins of these and other civic mints (*FITA*, 295–301). But his find-data are necessarily, for the most part, merely lists of individual coins that he happened to see in collections or publications. For a somewhat more systematic tabulation of the travel of local *aes* coins within the Iberian peninsula, see below, n.506.

**489** Tom B. Jones, *op. cit.* (n.484), 318, 323; cf. T. R. S. Broughton, *ESAR* IV, 886–7. There are valuable discussions of the rôle of this civic *aes* in currency circulation during this period by A. R. Bellinger (*Dura* VI, 188–210; *Essays in Roman Coinage presented to Harold Mattingly* (1956), 137–48; *Troy: The Coins*, 37–45, 103–4, 187–94); H. Seyrig (*Rev.num.* 1958, 171–7, reviewing *Dura* VI); and L. Robert (*Monnaies antiques en Troade* (1966), reviewing *Troy: The Coins*, especially 110–14). Reports of considerable coin finds in the course of excavations include those relating to Dodona (Carapanos, *Dodone et ses ruines* (1878), 115 ff.; Evangelidis, Πρακτικά 1952; Varoucha-Christodoulopoulou, Πρακτικά 1955); Elis (Karamesini-Oikonomidou, Ἀρχαιολογικὴ Ἐφημερίς 1963); Corinth (Edwards, *Corinth* VI (1933), *Hesperia* 6 (1937)), the agora at Athens (Shear, *Hesperia* 5 (1936), and, for the Roman coins, Thompson, *The Athenian Agora* II (1954)); Troy (*Troy: The Coins*); Sardes (Bell, *Sardis* XI (1916); Priene (Regling, *Die Münzen von Priene* (1927)); Tarsus (Cox, *Tarsus* I (1950); Curium (Cox, ANS *Numismatic Notes and Monographs* 145 (1959)); Antioch (Waage, *Antioch* IV.2 (1952); Samaria (Kirkman, *Samaria-Sebaste* III (1957)).

**490** In Crete, Cyrene, Cyprus and Judaea part of the small change circulating in Tiberius' time was provided by *aes* issues that are, by convention, not classed as official, although they were evidently produced on instructions from provincial governors, if not from higher authority. In Crete the Roman authorities played some part in the provision of currency during the last decades of the Republic, civic issues having lapsed except at Cnossos, and they seem to have participated again in the organising of ostensibly civic issues, of silver as well as *aes*, in Tiberius' time: see E. S. G. Robinson, *BMC Cyrenaica* (1927), ccix ff. In Cyprus and Cyrene issues sponsored by the Roman authorities took the place of the Ptolemaic coinage, for under the Ptolemies there had been no civic coinages that could continue or be revived. In Judaea, from A.D. 6, they took the place of Herodian coinage, itself the successor of Hasmonean coinage (Kindler, *op. cit.* (n.148), 190–5). Similar issues were produced in Cappadocia and Commagene from A.D. 17, to take the place of royal coinage, but scarcity of find information prevents an assessment of their importance. (The attribution to Commagene of the issue in question, *RIC* I Tiberius, 43, is rejected by Grant (*NC*⁶ 9 (1949), 241), who holds that it was 'a very large coinage intended for circulation throughout the Eastern provinces' (*Roman Anniversary Issues* (1950), 57), a view supported by Helga Gesche (*Chiron* 2 (1972), 343), who mentions that 'mehrere Stempel' are known; further investigation seems to be required.) The institution of these coinages meant a further extension of the area within which people accustomed to the availability of a local supply of small change became dependent on Rome for a continuation of it, and in a complete assessment of Augustan and Tiberian monetary policy, from an economic rather than a political standpoint, careful investigation of them would be necessary. However, in considering the contribution made by official *aes* issues to currency circulation one can class them with civic issues inasmuch as their existence meant that the areas in which they circulated are not to be included among those in which the cessation of local issues created a demand for 'official' Roman *aes*. Thus, for instance, an *aes* hoard of A.D. 68 found in Palestine comprised six Seleucid coins, 244 Hasmonean, 208 Herodian, 202 procuratorial and twenty-five of year 2 of the Jewish revolt (*Israel Numismatic Journal* 1962, 106); and among *aes* coins of 27 B.C.–A.D. 59 found at Caesarea Maritima fifty-nine are Herodian, 159 procuratorial, none official (H. Hamburger, *Israel Exploration Journal* 20 (1970), 81 ff.).

**491**  Also Sardes? See below, n. 532.

**492**  Peter A. Clayton, *Iraq* 29 (1967), 143–54.

**493**  Chance finds by an Italian mission in Albania comprised 209 *aes* and four silver Greek coins of the fourth to the first centuries B.C. (116 from north-western mints), ten *aes* and three silver coins of the Roman Republic; no pre-Neronian imperial coins except for one *as* of Gaius (*Atti e Memorie del Istituto Ital. di Num.* 7 (1932), 58–75). There was no Roman republican or imperial *aes* among over 150 coins, mostly of *aes*, seen by Clarke or Hammond in villages of Epirus, or among the 396 coins in the Jannina museum which Hammond catalogued in 1939 (N. G. L. Hammond, *Epirus* (1967), 715–31).

**494**  Gabriel Camps, *Libyca* 8 (1960), 203–9. Camps refers to the travel of these coins far beyond Numidia, particularly to their occurrence in Yugoslav hoards of *c.* 100 B.C. (*GCH*, 556–9, 643–4): add the occurrence of two on Delos, reported by Svoronos, *Journal international d'archéologie numismatique* 10 (1906), 191 ff.

**495**  Jean Mazard, *Bulletin d'archéologie marocaine* 4 (1960), 116.

**496**  Most of the published evidence is summarised in Table II. Maurice Euzennat, *VIIIe Congrès* (see n.365), 261–78, refers to some other coin finds.

**497**  And to a lesser extent by *aes* issues of Spanish towns, above all Gades. See Jean Marion, *Antiquités africaines* I (1967), 115–18. (For our purpose it is not important whether Lixus and Semes are to be identified, as Mazard, *Corpus Nummorum Numidiae Mauretaniaeque* (1955), 59–61, following Müller, has argued.)

**498**  Scramuzza, *ESAR* III, 306–10; Grant, *FITA*, 474–5. But persistence of civic *aes* in circulation down through the first century B.C. is shown by a hoard found in a house at Megara which had evidently been occupied until the final abandonment of the town in the thirties B.C., containing forty-three coins of Syracuse, two of Catana, one of Rhegion and one of Henna with the legend MVNATIVS II VIR (Villard, *Mél. d'Arch. et d'Hist. de l'École Fr. de Rome* 63 (1951), 47–8; *GCH*, 2252); Cicero (II *in Verrem* 3. 181), quoted above, n.123, was no doubt referring only to silver.

**499**  See *RRCH*, 66, 68, 69, 96, 99, 122, 127, 128; F. Villard, *op. cit.* (n.498); R. R. Holloway, *Congresso internazionale de numismatica* (Roma, 1961) II, 135–50.

**500**  Mommsen, *Geschichte des römischen Münzwesens* (1860), 663–7; Grant, *FITA*, 3 ff. The resultant currency situation is reflected in three hoards of *aes* coins: one containing thirty-eight Roman *asses* of the second century B.C. and twenty-seven of these Panormos coins (Aldina Tusa Cutroni, *AIIN* 3 (1956), 210 = *RRCH*, 137); another containing a coin of Ebusus, a *pentonkion* of the Mamertini of Messana, nine republican *asses*, thirty-nine of the Panormos coins, and one Augustan Roman *as* (Cutroni, *ibid.*): the third containing five coins of Syracuse under the Romans, six republican *asses* of the second century B.C., twenty-five of the Panormos coins, and one Augustan Roman *sestertius* (Maria Teresa Currò Pisanò, *AIIN* 9–11 (1962–64), 225; *GCH*, 2253; more fully, *RRCH*, 494). Mamertine *pentonkia* have turned up also in excavations at Halaesa and Solus, along with Roman *aes*, some of both halved (Gianfilippo Carettoni, *N.Sc.*[8] 13 (1959), 293 ff.; 15 (1961), 266 ff.; Aldina Tusa Cutroni, *Kokalos* 6 (1960), 110–23), which points to circulation side by side down into Augustus' reign (cf. Appendix A).

**501**  Grant, *FITA*, 199; cf. 295.

**502**  *AIIN* 2 (1955), 192–5; 4 (1957), 221–3; 5–6 (1958–59), 312–13. Seven coins struck by Panormos under Augustus and Tiberius were found, as against three *asses* and one *quadrans* of Augustus and two *asses* of Tiberius from Rome, along with earlier and later Roman *aes*.

**503**  See the haphazard but valuable register of finds compiled by Felipe Mateu y Llopis (*Ampurias* 4 (1942); 10 (1948; 13 (1951); *Num.hisp.* 1 (1952)–11 (1967): cf. the find of eleven Roman *aes* coins of the second and early first centuries B.C. with over seven hundred Spanish *aes* coins in two hoards deposited about the time of the Sertorian war at the native stronghold of Azaila (Pio Beltran, *Bol. arqueol. del sudeste español* 2 (1945), 135 ff.; for the date cf. A. Beltran, *Caesaraugusta* 23–24 (1964), 79 f.); G. K. Jenkins, *NC*[7] 12 (1972), 324–5; *RRCH*, 220; *GCH*, 2349.

**504**  At Caceres (Castra Caecilia) seventy Roman and 138 Spanish *aes* coins were found (*Archäologischer Anzeiger* 1928, 12–14; 1930, 54–8; 1932, 346–8); at Coimbra (Conimbriga), four republican *asses* and one half, and about sixteen pre-Augustan Spanish *aes* coins (Isabel Pereira, Jean-Pierre Bost and Jean Hiernand, *Fouilles de Conimbriga* III: *Les Monnaies* (1974)).

**505**  See M. Gomez Moreno, *Miscelaneas* I (1949), 172–4; A. M. de Guadan, *Numismatica iberica e ibero-romana* (1969), 119–53.

**506**  Jannoray, *op. cit.* (n.131), 341–2; Jenkins, *Survey . . .* (see n.127), 215–16. There was also travel over long distances within the peninsula, especially from mints in and around the Ebro valley, illustrated by maps in *Fouilles de Conimbriga* III (see n.504), which unfortunately however give no indication of the quantities in question (36·8 per cent of the Spanish *aes* found at Conimbriga itself was from nearby Emerita; but that mint only came into being under Augustus).

**507**  Schulten, *Numantia* IV (1929); Mateu y Llopis, *Ampurias* 13 (1951), Hallazgos No. 378.

**508**  'Quant au rôle joué par les émissions hispano-romaines, il apparaît de toute première importance . . . La part du monnayage municipal s'accroît sensiblement sous Tibère et atteint alors son apogée' (*Conimbriga* III (see n.504), 214, 218: twenty-six clearly Tiberian Spanish *aes* coins found, against twenty clearly Augustan; altogether over 100 Spanish *aes* of the time of Augustus and Tiberius, against nine *aes* of that period from outside the peninsula). Cf. M. Grant, *NC*[6] 9 (1949), 93–106; A. J. Parker, *NC*[7] 10 (1970), 327. Parker goes so far as to say that '*aes* of Rome or Gaul for the first three emperors is almost unknown in mainland Spain. Claudian coins are common.' According to Grant, local issues declined in volume after about 2 B.C., but this view seems not to be shared by Parker: 'under Tiberius and Caligula these series continue . . . in full strength; some mints close, others open, but in general there seems to be no diminution in overall output.'

**509**  As Grant assumes, *FITA*, 123; doubted by Parker, *loc. cit.* (n.508). Use of a common obverse die at two mints, Calagurris and Celsa, has been detected (L. Villaronga Garrida, *Gaceta Numismatica* 7 (1967), 25), but this co-operation could as well be the result of local initiative as of central planning: cf. below, p. 64 and n.519.

**510**  See, for example, finds at Elche (Ilici: A. Ramos Folques, *Num.hisp.* 8 (1959), 133–49), excavation finds at Pollensa (Pollentia: *AEA* 27 (1954), 290–2), at Jerez (Hasta Regia: M. Estero Guerrero, *Excavaciones de Asta Regia, 1945–46, Informes y Memorias* 22 (1950)), at Juliobriga (A. Garcia y Bellido, *AEA* 29 (1956), 131 ff.), and in the Roman cemetery at Ampurias (Emporiae: Martin Almagro, *Las Necropolis de Ampurias* (1955)): cf. also the register of Mateu y Llopis (see above, n.503). A find at Pobla de Mafumet, near Tarraco, of more than 250 Claudian sesterces, 'almost all struck from the same die, packed in rolls in a jar' (Max von Bahrfeldt, *Blätter für Münzfreunde* 18 (1930–33), 754–5; cf. F. Mateu y Llopis, *Boletín arqueologico* 52 (1952), 49–53) has led numismatists to suspect either 'wholesale importation of Roman *aes* to Tarraco' during Claudius' reign (Parker, *loc. cit.* (n. 508)) or the establishment there of a branch of the imperial mint, so that the shortage resulting from the cessation of local issues could be met, in a province rich in metals, without incurring transport costs (Alberto Balil, *Historia economica y social de Espana*, 1: *La antigüedad* (1973), 325). The authors of *Conimbriga* III (see n.504) argue strongly (218–19) for production in Spain, to which they attribute forty-seven Claudian *asses* found by them, characterised by small flans and peculiarities of lettering (and probably twenty-two from earlier excavations), assigning to Rome only a *sestertius*, four *dupondii* and three *quadrantes*, the residue of the Claudian *aes*. They suggest that some local mints were reopened for this purpose, e.g. at Emerita, where the museum has thirty-four similar *asses*.

**511**  Grant, *FITA*, 296. In Syria and Palestine, for instance, 'the pre-Augustan pattern was little altered' (Sutherland, *Proceedings* . . . (see n.148), 90).

**512**  Bellinger, *Troy: The Coins*, 194. However, it must be borne in mind that the appearance in the east of new *aes* issues of monetary significance may be in part the result of the extinction of eastern silver coinages.

**513**  A. M. de Guadan, *Numismatica iberica e ibero-romana* (1969), 110, 187–90, 205. I have not seen M. Ruiz Trapero, *Las acuñaciones hispano-romanas de Calagurris* (1969), mentioned by Jenkins, *Survey* . . . (see n.159).

**514**  This small contribution almost vanishes if one allows for the probability that those who undertook responsibility for commemorative issues of modest size will seldom have bought metal for the purpose, finding it less troublesome to buy and melt down a sufficient quantity of coins. For *aes* minting on a larger scale this is much less likely to have been done, for the striking of new metal could yield a profit to communities that felt confident of getting their coins accepted in the international money market at something approaching their 'face value' (see Dittenberger, *Orientis Graecae Inscriptiones Selectae*, 339. 43 ff., often quoted, because of the rarity of written evidence on such matters).

**515**  Grant, *APT*, 38. But on Spain see above, n.510.

**516**  Wruck, who was making a special study (never published) of Syrian civic coinages, held that a decline came with the accession of Tiberius: in his view, the Syrian cities did not strike coins in anything like the same quantity under Tiberius as they had under Augustus (*Die syrische Provinzialprägung von Augustus bis Traian* (1931), 42). But his words, and his reference to *BMCRE* I as providing evidence for a parallel contraction of official *aes* coinage, lead one to suspect that, like Frank, he confused number and size of issues. (Sutherland, *op. cit.* (n.511), 90, confirms that in Phoenicia and Palestine there were fewer issues than under Augustus, in particular none at Tyre; but he refrains from asserting that total output was markedly reduced. Mattingly held a similar view with regard to coinage in Spain and Africa: as a result of fear inspired in Tiberius by the nationalist movement in Gaul, he 'more and more discouraged local town issues in these two provinces' (*BMCRE* I, p. xviii). However, Grant maintains that, if one compares Tiberius' reign with Augustus' last sixteen years, 'there is no sign of a diminution of local coinage anywhere in the West', and that in the case of colonial and municipal mints in general, 'we reach a somewhat similar conclusion if we look, not at the number of mints but at the extent of their output', while our knowledge of peregrine mints is insufficient to demonstrate any decline (*APT*, 35–40, cf. 140–2).

**517**  See pp. 62–3: cf. n. 474.

**518**  Bellinger, *Troy: The Coins*, 187, 190.

**519**  Konrad Kraft, *Das System der kaiserzeitlichen Münzprägung in Kleinasien* (1972), presenting the evidence for the findings which he had adumbrated earlier, *XI^e*

*Congrès International des Sciences Historiques*, 1960, *Résumés des communications*, 63–4: cf. Bellinger, *Dura* VI, 190.

**520** Kraft, *Das System* . . ., 63–6, refers to 'ganz grobe und bruckstückhafte Andeutungen' that the system of workshops serving large delivery-areas (nineteen) existed already in this period: e.g. under Claudius one mint served at least fifteen places in Phrygia, extending over an area of 240 km from north to south and 150 km from east to west. Co-operation on a smaller scale in pre-Roman Asia Minor had already been proved by L. Robert, *Villes d'Asie mineure* (1935), 188 ff. (ed. 2 (1962), 366 ff.). For a case from Spain see n.509.

**521** A. J. Parker, *NC*⁷ 10 (1970), 326, referring to the republican period. He also points out (327) that the persistence of certain anomalous issues, such as those of Carteia, into imperial times shows that 'the view that all the imperial mints of Spain functioned as a monetary unit is untenable'. But with respect to eastern issues Bellinger shares the view of Grant: 'with Augustus', he says, '. . . we can be sure . . . that now we do meet a general plan' (*Troy: The Coins*, 194). Many of the communities that issued coins were *coloniae* or *municipia*, and these, being in a sense constituent parts of the Roman body politic, clearly did require permission to do so, hence the occasional formula *permissu Augusti*, or the like (at Paestum, exceptionally, S.C.). Even so, it seems to me less certain than is often supposed that the *size* of their issues was dictated, as part of an imperial monetary plan.

**522** M. J. Price, *Hesperia* 36 (1967), 367 f. argues that Corinth may have entered into such arrangements in the second century B.C.

**523** Grant's detailed examination, *FITA*, 4–84, is primarily concerned with their political significance.

**524** Sutherland, *CRIP*, 11, referring to issues attributed to subordinates of Julius Caesar.

**525** *Ibid.*, with reference to all the issues of this period.

**526** *FITA*, 11–13. This issue, and those exemplified by several of the rarer and more puzzling coins which Grant has discussed, may have been purely commemorative in intent.

**527** They constitute the third and fourth of those series which Grant has identified as the six main *aes* coinages of Augustus (*FITA*, 70 ff., 91 ff.; *SMACA*, 1 ff.), that is, 'series which were intended to possess a wider scope than a single province or part of a province' (*SMACA*, 1; cf. Bellinger, *Dura* VI, 190, 202).

**528** This series forms the subject matter of Wruck's book, referred to above, n.516; he believed that it was intended for circulation in Syria only.

**529** Only a small minority are of known provenance, since 'there is still (with encouraging exceptions) little of the careful recording of finds which often occurs in the West' (*SMACA*, 17). See Grant's lists, *FITA*, 98 ff., *SMACA*, 17: add Curium (two: Dorothy H. Cox, *Coins from the Excavations at Curium*, 1952–53 (ANS *Numismatic Notes and Monographs* 145 (1959)); Antioch excavations (eleven: Waage, *Antioch* IV 2 (1952)); Dura (fourteen: *Dura* VI).

**530** See Grant's lists, *FITA*, 102 ff.; *SMACA*, 18; add Antioch (twenty), Curium (five), Dura (three), Delos (two: *Journal international d'archéologie numismatique* 13 (1911), 75 ff.), Elis (one: see n.490), Dodona (four: *ibid.*), Pompeii (one: *N.Sc.* 1899, 203–5), Magdalensberg (*Carinthia* I. 149 (1959)—half of an *as*, 'barbarian'), Ajtoska Banja (two halves: *Izv.BAI* 20 (1955), 579–80), northern Rhaetia (two: *FMRD* I, 1043, 1252: one of these being Grant's 'Oberhausen' coin), Mainz (one: *FMRD* IV, 1148), Vindonissa (one: Kraay, *Vindonissa*).

**531** Civic issues of Antioch and Corinth could perhaps be shown to have travelled as widely in the east, but I know of only one Corinthian imperial piece found in Germany (*FMRD* II, 1086).

**532** The scarcity of excavation finds has to be set against the impression made on Grant by his 'inspection of collections such as Zagreb, Sofia, Afyonkarahisar and

Antakya and of the contents of Turkish bazaars' which led him to regard disbelief in the importance he attributed to these series as 'entirely wrong' (*SMACA*, 126 n.1). One awaits eagerly the publication of the coin finds from the current excavations at Sardes, in order to assess the significance of the isolated datum (Buttrey, *AJA* 76 (1972), 32 n.10) that nineteen halves of *asses* of our second series have been found (the earlier excavators found only two *asses* of this series: see *Sardis* XI (1916)).

**533**  It may have been produced, in part at least, at the same mint, or at least in the same city, as some of the *cistophori*: cf. Mattingly *BMCRE* I, pp. cxix, cxxii.

**534**  Mattingly and Sydenham, *RIC* I, p. 52; cf. *BMCRE* I, p. cxxv, following Froehner, *Mélanges d'épigraphie et d'archéologie* 22 (1875), 76: an interpretation that fits in with a coherent view of Augustan *aes* coinage, according to which Augustus was trying to find ways and means of seeming not to claim the right to strike *aes* coins as an imperatorial prerogative, like the well-established imperatorial right to issue coins of precious metal. Grant has argued that some of the mints producing coins of this series, with this legend, lay outside the province of Asia (*SMACA*, 114–16; *FITA*, 106–7: cf. Sutherland, *CRIP*, 43; a mint in Antioch is accepted by Bellinger, *AJA* 51 (1947), 339, and one in Cyprus by Cox, *op. cit.* (n.529), 113 n.9); but that may be thought a less decisive objection than the lack of parallels for *Caesaris auctoritate*, proposed by Grant. Though this problem cannot be pursued further here, it may be noted that the *asses*, the coins of this series most commonly found, do not bear the legend CA.

**535**  Cf. Mattingly, *Roman Coins²*, 191. Adherence to this interpretation involves the rejection of Kraft's hypothesis that the letters SC on the *aes* of the Roman mint, and on these coins of the series under discussion, refer merely to the senatorial decree which conferred on Augustus honours to which the coin types allude (cf. also Wruck, *op. cit.* (n.516), 5), a hypothesis which is largely persuasive: Kraft rightly stresses Augustus' anxiety to advertise his relationship with the Senate; but does not seem to me to explain adequately the size of the letters in proportion to the symbols. It would remain to consider why there should have been two eastern series, but this is not the place for suggestions, especially as the chronology of both series is still controversial.

**536**  Under Tiberius SC coins were produced, in Grant's opinion, at several mints besides Antioch (*FITA*, 100; *SMACA*, 125): for Wruck, *op. cit.* (n.516), 5, Antioch was the only mint under Augustus and Tiberius.

**537**  For an earlier eastern issue under Tiberius, which may also have been large, see above, n.490.

**538**  Cessation of Roman official issues in the eighties: Grueber, *British Museum Catalogue of Coins of the Roman Republic* (1910), I, 359; *CRR*, p. xxxiv. Spasmodic issues of *aes* were made by Roman generals or their deputies in and after the forties in various places outside Italy, to meet military needs, but, to judge from finds, hardly any part of these issues reached Italy, apart from Sextus Pompeius' issue in Sicily. The colony of Paestum, which for some reason had continued to strike small *aes* coins after the coinages of other Italian communities had ceased, went on producing issues after the eighties (Mommsen, *Geschichte des römischen Münzwesens*, 338), and a fair amount of this Paestan *aes* seems to have been in circulation at Pompeii (see, for example, *AIIN* 2 (1955), 189–92; 4 (1957), 198–200; 5–6 (1958–59), 270–8), but it does not appear to have circulated further afield, and production was no doubt on quite a small scale.

**539**  Crawford, *JRS* 60 (1970), 47. Reference to another possible explanation is made in Appendix A. Buttrey's view is that 'there was already enough in circulation. Certainly the older sextantal and uncial *asses* went on circulating in enormous quantities decade after decade, into the first century of our era' (*AJA* 76 (1972),

40 n.56). But the fact that these went on circulating does not seem to prove that there was no shortage prior to the inception of Augustus' *aes* coinage.

**540** *CRR*, 1335–36. For instance, in a hoard of 719 Roman *aes* coins extending down to A.D. 97, found in 1961 near Bolsena, there were twenty-one of these coins, as against ninety-six republican *aes* coins and 372 from the whole of Augustus' reign: Jean-Pierre Callu and F. Panvini Rosati, *Mél. d'Arch. et d'Hist. de l'Éc. Fr. de Rome* 76 (1964), 1–96, esp. 63–4; and coins recovered from the river Liri included ten of them, against 331 (many of smaller denominations) and fifty-four: Bruce W. Frier and Anthony Parker, *NC*[7] 10 (1970), 89–109.

**541** In Italy the coins most commonly halved were republican *asses* and those of Sextus Pompeius and of Octavian (*CRR*, 1335–36). Thus finds in the river Liri (among which coins of small denominations may be abnormally numerous) included ninety-one whole republican *asses*, twenty-four halves and one quarter, two whole *asses* of Sextus Pompeius and one half (*NC*[7] 10 (1970), 89 ff.); finds in American excavations at Cosa included eighty-nine whole *asses* and nineteen halves (in the American Academy at Rome: Buttrey, *AJA* 76 (1972), 39).

**542** Site finds suggest that an even larger proportion of *quadrantes* than of larger *aes* coins remained in Italy. They are relatively most numerous in finds from Pompeii (1,827 Augustus–Hadrian, against 4,274 *asses* and *dupondii*: Breglia, *op. cit.* (n.424)) and the river Liri (thirty-five of Augustus, against fifty *asses* and *dupondii*: see n.540); cf. nn.462, 475. We can only guess for what purposes they were produced.

**543** Kraay, *Vindonissa*, 27, 33 n.46.

**544** For this system see G. R. Watson, *Historia* 5 (1956), 339–40.

**545** *RIC* I, 55.

**546** Denis van Berchem, *Les Distributions de blé et d'argent à la plèbe romaine sous l'empire* (1939), 163.

**547** *Ibid.*, 167–8.

**548** *RIC* I Augustus, 369–71: see below, n.571.

**549** Kraay, *Vindonissa*, 28. Evidently he takes it for granted that *aes* coins might be used for *congiaria* or donatives, for elsewhere (*Mattingly Essays* (see n.54), 133, 136) he suggests that countermarks may sometimes have been applied to existing coins on such occasions, in lieu of the minting of new coins, e.g. to Augustan coins the countermarks TIB, TIB IM, TIB AVG in connection with 'the payment to the troops of the bequests of Augustus'.

**550** Van Berchem, *op. cit.* (n.546), 123.

**551** Grant could point to only one example found in Italy (more precisely, in Cisalpine Gaul) of each of the two eastern *aes* series discussed above; only one example, also, of the *aes* of Nemausus, which he regards as another of the main *aes* coinages of Augustus (add one of our second eastern series, from Pompeii: see n.530). Examples of the huge Lugdunum series, though less scarce than these eastern coins, are also relatively scarce south of the Alps. Grant notes two, another was found at Minturnae (cf. n.425), another two in recent excavations at Luni (against ten from the Roman mint: *AIIN* 12–14 (1965–67)), but there were none in the Pozzarello (Bolsena) hoard of 719 Roman *aes* coins, which included 372 of Augustus from the Roman mint (J.-P. Callu and F. Panvini Rosati, *op. cit.* (n.540), 52 ff.), none in a Pompeian hoard of *denarii* and *aes*, which included thirty-five Augustan *aes* coins from the Roman mint (*N.Sc.* 1882, 320–1), none among the coins recovered from the river Liri at Minturnae (see n.540), none from excavations at Aquileia, which produced five Augustan and nine Tiberian *aes* coins from the Roman mint (G. Brusin, *Gli scavi di Aquileia* (1934)). Similarly, among published finds from the Magdalensberg in Noricum, there were only seven or eight (and four Nemausus *asses*) against a hundred or so Augustan *aes* coins from the Roman mint (cf. n.425).

**552**  It is thus somewhat misleading to state that despite the travel (outside Italy) of 'occasional examples of Augustan *aes* . . ., finds in Gaul are predominantly of the mint of Lugdunum' (David W. MacDowall, *NC*⁷ 7 (1967), 44).

**553**  Sutherland, *CRIP*, 48 (in the context of wide-ranging hypotheses concerning Augustus' monetary policy and other aspects of his regime); cf. Grant, *FITA*, 91 ff.

**554**  Thus, for instance, among Augustan *aes* coins found in the Fourvière (Lugdunum) excavations, there were five Nemausus coins, one civic *semis* of Copia (Lugdunum) (cf. *FITA*, 208), four official Lugdunum *asses*, but no coins from the Roman mint: *Gallia*, Supplément IV (1951), 81. Likewise no Augustan coins from the Roman mint were included in the finds from the River Mayenne (n.416), Font-Garnier (Charente-Inf.) (n.129), Hussigny (Meurthe-et-Moselle) (n.458), Montmaurin (Haute-Garonne) (*Gallia*, Supplément X (1969), 335 ff.) and only one in the find from Port Haliguen, Quiberon (n.458). Even at Augusta Raurica finds of Augustan *aes* from the Roman mint, though quite numerous, are less numerous in relation to finds of Lugdunum *aes* than at Vindonissa—the proportion being approximately 4:6 as against 6:4 (Hugo Doppler, *Provincialia, Festschrift für Rudolf Laur-Belart* (1968), 71–2). (But at Glanum Roman *aes* dominates: *Gallia*, Supplément I (1946); XI (1958).)

**555**  Chantraine (*Novaesium* III, 34) speaks of it as 'circulating mainly in the time of Tiberius' (cf. Kraft, *Mainzer Zeitschrift* 46/47 (1951–52), 30). But one must not try to draw too precise conclusions from these find statististics: see Wells, *op. cit.* (n.199), 283–6.

**556**  Cf. Anne S. Robertson, *NC*⁷ 8 (1968), 66, on 'the evidence . . . that in spite of the cost of transporting heavy *aes* coins in bulk, consignments of *asses* at least were delivered from the main mints to Britain for the payment of troops'.

**557**  That is what Kraay, for instance, appears to assume in *Vindonissa*.

**558**  Cf. n.556. However, T. V. Buttrey seems not to share Robertson's view, for he remarks that for the Rhine armies, after the closing of the Lugdunum mint, 'coins had to be provided from the mint at Rome, and indirectly at that, through movement in normal circulation' (*AJA* 76 (1972), 42).

**559**  Including the possibility that part of some Tiberian issues traditionally ascribed to the Roman mint was struck elsewhere: see n.571.

**560**  Thus in the seventeenth century, when there were frequent shortages of money, 'faute de mieux, on voyait même de gros paiements faits en billon' (Jean Meuvret, *Annales* 15.1 (1960), 571, reviewing Frank Spooner, *L'Économie mondiale et les frappes monétaires en France, 1493–1680* (1956)): and in Priene in the late second century B.C. 'bei dem fast völligen Mangel an Silbergeld das Publikum nach der Bronze als Hauptumlaufsmittel griff und sie sorglich thesaurierte, weil schlechtes Geld eben besser als gar keines ist' (Regling, *Die Münzen von Priene* (1927), 175).

**561**  Bellinger has pointed out (*Mattingly Studies* (see n.54), 148) that 'the coining of bronze was a valuable privilege since the face value of the coins was greater than their bullion value. In the case of "imperial" issues the profit went to the emperor', going on to suggest that 'Augustus' primary purpose in creating his international [*aes*] currency was fiscal'. It has indeed been suggested that in the last years of his reign the average weight of the *as* was reduced considerably, from 11·26 g to 10·40 g: see J.-B. Giard, *Rev.num*⁶ 10 (1968), 79, 96–8. (*Denarii* at a premium: n.475.)

**562**  Mattingly referred to these as 'the coins of Tiberius himself' and 'the coins of his son Drusus' (*BMCRE* I, p. cxxxii), meaning thus to distinguish them from coins struck during Tiberius' reign but not bearing the portrait of either: this is one of those conventional numismatic usages that are somewhat confusing to the layman. It is likewise customary, and confusing, as Guey has pointed out (*XI*ᵉ *Congrès International des Sciences Historiques*, Stockholm, 1960, *Rapports* II, 55) that the word 'coins' has to be understood here, as we shall see, to mean what Frank called 'issues', and what Guey has proposed calling 'varieties'.

**563** Mattingly, *loc. cit.* (n.562). This has recently been disputed by Michael Grant, who has argued (*Roman Anniversary Issues* (1950), 31 ff.) that many Tiberian issues were not made in the years of tribunician power indicated in the legend, but C. H. V. Sutherland has shown (*CRIP*, 191–5, 198) that there are 'some strong arguments against the "deferred" view', except in so far as there may have been a time-lag due rather to 'a delay in distribution than in actual production'.

**564** *Aes* was minted officially in Syria in A.D. 31/32 (above, n.556): but no one would suggest that this could have had any effect on supplies in Italy; it merely illustrates the care of the authorities to make provision for the armies as and when required.

**565** Mattingly, *BMCRE*, I p. cxxxiii.

**566** *Divus Augustus Pater: RIC* I, p. 95 Nos. 1–6 (his *providentia*: No. 6); Agrippa: *RIC* I, Tiberius 32.
For the size of these issues see Table III.

**567** 'It is probable that these coins [the various issues in honour of Augustus] were issued largely for the West of the Empire, but at the mint of Rome; the same is true of the *asses* of Agrippa': Mattingly, *BMCRE* I, pp. cxxii–cxxiii.
Of the 'Providentia' *asses* found at Vindonissa, about 250 are well enough preserved to have enabled Kraay to divide them into two main groups; about eighty, of finer style, might be ascribed, he believes, to the mint of Rome, the other 170 or so to a mint nearer Vindonissa, especially as die links, otherwise rare in this issue, suggest a local mint. Of the 'Agrippa' *asses*, the ninety that are well preserved again, in his view, fall into two groups, twenty-seven that might be Roman, sixty-three that might be from the same provincial mint, though better in style than the 'Providentia' *asses* ascribed to it (Kraay, *Vindonissa*, 34–5; cf. *JRS* 53 (1963), 177). (Wells, *op. cit.* (n.199), 277, states categorically that the 'Providentia' issue was 'struck not only in Italy but also, despite the legend, in the provinces', but to Jameson, who divides the 'Agrippa' *asses* into three groups (see Appendix C), 'it appears probable that the coins of both these issues were struck in Rome.') There was no need in Gaul for a fresh issue before the early twenties, because production of an issue of Lugdunum 'altar' *asses*, in the name of Tiberius (*RIC* I Augustus, 369–71) had begun at the very end of Augustus' reign—one of the largest issues of the first century (though it included some overstriking of worn Nemausus *asses*, creating *asses* that were still abnormally heavy, despite the wear, and that have therefore been taken for *dupondii*: see Chantraine, *Novaesium* III, 16–17). This whole vast issue would appear to have been produced in the short period between Tiberius' seventh acclamation as *imperator*, in A.D. 12 (Hohl, *Sitzungsberichte der Deutschen Akademie der Wissenschaften, Berlin, Klasse für Gesellschaftswissenschaften*, 1952) and Augustus' death—in which case most of it must have gone into store. (Kraay has suggested (*Vindonissa* 28) that it might have continued for a time after Tiberius' accession, but this would not affect our argument.)

**568** For the scarcity in Italy of *aes* struck under Augustus in the west outside Italy, see n.551. For the relative abundance in Italy of 'Providentia' *asses* and 'Agrippa' *asses*, see Table III.

**569** *RIC* I, p. 100, following E. A. Sydenham, *NC*⁴ 7 (1917), 258–78, who was for the most part developing views expressed by L. Laffranchi (*Rivista italiana di numismatica* 23 (1910), 21 ff.).

**570** See Appendix C.

**571** See Appendix C.

**572** It is curious, therefore, that Sutherland still lays stress on the issues of A.D. 34–7 as 'the resultant new coinage of *aes*', struck 'in the face of a severe economic crisis' (*CRIP*, 103), especially since, as we have seen (n.568) he is inclined to attribute the 'Agrippa' *asses* to Gaius. 'There is much to be said for the view that production [of *aes* coinage] proceeded without interruption under Tiberius' (Kraay, *Vindonissa*, 10).

**573**  The *dupondii* of the Roman mint which are dated only by reference to Tiberius as IMP VIII (*RIC* I Tiberius, 30–1) could have been produced at any time between A.D. 18 and Tiberius' death (and have been assigned to A.D. 34–7 by Grant, *Roman Anniversary Issues* (1950), 47 f.) but the two issues are die-linked, and Sutherland assigns one to A.D. 23 on historical grounds (*JRS* 28 (1938), 137; cf. *CRIP*, 98 f.). They were in any case small (see Table III).

## Conclusion: notes 574–579

**574**  Gaius and Claudius may have followed suit. The abundance of imitations of Claudian *aes* coins, in not only Spain (see n.510) but also Gaul and Britain, might appear to point to the opposite conclusion, but their very abundance, not least in military contexts, suggests that production was tolerated, if not sponsored, by the imperial authorities. At Dura 'the peak of the early Roman coins is under Claudius' (*Dura* VI, 203); at Thamusida 'the very abundant coins of Claudius I circulated so long as *aes* coins of that size were in use' (R. Rebuffat, *Thamusida* II (1970), 55).

**575**  It is perhaps of some use to compare the quantity of Augustan *aes* found on some particular site or in some area or included in a hoard with the quantity of Tiberian *aes* found. The quantities have been expressed in terms of *asses*, Nemausus coins being counted as *asses*; halved *asses* have been counted as *semisses*. Coins struck by local authorities in the provinces (with the exception of those of Nemausus) have been excluded from the reckoning; so have doubtful and allegedly barbarian coins. 'Agrippa' *asses* have been listed separately. The figures are, of course, only approximate.

|  | Augustus | Tiberius | Agrippa |
|---|---|---|---|
| *FMRL* | 256 | 31 | 21 |
| *FMRD* | 1,381 | 714 | 263 |
| Neuss 1955–62 (*Novaesium* III) | 916 | 130 | 25 |
| Vindonissa | 2,424 | 3,574 | 199 |
| Puy-de-Dôme (Flavian hoard of 122 *aes* coins: see n.472) | 28 | 12 | 11 |
| Pozzarello (hoard of 719 *aes* coins to A.D. 97: see n.540) | 471 | 67 | 19 |
| Magdalensberg (see n.425) | 136 | 40 | 15 |
| Minturnae (see n.425) | 15 | 26 | 6 |
| River Liri (see n.540) | 48 | 59 | 7 |

The Neuss figures, set alongside the *FMRD* figures, would suggest, *prima facie*, as the finds from earlier excavations had already suggested to Strack (*Bonner Jahrbücher* 108/109 (1902), 424) that occupation was on a smaller scale during part of Tiberius' reign: but Chantraine disputes this (*Novaesium* III, 34). The Pozzarello figures do suggest that in Italy much less, per annum, was contributed to the stock of *aes* currency by Tiberius than by Augustus. But the figures from the Minturnae area conspicuously fail to confirm this. These various discrepancies are a salutary reminder that 'bei dem geringen Wandern der Bronzemünzen . . . örtliche Gegebenheiten von Einfluss sind' (Chantraine, *ibid.*).

**576**  Suetonius (Tib. 47 f.) is malicious: see e.g. Tac., *Ann.* 1.75, 2.47, Dio 57.10.

**577**  Kraay, *Vindonissa*, 8; Chantraine, *Novaesium* III, 11. This can be brought out most clearly in a table analysing, in terms of *asses*, the large mass of published *aes* coins of the early imperial period found at Vindonissa and at Neuss in the excavations of 1955–62: see Table IV. (A separate column has been provided for halved *asses*, each half being reckoned as a *semis*. The *aes* coins of Nemausus, which have been included among coins of Augustus and which were frequently halved, are counted as *asses*.) What emerges unmistakably is the steadily increasing use of *dupondii* and *sestertii*. (Even if the imperial bronze coinage was not fiduciary (see n.475) this would not affect the present argument.)

**578** 'From the middle of the third century B.C. an ever increasing stream of coin and bullion flowed into the Roman treasury from countries overseas . . . The chief result of this vast influx of coin and bullion was that the Roman people paid little or nothing for the initial conquest and the continued garrisoning of their expanding Empire . . . There is no evidence to estimate how much of the profits of the provinces went to the treasury, and how much into the pockets of the Roman upper class, but there are a number of figures which suggest that private profits greatly exceeded public revenue' (A. H. M. Jones, *op. cit.* (n.185), 81–2, 86.)

**579** 'Economic theory is little understood today and we can hardly credit the Roman financiers with even our limited knowledge. The immediate need was always their guide. They took such measures as it dictated and had to bear the consequences as best they might' (Mattingly, *Roman Coins*², 86).

# APPENDICES

## A Halved coins

All the halved coins found in Italy and the great majority of those found in Sicily (where Mamertine *pentonkia* were also cut; Buttrey, *loc. cit.* (n. 465), 39–40, cf. n.500) and in Gaul away from the military zone are bronze *asses* which were struck by the republican government, by the sons of Pompey, by Octavian, or by Gallic *coloniae*. All except Octavian's have as obverse type a Janiform head, or two heads back to back; they were nearly always cut between the heads. Halves of such coins occur also in the military zone along the Rhine and at Oberhausen and on the Magdalensberg (n.466), but so do halves of Augustus' new smaller, lighter copper *asses* (except at Oberaden, where the new *asses* are not represented, except by one fragmentary piece) and a few halves of Tiberian *asses*. Halves of these smaller *asses* do not occur at all in Italy and Sicily and they are much less common elsewhere in Gaul than halves of the larger *asses* (though Buttrey, *ibid.*, 41 and n.58, seems to be wrong in stating that they are unknown in southern France: relevant published evidence is scanty, but of the eight Augustan pieces found in the excavation of a Gallo-Roman villa at Montmaurin (Haute-Garonne) one and four halves were Nemausus coins, two and a half were Lugdunum altar *asses*: M. Labrousse, *Gallia* Supplement xx (1969), 335 ff.).

Buttrey has concluded, after a very engaging presentation of much of the evidence and the earlier discussions, that we have here phenomena separate in significance and separated in time 'by roughly half a century' (*ibid.*, 40). He agrees that the only plausible explanation of the halving of the lighter *asses* is that it was done to meet a demand for *semisses* (in his view, only among soldiers), but he suggests that the halving of the heavier *asses* was a sequel to a retariffing of them as *dupondii*, officially decreed when the production of the new *asses* began.

This raises several difficulties, which can be mentioned only briefly here. It is not an objection that we know nothing of such a retariffing; we have so little information on monetary matters beyond what we can extract from the coins themselves. But there are the practical difficulties that would have been involved in retariffing millions of coins, by no means negligible in purchasing power, without withdrawing them. For instance, those who were first to hear of the impending edict could have hurried to change *denarii* into *asses*, using their inside knowledge like the friends of Solon in Androtion's story (Aristotle, *Resp. Ath.* 6. 2). *Prima facie*, such a retariffing would have had the advantage of vastly expanding, at a stroke, in terms of purchasing power, the supply of money in everyday use (a point which Buttrey does not make, since he does not believe that there was any shortage of *aes* currency); but prices would probably have been pushed up as a result. Augustus made his new light *as* and his relatively even lighter *dupondius* acceptable as such by striking them in copper and *orichalcum* respectively, instead of *aes*; to make people, other than those who had cornered a large supply of old *asses*, willing to believe that coins that had always been recognisable and recognised as *asses* were now worth double would not have been as easy. It was probably because, early in the first century B.C., after many reductions had been stomached, people would not accept as *asses* new bronze coins of a much lower weight—semuncial *asses*—that production of *aes* ceased altogether, continued production of uncial *asses* having perhaps become too costly (cf. Mattingly *Roman Coins*[2], 27; Grant, *FITA*, 3: though Buttrey, *op. cit.*, 40 n.56, objects that 'there is no evidence for this at all'): and it was probably for the same reason, as Grant has argued (e.g. *SMACA*, 4–7) that Julius Caesar made the first experiments in the use of a different alloy, *orichalcum*, that might appear more valuable.

And what would have been the effect of the retariffing on western civic issues generally, especially those of Spain?

Moreover, there is no need to suppose that the halving of the heavier *asses* had practically ceased before the halving of lighter *asses* began. The finding of lighter *asses* at Oberhausen—163, and fifty-two halves—shows that the phenomena cannot be separated by more than, roughly, one quarter of a century; but surely the simplest explanation is that the larger, two-headed *asses*, which lent themselves so well to halving, were halved wherever and whenever they were available in sufficient quantity to meet whatever demand there was for *semisses*—not least after the smaller *asses* became freely available. It is quite conceivable that halving of them continued for as long as the halving of the smaller *asses*: that is, indeed, what is suggested by the fact that the proportion of the larger *asses* that had been halved is far higher (74 per cent) in the latest of the camps, Vindonissa, founded at a time and place at which lighter *asses* would be circulating freely, than in the earlier camps, Oberaden (28 per cent) and Haltern (37 per cent) (but see n.466 for another factor in this difference). The demand for *semisses* may have been more prolonged in Gaul, as on the frontier, than it was in Italy, but in Gaul most of the demand was in effect met by the continued production of *asses* at Nemausus; in the camps the smaller *asses* that were sent to them (cf. n.556), alongside those that travelled to them in normal circulation, constituted an ever-increasing proportion of the supply, so there had to be some recourse to these for halving: likewise at the town on the Magdalensberg, to which money must have flowed from Italy rather than from Gaul.

So it does not seem necessary to abandon the view that *asses* were halved in order to provide coins worth half an *as*, for which there was for some time, in some areas, a demand which the Roman authorities did not trouble to satisfy.


## B   Bigati

According to Pliny (*NH* 33. 46) and, seemingly, Festus (*Excerpta Pauli*, p. 98M), *bigati* and *quadrigati* were so called because the (reverse) type depicted a *biga* or a *quadriga*. The only other Roman writer to use the term *bigatus* is Livy; he uses it to designate Roman silver money in nine passages, one (23. 15. 5) relating to an episode in 216 B.C., the other eight reporting spoils won in Gallia Cisalpina or in Spain and carried in triumphs between 197 and 190. Most scholars think that he intended it to bear the meaning which Pliny and Festus, and presumably Festus' source Verrius Flaccus, attached to it. However, it is now almost certain that no Roman coins bearing this type, and indeed no *denarii* at all, were in circulation as early as 216 B.C. We must therefore dismiss the use of the word in the first passage as an anachronistic error. But the other passages also constitute a problem, for it is hard to see why all or most of the Roman coins that fell into the hands of victorious

Roman generals in those regions in the 190s should have borne this type (which, indeed, some numismatists believe not to have been used at all before 190), rather than the Dioscuri type most commonly used on early *denarii*.

Mattingly therefore suggested an alternative interpretation (*JRS* 35 (1945), 76 n.47). *Bigatus*, he thought, might have become a popular nickname for the *denarius*, like the 'half-crown' of pre-decimal British currency (he did not alude to this parallel), without reference to the type, simply because the *denarius* weighed half as much as a coin which it superseded, which Livy refers to as a *quadrigatus* in three passages relating to 216 B.C. (22. 52. 3, 54. 1, 58. 4), and which modern numismatists also call by that name. (Since, however, Mattingly believed, in 1945, that no *denarii* had been struck before 187, he suggested that the term *bigatus* was, to begin with, applied to the coin now generally called the *victoriatus*.) It is note-worthy that the *quadrigatus* was, in fact, quite often halved in southern Italy and Sicily before the minting of the smaller coins began (e.g. *RRCH*, 48, 58, 61, 93: this was pointed out by Leslie R. Neatby, *AJA* 1951, 241 ff.).

If this theory is correct, the word *bigatus* was perhaps already misunderstood by Livy (if he stopped to think what it meant): not surprisingly, for as we have seen, already by the time of Verrius Flaccus it seems to have been taken to refer to the type. However, Rudi Thomsen, who has conveniently summarised views expressed down to 1955 on this question (*Early Roman Coinage* I (1957), 210–47), has emphasised a difficulty involved in Mattingly's theory, that in the eight Livian passages referring to triumphs between 197 and 190 B.C. the word is used in what appear to be *verbatim* extracts from official records (*op. cit.*, II (1961), 184–97: the view that Livian passages of this kind are derived from official documents gains support from the work of Gast, 'Die zensorischen Bauberichte bei Livius und die römischen Bauinschriften' (Diss. Göttingen, 1965)).

Moreover, Mattingly's theory does not explain why Tacitus chose to use the word. If he had supposed it to be simply a nickname of the *denarius*, applicable to all *denarii* alike, his remark would be senseless.

Presumably, therefore, Tacitus, like Verrius Flaccus and Pliny, took the word to refer to the type. But why should Germans have preferred *denarii* which bore on the reverse a representation of a *biga*? It is intelligible that they should have favoured coins that were clearly distinguishable from the issues, beginning with Julius Caesar's in Gaul, that were found to contain a high proportion of plated coins (see n.217), and at the time at which Tacitus wrote the *Germania* their suspicion might well have embraced Flavian coins, which were in fact more dependable, since they could not readily be distinguished by the illiterate from earlier, more dubious imperial coins. But why should they have preferred coins depicting a *biga* to the numerous early *denarii* that bore one or other of two equally distinctive types, a *quadriga* or the Dioscuri on horseback? To escape from this difficulty, Much, commenting on *Germania* 5. 5 (see n.212), suggested that coins with a *quadriga* type could have been called *bigati*, and Seltman (*NC*[6] 4 (1944), 79) argued that the horses of the Dioscuri could be described as a *biga*, but neither proposal is wholly convincing.

It would be convenient to suppose that Tacitus intended his two words to cover republican silver in general: as we have seen, there would have been some reason for such a preference, and there would have been no great difficulty in catering for it, although the evidence does not permit us to affirm that there was in fact an abnormally high proportion of republican silver among the Roman coins used in trade with the Germans down to the time of Tacitus. However, it is hard to believe that he would have used strange old words quite so carelessly and ambiguously.

## C  The dates of two main *aes* issues

The possibility that the great issue of *asses* in honour of Agrippa (*RIC* 1 Tiberius, 32) should be assigned to Gaius' reign was recognised by Mattingly (*BMCRE* 1 p. cxxxiii), but in recent years Michael Grant (e.g. *NC*[6] 8 (1948), 125–6) and C. H. V. Sutherland (e.g. *CRIP*, 102) have come out strongly in favour of this view, and several other scholars have advanced arguments in support of it. 'These undated pieces,' Sutherland wrote, 'whose abundant frequency has for long made them a puzzle to interpret, were more probably struck under Gaius, to judge from the date of other coinages which reproduce this design', although he regarded it as 'just possible' that they came out 'at the very end of Tiberius' principate' (*CRIP*, 102 n.2). Since Sutherland wrote, Anne Robertson (*Roman Imperial Coins in the Hunter Coin Cabinet* 1 (1962), p. lxv) has added a technical argument in favour of inception under Gaius—the fact that the obverse and reverse types on these coins are regularly at 180° in relation to one another, for this did not become the regular die-arrangement for *aes* coinage before Gaius' reign (it was usual in the middle year of Tiberius' reign, but not dominant). These arguments have convinced D. W. MacDowall (*NC*[7] 7 (1967), 47 n.5) that 'the majority of issues must have been Caligulan', while J.-B. Giard believes that attribution of the whole issue to Gaius is, at present, the most probable hypothesis, on grounds of community both of style and of countermarks (*Rev. num*[6]. 10 (1968), 80–1). H. Chantraine holds that the find evidence also points to inception after Tiberius' death (*Novaesium* III, 13).

However, Sydenham had already urged (*NC*[4] 17 (1917)) that Gaius' reign was too short for 'so vast an issue', and after the publication of Sutherland's book Carl Küthmann argued afresh in favour of attributing the whole issue to the reign of Tiberius, other *aes* issues being, in his view, ample in number and size to fill Gaius' reign (*Schweizer Münzblätter* 4 (1954), 73–7). He suggested that the coins of Caesaraugusta in Spain which Sutherland gave as his example of coins reproducing the design of the Agrippa *asses* were probably struck, not under Gaius, as Sutherland held, but under Tiberius, in A.D. 37, and that the appearance of countermarks of Claudius' reign on some of the Agrippa *asses* (Kraay, *Vindonissa*, 48) is not at all surprising, the reign of Gaius having been so short. He suggested also that the reign of Tiberius is the most likely historical context for this advertising of Agrippa, since there was a strong personal tie, through Vipsania, between Agrippa and Tiberius (C. E. Stevens has quoted Velleius (2. 127) for Agrippa's high standing *c*. A.D. 30 (*NC*[7] 3 (1963), 262)) but, despite the fact that Gaius was Agrippa's grandson, none between Agrippa and Gaius (cf. Suetonius, *Gaius*, 23). Professor H. B. Mattingly has said, in conversation, that he still regards these historical considerations as weightier than the numismatic arguments against inception under Tiberius. He believes that the bulk, at least, of this issue was produced between 23 and 31 (cf. n.576), while Seianus was influential. Unfortunately the political question, *cui bono*?—who is most likely to have wished to advertise Agrippa, above all to the troops on the Rhine and the Danube frontiers, and at what period?—can not be given an answer that will convince everyone, as is shown by the diversity of the views about personal relationships at this period that have been put forward (see, for instance, Ann Boddington, *AJP* 84 (1963), 1–16).

Shelagh Jameson, however, has argued, on the evidence of the die-axis and of 'hybrids' that occur, that one of the three groups into which she believes the issue can be divided began to be produced in about 22 or 23; minting 'will have covered a span of several years' (*NC*[7] 7 (1967), 95–124). But Professor Robertson, as we have seen, draws a different conclusion from the die-axis, and John Nicols (ANS *Museum Notes* 19 (1974)) has shown the flimsiness of the 'hybrid' evidence. Moreover, the fact that eighteen halves of *asses* of the other great issue, celebrating the *providentia* of Augustus, were found at Vindonissa, but no halves of these *asses* is, as he says, 'fairly strong evidence against assigning a mid-Tiberian date to the Agrippa *as*' (cf. Appendix A and Table III).

If one weighs up the numismatic and the historical arguments, no one of which is decisive, it seems most likely that production of these *asses* began in the later years of Tiberius' reign, already with the intention, at least, that the issue should be large. However, C. M. Kraay, while believing that the major part of it, including all the coins struck in Rome, belongs to Tiberius' last years, has pointed to find evidence indicating that in Gaul some production continued for much longer (*Vindonissa*, 10, 35); and Jameson attributes her other two groups, mainly on stylistic grounds, to the reigns of Gaius and Claudius respectively. But Giard regards any seemingly Claudian examples as unofficial imitations (*Rev. num.*[6] 10 (1968), 80–1), and Nicols argues that the find evidence indicates that under Claudius these *asses* 'were not struck in any significant numbers' (*op. cit.*, 82).

The view of Laffranchi, Sydenham and Mattingly that the other great issue of *asses* discussed above, the issue celebrating the *providentia* of Augustus (*RIC* I, p. 95.6) 'should be assigned on account of their finer style . . . most probably to the years A.D. 23–32' (see n.567) has since been defended by C. H. V. Sutherland with additional technical and stylistic arguments (*NC*[6] I (1941), 97–116: 'A.D. 22/23–30 ?'; cf. *CRIP*, 99 n.1: 'produced in the mid or late twenties'). It has been accepted by Anne Robertson (*op. cit.* (n.556), pp. liv ff.), by J. B. Giard (*Rev. num.*[6] 10 (1968), 110), and for use in *FMRD* (see Hans Gebhart and Konrad Kraft, *JbNumG* 7 (1956), 26). However, Michael Grant (*Roman Anniversary Issues*, 62–3) and Harald Küthmann (*Mitteilungen des historischen Vereins vom Pfalz* 58 (1960), 69 (*non vidi*) would date its inception somewhat later, *c.* A.D. 30, and Sir Ronald Syme (*Tacitus* (1958), 754) has suggested that it is related to the destruction of Seianus. Kraay, while accepting the most widely favoured date, the early twenties, for its inception, believes, on the strength of 'rare examples (of non-Roman style but not barbarous) overstruck upon *asses* of Caligula' that 'some production continued' in Gaul, if not at Rome, 'at least into his reign' (*JRS* 53 (1963), 177, cf. *Vindonissa*, 10, 29, 35).

# TABLES

**Table I** Gold and silver hoards and settlement finds.
Unless otherwise stated, numbers relate throughout to *denarii* or (*aurei*).

| Hoards | A | B | C | D | E | F | G | H | I | J | K | L | M | N | O | P | Q | Other coins and additional data |
|---|---|---|---|---|---|---|---|---|---|---|---|---|---|---|---|---|---|---|
| 1 Maille | 422 | 409 | 4 | 6 | – | – | 3 | 1 | 1 | – | | | | | | | | |
| 2 Metz | 258 | ←—199—→ | | 3 | – | – | 54 | 3 | 1 | – | | | | | | | | |
| 3 Gallignano | 441 | 365 | 54 | 11 | – | – | 8 | 7 | 3 | 14 | | | | | | | | 1 *RIC* Aug., 372 |
| 4 Olbia | 870 | 713 | 108 | 20 | – | – | 18 | 7 | – | 28 | | | | | | | | |
| 5 Penmacor | 84 | 61 | 5 | 2 | – | – | 11 | 5 | 5 | 71 | | | | | | | | |
| 6 Ambenay | (192) | (19) | – | (8) | – | (7) | (28) | (5) | (124) | 3 | | | | | | | | (1) *RIC* Aug., 372 |
| 7 Tibru | 194 | 138 | – | 5 | – | 1 | 25 | 6 | 17 | 1 | | | | | | | | 1 Hadrian, 1 Antoninus *denarii* |
| 8 Strimba | 212 | 198 | – | 4 | – | 1 | 2 | 2 | 5 | 2 | | | | | | | | 3 barbarous *denarii* |
| 9 Este | 285 | 200^a | 50 | 2 | – | 1 | 13 | 7 | 13 | 17 | | | | | | | | 1 Augustan *aes*; ^a including 2 *quinarii* |
| 10 Pravoslav | 58 | 33 | – | 3 | – | – | 8 | 11 | 3 | 3 | | | | | | | | |
| 11 Seppenrode | 56 | 31 | 5 | – | – | – | 2 | 3 | 3 | 14 | | | | | | | | |
| 12 Aquileia | 560 | 392 | 66 | 8 | – | – | 28 | 11 | 26 | 28 | | | | | | | | 1 *RIC* Aug., 372 |
| 13 Haltern | 184 | 84 | 8 | 2 | – | – | 8 | 3 | 8 | 71 | | | | | | | | |
| 14 Polaniec | 147 | 139 | – | 1 | – | – | – | 3 | 1 | 3 | | | | | | | | |
| 15 Krusevo | 97 | 71^a | 12 | 3 | 2 | 1^b | 4 | 1 | 1 | 2 | | | | | | | | ^a including 5 *quinarii*; ^b *RIC* Aug., 62 |
| 16 Ribnik | 335 | 234 | 65 | 6 | – | 4^b | 16 | 2 | 10 | 2 | | | | | | | | |
| 17 Vicopisano | 177 | 95^a | 37 | 2 | 2 | 4^b | 5 | 10 | 5 | 17 | | | | | | | | ^a including 21 *quinarii*; ^b including 1 *RIC* Aug., 12 |
| 18 West Sicily A | 30 | 20 | 1 | 1 | – | – | 2 | 1 | 1 | 1 | 2 | 1 | | | | | | |
| 19 West Sicily B | 33 | 25 | 1 | 1 | – | – | 2 | 2 | 1 | 1 | 2 | – | | | | | | |
| 20 Fotos | 271 | 259 | 1 | 1 | – | – | 3 | 1 | 1 | 1 | 4 | – | | | | | | |
| 21 Onna | 258 | 182 | 36 | – | – | – | 4 | 1 | 2 | 13 | 20 | – | | | | | | 2 unidentified Augustan *denarii* |
| 22 Feins | 53 | 27 | 8 | 1 | – | – | 1 | – | 2 | 10 | 4 | 1 | | | | | | |
| 23 Mainz A | 53 | 30 | 6 | 1 | – | – | 2 | – | 1 | 11 | 2 | – | | | | | | |
| 24 Lakenheath | 67 | 36 | 5^a | 1 | – | – | 1 | – | 6^a | 6^a | 16 | – | 2 | (4) | | | | 415 British. ^a 1 of each plated |
| 25 Bredgar | (34) | (1) | – | – | – | – | (1) | – | (3) | (8) | (15) | (2) | 2 | 1 | (35) | (2) | | |
| 26 Emona | 31 (1) | 21 | 5 | – | – | – | – | – | 1 | 2 | 1 | – | 1 | 1 | 1 | | | 16 *aes*, Tiberius–Claudius |
| 27 Utrecht | (50) (1) | – | – | 1^b | – | – | (1) | – | – | – | (4) | – | – | (8) | | (2) | | |
| 28 Ostia | 34 | 20^a | 2 | 1^b | 2 | – | – | – | – | 2 | | – | – | – | | 6 | 2 | ^a including 3 *quinarii*; ^b plated |
| 29 Pompeii A | 78 | 48 | 18 | 1 | 1 | 1 | 1 | – | 1 | 2 | | – | – | – | 8 | 1 | 6 | |
| 30 Pompeii B | 216 (45) | 12 | 54 | – | – | – | – | – | – | 1 | | – | – | – | 8 | 8 | 133 (26) | 18 *aes*, Tiberius–Vespasian; 1 republican, 1,048 imperial *aes* |
| 31 Pompeii C | 87 (1) | 56 | 19 | – | – | – | 2 | – | – | (1) | | (3)^a | (1) | (2) | (12) | – | 9 | ^a *quinarii aurei* |
| 32 Pompeii D | 49 (61) | 33 | – | – | – | – | – | – | 1 | – | | – | 1 | (2) | 1 (37) | (1) | 3 (16) | 14 unidentified *denarii* |
| 33 Budge Row | 74 | 26 | 11 | 2 | – | 1 | 1 | 1 | 1 | 3 | 5 | – | | | 2 | (5) | 18 | 7 Vespasian *aes* |
| 34 Mainz B | 14 (9) | 7 | 1 | 1 | – | 1 | 1 | 1 | 1 | 1 | 1 | – | | | (7) | 4 | (2) | |

| Hoards | A | B | C | D | E | F | G | H | I | J | K | L | M | N | O | P | Q | Other coins and additional data |
|---|---|---|---|---|---|---|---|---|---|---|---|---|---|---|---|---|---|---|
| 35 Rheingönheim | 142 (1) | 74[a] | 24 | - | - | 1 | - | - | 1[b] | 1 | 6 (1) | - | - | 3 | - | 31 | 1 | [a] including 9 *quinarii*; [b] plated |
| 36 Friume | 398 (1) | 163 | 47 | - | - | - | 6 | - | 6 | 57 | 58 | - | 2 | 3 | 1 | 10 | 34 | 1 Titus *aureus*, 7 Titus, 1 Domitian, 41 unidentified *denarii* |
| **Sites** | | | | | | | | | | | | | | | | | | |
| **Neuss, 1955–62** | | | | | | | | | | | | | | | | | | |
| AR: good | | 13[a] | 3 | - | 3 | 1 | 2[a] | 1 | - | - | 2 | - | - | 1 | - | - | - | [a] including 1 *quinarius*; [b] cistophorus, *RIC* Aug., 13. 1 unidentified Augustan *denarius* (plated), 2 unidentified *denarii* (plated) |
| plated | | 3 | 2 | 1 | 1 | 1[b] | - | 1 | 2 | 4 | 5 | - | - | 3 | - | - | - | |
| **Vindonissa** | | | | | | | | | | | | | | | | | | |
| AV | | | | | | | | | | | | | (1) | (2) | | | (1) | [a] including 16 *quinarii* |
| AR: good | | 85[a] | 18 | 2 | 5 | - | 2 | - | 2 | 16 | 7 | 1 | 1 | 3 | | 5 | 18 | |
| plated | | 6 | 6 | 1 | - | - | 2 | 3 | 2 | 8 | 3 | 1 | 1 | 1 | | 2 | 2 | |

A   Identified Roman AR and AV coins
B   Republican, other than C and D
C   Legionary (Marcus Antonius)
D   Octavian (Imp. Caesar, Caesar Divi filius) included in *RIC* I
E   *Quinarii*, *RIC* Aug., 18
F   Augustus, East
G   Augustus, 'Spain'
H   Augustus, Rome
I   Augustus, Gaul, except J
J   Augustus, *RIC* Aug., 350
K   Tiberius, *RIC* Tib., 3
L   Tiberius, others
M   Gaius
N   Claudius
O   Nero
P   Civil wars, Galba, Otho, Vitellius
Q   Vespasian

Table I: Reference to publications.

1   *Rev.num.*[6] 5 (1963)
2   *ZfN* 9 (1882), 11 (1884)
3   *NSc* 1930
4   *NSc* 1904, *AIIN* 7–8 (1960–61)
5   *Coimbriga* 2–3 (1961)
6   E. de la Grange, *Notice* . . . (see *RRCH* 507; Mr Crawford kindly lent me his copy of the annotated copy in the British Museum)
7   *Apulum* I (1939–42), 11 (1973)
8   *SCN* 2 (1958)
9   *NSc* 1899
10   *Izv BAI* 27 (1964)
11   *FMRD* VI 4039
12   *NSc* 1928
13   *FMRD* VI 4056
14   *Rocznik Muzeum Swietokrzyskiego* 6 (1970)
15   *JhÖAI* I (1898)
16   *Numismatika* 1933
17   *NSc* 1920
18, 19   *AIIN* 5–6 (1958–59)
20   *Materiale si cercetari arheol.* 2 (1956)
21, 22   Van Es, *De romeinse Muntvondsten uit de drie noordelijke Provincies* (1960)
23   *FMRD* IV 1150
24   *British Numismatic Journal* 9 (1959–60)
25   *NC*[6] 19 (1959)
26   *Situla* 8 (1965)
27   *Jaarboek voor Munt- en Penningkunde* 47 (1960)
28   *NSc* 1948
29   *AIIN* 5–6 (1958–59)
30   *NSc* 1901
31   *NSc* 1911
32   *AIIN* 5–6 (1958–59)
33   *NC*[6] 20 (1960)
34   *FMRD* IV 1151
35   *FMRD* IV 2212
36   *Coimbriga* 2–3 (1961)

**Table II**  Finds on African Sites

| | Sites | | | | | | |
|---|---|---|---|---|---|---|---|
| Minting authorities | Volubilis | Valentia Banasa | Thamusida | Souk-el-Arba and interior | Provenance unknown | Tamuda | Mogador |
| *Numidia* | | | | | | | |
| Kings | 13 | 23 | 2 | 3 | 13 | 73 | – |
| Carthage | 2 | – | – | – | – | – | – |
| Babba | 1 | – | – | – | – | – | – |
| Bulla Regia | 3 | 1 | 2 | – | 1 | – | – |
| Camarata | 2 | 1 | – | – | – | – | – |
| *Mauretania* | | | | | | | |
| Bogud | – | 2 | 1 | – | – | – | – |
| Bocchus (and interregnum) | 2 | – | – | 1 | 1 | – | – |
| Juba II | 51 | 81 | 11 | – | 39 | 30 | 5 |
| Juba II/Ptolemy | 1 | 10 | 1 | – | 11 | – | – |
| Ptolemy | 6 | 7 | 3 | – | 1 | 18 | – |
| Iol Caesarea | 1 | 3 | – | – | 4 | 16 | – |
| Tingis | 10 | 6 | 1 | – | 10 | 101 | 1 |
| Lixus | 9 | 26 | 5 | – | 11 ⎫ | 27 | 3 |
| Semes | 77 | 62 | 14 | 2 | 50 ⎭ | | |
| Sala | 4 | 1 | 5 | 1 | 1 | – | – |
| Other towns | 22 | 12 | 7 | 1 | 31 | – | – |
| *Spain* | | | | | | | |
| Gades | 10 | 18 | 37 | – | 12 | 22 | 4 |
| Carteia | 5 | 3 | – | 1 | 1 | 6 | 1 |
| Others, autonomous | 3 | 4 | 1 | 1 | 1 | 14 | – |
| Others, imperial | 4 | 4 | 1 | 1 | 2 | – | – |
| *Gaul* | | | | | | | |
| Nemausus | – | 1 | – | – | – | 1 | 1 |
| *Rome* (silver/aes) | | | | | | | |
| Republic | 11/2 | 7/4 | 16/4 | – | 6/12 | –/14 | – |
| Augustus | 1/2 | –/3 | 3/– | – | – | – | –/1 |
| Tiberius | –/3 | 3/11 | 1/8 | –/2 | –/2 | – | – |
| Gaius | –/4 | 1/2 | –/1 | – | –/1 | – | – |
| Claudius | –/62 | 1/143 | 1/29[a] | –/1 | –/65 | –/5 | –/2 |
| Nero | 2/8 | –/17 | 1/3 | –/1 | 1/5 | – | – |
| Indeterminate Julio-Claudian | –/32 | –/44 | –/26 | – | –/40 | – | – |

References: Tamuda: M. Tarradell, *AEA* 22 (1949) 86–100; Mogador: A. Jodin, *Les Établissements du Roi Juba II aux Iles Purpuraires (Fouilles du Service des Antiquités du Maroc, 1967)*, 237–52; others: J. Marion, *Antiquités africaines* 1 (1967), 99–118. The 'interior' sites are within the area bounded by Arbaoua, Thamusida, Rabat and Meknes. Those of unknown provenance are from various digs, including Volubilis and Valentia Banasa. The contents of Cherchel and Tipasa museums remain unpublished (J. Mazard, *Libyca* 4 (1956), 57).

[a] A much higher Claudian total emerges from figures given, for excavations to 1955, by Marion, *Bull. d'arch. maroc.* 4 (1960), 454–6 (50) and, for excavations since 1960, J.-P. Callu, *Thamusida* 1 (1965) (27).

**Table III** Tiberian *aes* issues

| | Towns | | Camps | | | Votive Deposits | | | | Hoards | | Miscellaneous | | |
| RIC I Tiberius | Minturnae (n.425) | Magdalensberg (n.425) | Neuss (n.26) | Hofheim (n.26) | Vindonissa (n.26) | River Liri (n.540) | Augst (n.554) | River Mayenne (n.416) | River Aisne (n.473) | Pozzarello (n.540) | Puy-de-Dôme (n.472) | FMRD | FMRL | Total |
|---|---|---|---|---|---|---|---|---|---|---|---|---|---|---|
| 14–17 *Asses* | 2 | – | 2 | 1 | 18 | 4 | 4 | 2 | 1 | 2 | – | 16 | – | 52 |
| 11–13 *Asses* | – | – | – | – | – | – | – | 1 | – | – | – | 1 | 4½ | 6½ |
| *Semisses* | – | – | – | – | – | – | – | 3 | 6 | – | – | 1 | 3 | 13½ |
| p. 95.2 *Asses* | 2 | 3 | 10 | 1 | 60½ | 4 | 5 | – | – | 2 | – | 36 | – | 123½ |
| 18–28 *Sestertii* | – | – | – | – | 7 | 3 | – | – | – | – | – | 6 | – | 16 |
| *Dupondii* | – | – | – | – | 16 | 3 | – | – | 1 | 2 | – | 4 | – | 28 |
| *Asses* | 2 | 7 | 3 | 2 | 30½ | 5 | 1 | 4 | 1 | 5 | 1 | 29 | 2 | 92½ |
| p. 95.4–5 *Dupondii* | – | – | – | – | – | – | – | – | – | – | – | 2 | 1 | 3 |
| p. 95.7 *Dupondii* | – | – | 1 | 1 | 2 | 1 | – | 1 | – | 1 | – | – | – | 7 |
| p. 95.6 *Asses* | 4 | 13 | 110½ | 88 | 582½ | 8 | 65 | 8 | 17 | 18 | 7 | 442½ | 8 | 1370½ |
| 30–31 *Dupondii* | – | – | – | – | – | – | – | – | – | – | – | 1 | – | 1 |
| p. 95.1 & 3 *Asses* | 4 | 5 | 1 | 1 | 44 | 10 | 2 | 10 | 3 | 11 | 2 | 59 | – | 150 |
| 37–42 *Sestertii* | 1 | – | – | – | 2 | – | – | – | – | 3 | – | 1 | – | 7 |
| *Asses* | 4 | 3 | – | – | 11 | 5 | – | 4 | 4 | 11 | – | 19 | 1 | 65 |
| 32 *Asses* | 6 | 17 | 25 | 40 | 180 | 7 | 11 | 113 | 100 | 19 | 11 | 269½ | 21 | 819½ |

**Table IV**  *Aes* coins found at Neuss (1955–62) and Vindonissa

(*a*) Finds classified by denominations (to A.D. 96)

| | | *Quadrantes* and *Semisses* | Halves of *Asses* | *Asses* | *Dupondii* | *Sestertii* | Total value, in *asses* |
|---|---|---|---|---|---|---|---|
| Republic | N | I *uncia* | 25[a] | 7 | – | – | 19 |
| | V | – | 313 | 79 | – | – | 235 |
| 43–28 B.C. | N | – | 67[a] | 20 | – | – | 53 |
| | V | – | 27 | 10 | – | – | 23 |
| Augustus (incl. | N | 8 | 190 | 737 | 21 | 10 | 918 |
| Nemausus) | V | 135 | 475 | 1826 | 113 | 19 | 2400 |
| Tiberius | N | – | 2 | 127 | I | – | 130 |
| | V | – | 22 | 788 | 5 | 9 | 845 |
| Agrippa | N | – | – | 25 | – | – | 25 |
| (*RIC*, Tib. 32) | V | – | – | 190 | – | – | 190 |
| Gaius | N | – | – | 95 | 8 | 7 | 139 |
| | V | 2 | I | 338 | 58 | 30 | 575 |
| Germanicus | N | – | – | – | 10 | – | 20 |
| (*RIC*, Tib. 36) | V | – | – | – | 48 | – | 96 |
| Claudius | N | – | – | 35 | 36 | II | 151 |
| | V | 7 | 2 | 158 | 40 | 56 | 465 |
| Nero | N | 5 | – | 10 | 8 | I | 31 |
| | V | 5 | 7 | 143 | 21 | 13 | 242 |
| A.D. 68–96 | N | I | – | 32 | 10 | 4 | 68 |
| | V | 19 | I | 215 | 136 | 77 | 802 |

*Note:* [a]Also eighteen indeterminate: divided equally between these periods for Table (*b*).
Nineteen halves of *dupondii* and *sestertii* from Vindonissa have been omitted.

(*b*) Proportion of quantity of each period represented by different denominations (%)

| | Fractions | *Asses* | *Dupondii* | *Sestertii* |
|---|---|---|---|---|
| Republic | 66 | 34 | – | – |
| 43–28 B.C. | 61 | 39 | – | – |
| Augustus | 11 | 77 | 8 | 3½ |
| Tiberius | 1 | 94 | 1 | 3½ |
| Gaius | 0 | 66 | 16 | 18 |
| Claudius | 0 | 26½ | 36½ | 36½ |
| Nero | 2½ | 56 | 21 | 20½ |
| A.D. 68–96 | 1 | 28½ | 33½ | 37 |

Halves of *asses* have been counted as *semisses*. 'Agrippa' *asses* have been divided equally
between Tiberius and Gaius. 'Germanicus' *asses* have been assigned to Claudius.

**Table V** Finds in south India. Numbers indicate denarii, (aurei) and (defaced aurei). Hoard numerations from *Aspects* (see n.378). W = *Anc. Ind.* 56; B = Seshadri; N = Nasthullapur; A = Akkanpalle; Is = stray finds; Ex = excavation finds. Quoted details are from Thurston and Sewell (see n.378).

| | Augustus | Tiberius | Augustus and Tiberius | Gaius | Claudius | Nero | Vespasian | Domitian | Nerva | Trajan | Hadrian | Antoninus Pius | Marcus Aurelius | Later | Further particulars |
|---|---|---|---|---|---|---|---|---|---|---|---|---|---|---|---|
| N | 11 | 28 | | | | | | | | | | | | | Augustus: *RIC*, 350; Tiberius: 27 *RIC*, 3; 1 *RIC*, 2 |
| 9 | ? | ? | 1,390 | | | | | | | | | | | | Augustus: *RIC* 350; Tiberius: mostly *RIC* 3 |
| 10 | – | 2 | | | | | | | | | | | | | |
| 15 | 27+ | 90+ | 233 | | | | | | | | | | | | 'Large numbers', all *RIC* Aug, 350 or Tiberius *RIC*, 3 |
| 19 | ? | ? | ? | | | | | | | | | | | | |
| 20 | ? | ? | 4 | | | | | | | | | | | | 'Large numbers' |
| 36 | ? | | | | | | | | | | | | | | |
| 37 | ? | | | | | | | | | | | | | | |
| 39 | – | 11 | | | | | | | | | | | | | |
| 43 | 121 | – | | | | | | | | | | | | | |
| B | 18 | 230 | | | | | | | | | | | | | Augustus: *RIC*, 350; Tiberius: 229 *RIC*, 3; 1 *RIC*, 2. Also 8 unidentified |
| A | ? | ? | 1,531 | | | | | | | | | | | | Mostly *RIC* Aug, 350 or Tiberius, 3; 55 imitations. All but 26 defaced. Mostly Augustus or Tiberius |
| W | (1) | | 163 in all → | | | | | | | | | | | | Tiberius: *RIC*, 3 |
| 16 | (1) | | → | | | | | | | | | | | | 'Thousands', Augustus to Nero |
| 17 | 189 | 329 | | 8 | 18 | 3 | | | | | | | | | Augustus: 188 *RIC*, 350; Tiberius: 328 *RIC*, 3 |
| 42 | 135 | 381 | | 3 | 5 | 1 | | | | | | | | | Augustus: 133 *RIC*, 350; Tiberius: 378 *RIC*, 3 |
| 44 | | | | (3) | | | | | | | | | | | |
| 23 | | | (11) in all | | | | | | | | | | | | |
| 41 | | | (6) in all | | | | | | | | | | | | |
| 67 | (42) | (167) | | (14) | (142) | (133) | (3) | | | | | | | | Augustus: 22 *RIC*, 350; Tiberius: 161 *RIC*, 3 |
| 12 | (2) | (11) | | (1) | (11) | (17) | (5) | (2) | | | | | | | Details doubtful: see n.519 |
| 57 | 21 | (8) | | | 2/(1) | 2/(2) | | (1) | | (1) | | | | | |
| 33 | | | | | | | | (5) | (2) | | | | | | |
| 14 | | | | | | | | | | (1) | (1) | | | | |
| 21 | (7)+ | (30)+ | | (3)+ | (30)+ | (31)+ | | | | | | (1) ? | | | 'Hundreds …, very fresh new and pure.' Nero next most after Tiberius |
| 28 | | | | | ← 4 → | | | | | | | | | | |
| 31 | | | | | (52)+ → | | | | | (?) | (6) | (1) | | | |
| 32 | | | | | (3) → | | | | | (?) | (6) | (1) | | | Some of Trajan 'quite fresh and new' |
| 58 | | | | | | | | (1) | | (2) | (2) | (6) | (2) | (2) | Tiberius: *RIC*, 3, Commodus, 1, Caracalla, 1 |
| 46 | | | 23 (Tiberius → To Constantine) | | | | | (1) | | | | | | | |
| 11 | | | | | | | (1) | (1) | | (1) | (1) | (1) | | | → To Constantine |
| Is | 5 | 2 | 7 | | | | | | | | | | | | |
| | (1) | (1) | (2) | | | | | | | | | | | | |
| Ex | 1 | 4 | 5 | | | | (1) | (1) | | (1) | (1) | (6) | (2) | (1) | Plated *aureus* of Tiberius Augustus: *RIC*, 350 |

# INDEXES

*References in italics are to the numbers of the notes*

## I Index of citations

[Aristotle], *Oeconomica* 1345b 20: 18, *113*
Caesar, *Bellum Gallicum*
  1.39: *208*
  7.3.1, 7.55.5: *149*
Cassius Dio
  41.38: *10*
  51.21: 7, *28, 36*
  52.30: *112*
  56.18: 31f., *218*
  57.10: *576*
  58.21: 1ff., 14f., *4, 86, 90*
  58.22: *97*
  65.6: *29*
Cicero
  *Epistulae ad Atticum*
    2.6.2, 2.16.4: 5, *19*
    5.21.11–13: 9, *76*
  *Epistulae ad familiares*
    2.17.4: *19, 23*
    12.13.4: *183*
  *pro Fonteio* 5.11: 19, *133*
  II *in Verrem* 3.181: *123, 498*
Dio Chrysostom 79.5–6: *197*
Dittenberger
  *Orientis Graecae Inscriptiones Selectae*
    339: *514*
    629: *122, 183*
  *Sylloge Inscriptionum Graecarum*³ 218: *115*
Festus, *Excerpta Pauli* p. 98M: 141
Florus, 2.33: 8, *36*
*Gnomon of the Idios Logos* 106 (Riccobono, *Fontes Iuris Romani Anteiustiniani* I² 99): *392*
Horace
  *Epodes* 2: *81*
  *Satires* 1.2.14: *77*
*Inscriptions de Délos* 407, 442, 1432, 1439, 1443, 1449, 1450: *172*
Livy
  22.52.3, 22.54.1, 22.58.4, 23.15.5: 141f.
  34.21.7: *99*
I Maccabees 15.6: *113*
*Archives of Nicanor* (Tait, *Greek Ostraca in the Bodleian Library* I): *367*
Orosius 6.19: 7, *35*
*Periplus Maris Erythraei*
  6, 8: *366*
  19: *364*

  24, 28, 32: *367*
  39, 49, 56: *50, 406–7*
  49: *381*
Petronius, *Satyricon* 54.3: *94*
Pliny, *Naturalis Historia*
  6.52: *356*
  6.101: *48, 50, 375, 408*
  12.84: *48, 376*
  33.46: 141f.
  33.47: *25*
  34.4: *97*
  37.45: *255, 257*
Pliny, *Epistulae*
  3.19.8: *8, 81*
  6.19: *80*
Statius, *Silvae* 3.85–105: 23, *154*
Strabo
  2.1.15, p. 73: *356*
  2.5.12, p. 118: 47ff., *362, 374*
  3.2.10, p. 148: *97*
  4.6.10, p. 207: *258, 283*
  5.1.8, p. 214: *253, 258, 283*f.
  7.2.4, p. 294: *257*
  7.3.11, p. 304: *313*
  7.5.2, p. 314: *258, 283*
  11.2.17, p. 498: *356*
  11.3.4, p. 500: *356*
  15.1.30, p. 700: *381*
  16.4.18–24, pp. 776–81: 47, *364, 370*f.
  16.4.26, p. 784: 47, *367, 369*
  17.1.13, p. 798: 48, *149, 195, 362*
Suetonius
  *Divus Augustus*
    41: 7, *28, 36*
    75: *21*
    101: 11f., *3, 68*
  *Gaius*
    23: *143*
    37: 11f., *65*
  *Tiberius*
    47–8: *576*
    48: 1ff., 15, *5, 90, 93, 102*
    49.1–2: 15, *98*
Tacitus
  *Annales*
    1.75, 2.47: *576*
    2.62: 36, *261*
    3.18: *67*
    3.40: *191, 283*
    3.53: 28, *196*

## II General index

*aerarium*: *see* treasury
Agrippa: 38, 143
Alexander: *19, 29, 169*
Antony: 6, 41, *30*
Arminius: 32, *202*
army, Roman: 5, 7, 22ff., 33, 35f., 53, 55f.,
62f., 64, 65f., 70, 140f., 143, *18, 73, 156,
168, 231, 233, 252, 420, 433, 439, 444,
452, 466, 538, 564*
Augustus: 4ff., 8ff., 23, 28, 55, 58, 65, 67f.,
71, *21, 26, 34, 91, 112, 166, 457, 534f.,
575; see also* Octavian

bankers: 2, 19, 24, 27, 49, 66, *123*
Burebista: 39, 43, *305, 313*

Caesar, Julius: 1ff., 6, 12ff., 64, 141, 142, *6,
9, 73, 84, 90, 305, 466, 524*
Claudius: 16f., 25, *108, 574*
counterfeiting: 60; *see also* plated coins

debasement: 6, 25, *25, 30, 122, 166, 170, 396;
see also* plated coins
debt: *see* moneylenders
demand: 7, 9, 18, 24, 26, 37f., 44, 56, 59, 62,
65ff., 70, 140f., *38, 47, 111, 192, 334,
360, 381, 437, 444, 462, 490; see also* uses
of coins
dies, life of: 10, 43f., *55, 56*
Drusus (brother of Tiberius): 33, *218, 228*

exchange: commission on, 19, *123*; rates, 19,
49, *22, 122, 124, 148, 481*
expenditure of Roman government: 4, 6f.,
9, 10, 15, 16, 22, 23, 27
export of Roman money: 4, 18, 27, 28, 35,
40, 47, 50, 67f., *109, 110, 187, 198, 381,
383, 399, 407, 410*

finds of coins, interpretations: 6, 9, 10, 19,
25f., 32f., 34, 36f., 38, 39f., 41, 45ff., 48,
52ff., *26, 30, 44, 47, 50, 108, 306, 308,
311, 317, 341, 399, 439, 444, 532, 575;
see also* hoards
*fiscus*: *see* treasury

Gaius (Caligula): 11, 16f., 143f., *108, 166,
201, 411, 574*
Germanicus: 33, *183*

hoards, interpretations: 5, 6, 10, 17, 19, 21,
26, 33, 34, 36f., 40, 42f., 44f., 48ff., *16,
18, 40, 50, 52, 63, 107, 125, 166, 181,
183, 229, 233, 281, 287*

interest: 1ff., 7, 12f., *8, 9, 36, 75ff.*
issues, relative sizes: 8ff., 16, 22ff., 67ff., *44,
47, 50, 52, 54f., 58, 567, 573*, Table III
Italy, monetary supply: 2, 4, 12, 26, 52, 65ff.

land, landowners: 1ff., 7, 12ff., *27, 35, 74,
75, 80, 192*
Licinus: *8*

Marius, Sextus: 15f., 97
mines: 8, 12, 15f., 19, 25, 42, 47f., 97, 99,
*100, 121, 169, 381*
minting, economics of: 5, 60, 141, *22, 28, 514*
mints, Roman imperial: Lugdunum, 5, 7, 12,
23, 27, 58, 65, 67f., 144, *24*; Rome, 5,
7f., 23, 58, 65ff.
money, right of issue: *18, 58, 112, 114, 116,
118, 121, 247, 457*
money, non-Roman: *75*; of Philip, Alexander
and Lysimachos (including posthumous
issues), 21, 39, 41, 46f., 56, 75, *290,
318f., 360, 441*; Seleucid, 21, 24f., 26,
45f., *100, 121f., 166, 183, 349, 352, 354,
360, 396, 490*; Ptolemaic, 7, *33f., 487,
490*; Mithridatic, 21, 26, 61, *121, 182,
357, 360*; Parthian, 46, *122, 148, 349,
352, 354, 360*; Arabian, 47, *200, 365f.*;
Phoenician, 21, 25, 61, 75, *148, 183,
354, 360*; cistophoric, 5, 21, 24, 26,
179ff., *360*; Thasian, Macedonian and
Thracian, 21, 24, 29, 39f., *27, 121, 161,
182, 287, 293, 297, 303, 441, 444*;
Athenian, 19, 21, 26, 38, 41, 61, 75, *58,
121, 124, 145, 181, 360, 487*; of Apollonia and Dyrrhachion, 21, 26, 38, 40,
*121, 147, 161, 182, 285, 287, 297f., 303,
313, 320*; of other Greek states, 21, 53,
56f., 61, 63, *318ff., 354, 441, 444, 481,
486, 489, 493*; Sicilian, 62, *275, 498,*